FAR
DISTANT
ECHO

*A Journey by Canoe from
Lake Superior to Hudson Bay*

FAR DISTANT ECHO

A Journey by Canoe
from
Lake Superior
to
Hudson Bay

FRED MARKS · JAY TIMMERMAN

 VANTAGEPress

Cover design by Pauline Neuwirth
Interior photographs by Philip Shutter and Clayton Hofernik

Vantage Press and the Vantage Press colophon are registered
trademarks of Vantage Press, Inc.

FIRST EDITION

Published by Vantage Press, Inc.
419 Park Ave. South, New York, NY 10016

Manufactured in the United States of America

ISBN: 978-0533-164639

Library of Congress Catalog Card No: 2011909358

0 9 8 7 6 5 4 3 2 1

To Jean; I could not have completed the paddle without you. You said nothing of the stores of food and equipment cached throughout the house. You happily endured my mental preoccupation with the trek. When personal commitments became obstacles you picked up the slack and always remained resolute that I reach Hudson Bay. You were always my most steadfast advocate. Though you stayed behind, in my thoughts you were always there with me in my canoe.

—FRED

To my parents, for all their love and support, the scoutmasters I had as a youth growing up (as they were the ones who encouraged my love of the outdoors), and to the Northern Tier High Adventure Program, for their support, encouragement, and the opportunities given to me over the years.

—JAY

Contents

FAR
DISTANT
ECHO

A Journey by Canoe from
Lake Superior to Hudson Bay

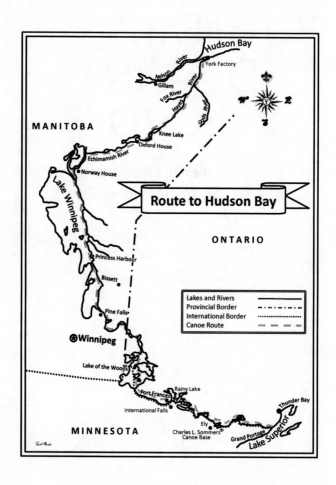

PROLOGUE

In 1670, from the mouth of the Hayes River on Hudson Bay, the Hudson Bay Company ruled a great fur trade empire. There, they built a fort—a trading center—most commonly known today as York Factory. The royal charter from Charles II gave them sole right to the fur trade in Hudson Bay's vast, amorphous, and unexplored drainage basin. Their territory was larger than many European countries. They named it Rupert's Land after their first governor, Prince Rupert. Unchallenged for over one hundred years, the company owned the fur trade business in central and western Canada. Although gone from Hudson Bay, the company is still in business today as Canada's largest department store chain. Shoppers can still find a myriad of merchandise at "The Bay."

Today on Hudson Bay, except for the ever-present wisps of long-forgotten fur trade ghosts, the lonely but stately white clapboard York Factory Depot is a sole, solitary sentinel to the Bay's former fur trade reign. Twenty-first century technology allows visitors to fly in. There are no roads to York Factory. The only other way to reach the depot from Rupert's Land is the same method used in 1670—by canoe.

Far to the southeast in Minnesota on Lake Superior's north shore near the Canadian border stands Grand Portage National

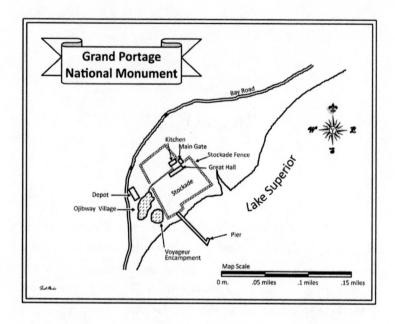

Monument. Its log stockade and buildings are a meticulous restoration of an old fort. It was the western, summer headquarters of the North West Company. Each spring, beginning in 1783 and ending in 1803, the company's trading partners led an armada from Montreal of up to two hundred, thirty-five-foot-long birch bark canoes. Each canoe, paddled by Montreal voyageurs, was loaded to the gunwales with trade goods. There were flintlocks, knives, beads, cloth, tobacco, and whisky. The actual list is much longer. The armada's quest was the beaver skin. Back in England, as done at the Hudson Bay Company, the North West Company sold the beavers' fine felt to make hats for the English and European gentry.

Simultaneously, the North West Company wintering voyageurs and traders headed east from scattered inland trading posts. In their twenty-five-foot birch bark canoes known as northern canoes—*canot du nord*—they carried the previous winter's furs. The two groups met at Grand Portage.

The way west is a trail called Grand Portage. Even in English, "portage" retains its French pronunciation—por-táge, with the accent on the last syllable. The path rises almost tortuously for eight and one half miles, bypassing the Pigeon River's lower falls. It ends in an open place in the forest on the river's bank. There used to be a stockade—Fort Charlotte. Nothing remains to note its location except a partially faded modern-day plaque with a one-page history. The Montreal voyageurs trekked across the portage every summer to Fort Charlotte. Each voyageur carried at least two ninety-pound packs. They earned a bonus if they could carry more.

While the Montreal voyageurs portaged to Fort Charlotte, the wintering voyageurs held a rendezvous on Lake Superior's shore. They sang. They drank and told tall tales. They danced and they renewed old friendships.

Grand Portage was not discovered by the North West Company. Around 1700 the French built a trading post there.[1] Before the white traders, explorers, and French missionaries came to Lake Superior, the Ojibwe and the Dakota Indians used this trail to travel west. In fact, the Ojibwe also called it Grand Portage—*Gichi-Onigami*.

But it was the North West Company that recognized the Portage's importance in backwoods commerce. In 1763 the French evacuated Canada after losing the French and Indian War—in Europe, it was called The Seven Years War. Their departure left

1 William Warren writes in *History of the Ojibway People* that the first trading post was built in the 1670s just a few years after the great 1671 French and Ojibway Convocation at Sault Ste Marie. Circa 1700 is the most widely accepted date for the construction of this French trading post.

a fur trading void with the Ojibwe. Enterprising Canadians, mostly Scotsmen, stepped in to fill the void. They first established informal seasonal trading partnerships. Eventually they realized that they would earn more money by combining their efforts. In 1783 they formed the North West Company. It became the greatest fur trade company that the world had ever seen, and its owners became frontier royalty. In fact, the North West Company partners referred to Simon McTavish, an original company leader, as the Marquis. They adopted "Perseverance" as their motto and ambitiously set forth to challenge their only competitor, the Hudson Bay Company.

Entering the stockade at Grand Portage National Monument today transports visitors through a genuine time portal back to the North West Company's golden age. In the center stands the Great Hall. It is a massive log building where the trading partners lived, ate, and ruled their empire. From the front porch over the pine-log stockade wall, you can still scan southeast and survey Grand Portage Bay and Grand Portage Island. Slightly farther to the east you can easily see Hat Point. The scene is the same as it was over two hundred years ago.

Behind the Great Hall at the end of a covered walkway is the log kitchen. Inside, a fire still burns for cooking. On cold days the fire partially warms the building. The aromatic pine-log smoke fills the senses. Around the fire, cooking pots hang on the wall. Neatly arranged on the shelves are spices, pemmican, and coffee. Around the walls are barrels and sacks of dried food.

There were more buildings at Fort William. We know where they were and what they were used for. Archeologists have found their foundations. Someday they may be rebuilt. For now, worn, sun-faded railroad ties frame the corners marking their locations.

South of the stockade is a voyageurs' encampment. A fire burns there, too, on cold days. Their neighbor is an Ojibwe village. The Indians have a small garden and several wigwams layered with large birch bark shingles. Nearby, a North West Company supply depot contains a thirty-nine-foot Montreal and twenty-five-foot Northern birch bark canoe. Both canoes hang lightly from the ceiling. On the floor is always a Northern canoe at some stage of construction.

Canoes were sealed with a mixture of pine resin, bear fat, and ash. A sample brown vial of rendered bear fat sits on a work-bench next to lumps of raw resin waiting for visitors to sniff—it has no more of an odor than canola oil. In the corner of the depot is a stack of barrels and canvas bundles that the northern canoe carried. Across present-day Bay Road is a museum, book store, and welcome center.

In 1803, because of American tariffs and border disputes, the North West Company moved their headquarters to Thunder Bay. The fort was not abandoned. It was moved log by log to the new location. The North West Company along with its voyageurs, traders and travelers no longer used Grand Portage to reach the Indians. Farther north the Kaministikwia River now became their route west.

The move was the North West Company's downfall. The Hudson Bay Company had become more aggressive in their trading tactics regaining lost ground. In 1820 the North West Company merged with the Hudson Bay Company. The North West name was gone, although as a business the Hudson Bay Company practices seemed to mimic the North West Company.

Roads and rails do not trace the historic fur trade routes, or even run roughly close or parallel to them. To explore the North West Company and Hudson Bay Company trade routes we decided over the summer of 2008, to canoe the more than 1,300 miles of connecting lakes and rivers. With paddle and pack we canoed and portaged from Lake Superior to York Factory on Hudson Bay. We knew Grand Portage. Jay and I had been there before. We would get to know York Factory.

—CHAPTER 1—

THE INITIAL STAGES

T'ousan' mile we mak' de travel—
t'ousan' mile an' maybe more,
an' I do de foolish prayin'
lak' I never pray at home,

"Chibougamou"
by William Henry Drummond

FRED WRITES:

People have asked why I first decided to undertake such a long canoe trek. Often, I answered flippantly, "Because it is there."

After considering it a little more seriously, it probably goes back to the spring of 1978. I was watching an interview with Freckles Brown at the Houston Rodeo on television. Earlier, in 1967 in Oklahoma City, Freckles had drawn a rank bull named Tornado. Tornado was infamous. In his six-year rodeo career over two hundred cowboys had climbed on his back. They were all thrown off. In addition to the cowboys Tornado threw, there were the cowboys who turned that bull out, admitting defeat without even trying to ride him.

In 1967, Freckles was the oldest bull rider on the rodeo circuit. He was one month shy of turning forty seven—ancient by bull-rider standards. He was not in the standing to win any money, but he climbed on Tornado's back anyway. When the arena dust settled, Freckles had ridden Tornado. Nobody remembers who won the bull riding champion buckle, but they remember Freckles.

ABC Sports aired a couple of still photographs while Howard Cosell described the historic ride. Cosell then interviewed Freckles on his most memorable of rodeo moments. In the way only Cosell could phrase a question or a sentence, he asked in his pointed, dry monotone, "Freckles, why did you still ride?"

Freckles looked squarely at Howard. With a slow, deliberate, Oklahoma cowboy twang he answered, "Howard, all my life all I want'd was to be a good cowboy. I guess I was still tryin'."

Freckles made an impression on me. I don't ride bulls; I paddle canoes. But his comment still applies. Be good at what you do and always strive to be better. Most importantly, don't walk away from a challenge! Now, like Freckles, I was older, maybe even ancient, but I still felt the need to improve. There was certainly more to learn about guiding and paddling in the North Woods. I was looking for and needed a new challenge. The challenge would be my quest for Hudson Bay.

Inadvertently, the French and later the North West Company created the United States border with Canada. The Treaty of Ghent, ending the War of 1812, and the 1783 Treaty of Paris, ending the American Revolution, both defined the border west of Lake Superior as, "the route most commonly used in the fur trade." This was where the men of the North West Company, the voyageurs—the Nor'westers—traveled. It was our trip's first leg. Our second leg, north on Lake Winnipeg and then down the Hayes

River, was the Hudson Bay Company's main route. The Hudson Bay men, the York Men, carried goods annually up and down the rivers and lakes. They first used canoes, but later changed to the significantly more commodious York Boats. I increasingly wanted personally to see and experience all of both routes. It quickly became something I knew I could do and wanted to do.

The North Woods have become my summer home. Even though I did not live there, I knew it through poetry. As a child I loved Longfellow's *Song of Hiawatha*. Its setting is there in the land of the Ojibwe on Lake Superior—Gichi-Gumi. Along with Hiawatha, I came to know the sights, sounds, and smells of his forests, lakes, and wildlife. Still today, I enjoy his adventures.

My first actual experience in the North Woods, in Quetico Provincial Park, was when I was sixteen. Our scout troop traveled to Ely, Minnesota to Charles L. Sommers Region Ten Wilderness Canoe Base. There, I was personally introduced to the lakes and forest. The water was clean. We could wade up to our knees and dip a cup into the water for a cool drink. In fact, each lake seemed to have a different taste. The water was cold. It stung and numbed our skin when we tried to swim. Above all, everywhere, we were surrounded by glorious forests. This was the most remote "bush" experience I had ever had, and I loved it. Even the mosquitoes and black flies were only mild irritants.

At the end of my first trip, the idea of exploring the Canadian woods lay mostly a dormant notion for well over thirty years although, when I sought an escape from the everyday doldrums, in my mind I often drifted back to Quetico. In my thoughts, I could still smell the tang of the fresh pine needles and the pungent campfire smoke. I could still feel the cool crisp summer breeze on my cheek. I could still hear the chirping of the birds and the barking squirrels, but returning always seemed so out of reach.

In 1999 I finally went back. My wife, Jean, and I took that overdue canoe trip. The water was just as clean and cold as I remembered. The bugs were still just a minor irritant. Most of all Quetico seemed a familiar place. Coffee and camp food tasted better by a smoking campfire. I slept deeply with the soft night sounds whispering in my ear. I went again the next summer with a friend. Then, I told Jean that I was going to apply to be a guide at Sommers Canoe Base. I knew that I could handle the physical requirements, but was uneasy thinking that they would not want an old man. To my joy they did. So began my retirement career guiding canoe trips. At first I thought that spending one summer in the bush would be satisfying enough. It was not. I longed to do something more. I wasn't sure what it was, but I kept going back.

My first encounter with a man on his quest for the Bay was with Dan Carter at Prairie Portage in Quetico Provincial Park in 2004. It was a short conversation. I asked where he was going. Most people you talk to at Prairie Portage have a destination of less than twenty miles away, and then they fish. Dan quietly pointed to his canoe. There it was on the side in big bold letters: "Superior to Hudson." I felt a little sheepish for not having noticed. It inspired me. In fact, I was impressed that he had made it alone as far as he did. I had not yet crossed Grand Portage, but knew that to solo across was no small feat. I wished Dan luck, but never saw him again.

The next spring I received an e-mail from a friend, Tom Copeland. We had worked together at Sommers Canoe Base. The note directed me to a website, the Hudson Bay Boys. Tom and two friends were also paddling from Lake Superior to Hudson Bay.

I saw Tom twice that summer. The first time was during staff training after he arrived from Lake Superior to resupply. The second time was also at Sommers after he returned from

Hudson Bay. We talked briefly. I knew then that I had to replicate Tom's trip.

In 2006 I tried to put a trip together for the summer of 2007, but it did not gel. Then in the summer of 2007, the trip began serendipitously with my return to Sommers. The stars lined up. The planets came together. Freckles rode Tornado. I would paddle to Hudson Bay.

I had not given up but was not sure who to go with or when it would happen. I was actually thinking of going alone. On one of my days on base while fixing trail stoves with Charles, he asked almost casually if I still wanted to paddle to Hudson Bay. "Sure," I said. It was that simple. Then I added something to the conversation: "I don't want a big group. It should only be the two of us." Charles agreed. We began immediately to plan, dividing up responsibilities. I don't think that it was said, but we both understood that it would take place the next summer.

We talked of keeping the expedition simple. In truth, it would be an expedition. A trip is only a weekend or maybe even a week. This would be several months. Neither of us wanted the typical freeze-dried, add-boiling-water, backcountry hiking food. We could do better and do it for less money. I offered to handle the food purchasing and packing. I also did not want a lot of sponsorship. If you have a sponsor, you cease to own the trip, and I wanted to own the trip. Charles was of the same mind.

Next in turn was the task of accumulating equipment. I already had most of it, but we needed a large crew pack, tent, and canoe. I bought all three used from the canoe base. The canoe was an eighteen-foot Kevlar Champlain. The tent was a used—well used—Eureka four man. The pack was a number three Granite Gear pack. Because of its gray color and its size, Sommers' staff always refer to them as gray whales. We seemed to be ready with the basics.

Our plans soon changed. Charles' brother, Jim, said that he wanted to go. It seemed to me at the time that we could all fit in my Champlain, but that we might also be able to find a fourth crew member, so I said, "Sure."

We talked to Karl. He said that he might be interested but that having just finished college, he truly needed to get a real job. I understood. That happened to me forty years earlier. We concluded our conversation with him adding that if he changed his mind, we needed to know by January so I could pack the right amount of food.

The base was throwing out some old tents. Rush, the Chief Outfitter, stacked them on the Bay Post's[2] porch with a big sign saying, "Free." I picked up a couple of extras in anticipation of an increasing crew size.

In late August, the 2007 canoeing season ended. During the drive home, my mind raced with all that had to be done. My immediate task was to come up with recipes and a menu. But then I thought, "First I have to come up with an itinerary so I know how much food to buy." I had outfitted numerous scout crews, with Sommers' support, plus some canoe trips of my own. In fact, some of the trip preparation process had become rote. However, now I had to plan for resupply and resolve whether it would be better to buy supplies along the way or pre-position food at various stops on our route. None of this was overwhelming; rather, decisions simply had to be made. I knew that Dan Carter had opted for the second choice. Tom Copeland had done a little of both. Reaching Missouri I decided that that the best option was to pre-position

---

2 The Bay Post is the base's outfitting building. Once the season starts, there is always a flurry of activity with crews coming and going.

food at Sommers, International Falls, Pine Falls, and Norway House, and to fill any shortages at those locations.

Returning home I told Jean it had come together. We would paddle to Hudson Bay. "It is a trip of a lifetime," I said. "Not many men have made the trip. At least, I don't know of any more than nine who have reached Hudson Bay starting at Lake Superior. If there are others out there, I can't find them."[3]

The nine I mentioned to Jean were canoeists of the last one hundred years. The first trip by a westerner from Lake Superior to Hudson Bay began in 1739. Joseph la France, an illiterate métis (half French, half Ojibwe) fur trader, was in danger of arrest by French authorities for operating as an unlicensed trader. He fled what was then New France—eastern Canada— for Rupert's Land in hopes of trading with the English on Hudson Bay. La France followed what is now Minnesota's northern border to Lake of the Woods. The next summer he paddled the Winnipeg River to Lake Winnipeg where, during the winter of 1740 to 1741, he lived with the Cree. The next winter he spent on Lake Manitoba. La France finally reached York Factory via the Hayes River in June 1742 with a large band of Indians and a payload of furs. Historically, his trip proved that there is a water route to Hudson Bay.

The route that Joseph la France traveled is the same route we

---

3 The nine that I know of are Dan Carter, Tom Copeland, Brian Dobry, Evan Durban, Steve Baker, Scott Andersen, Kip Barrett, Kees van der Wege, and Chris Gorton. Dan, Tom, Brian, and Evan portaged over to Gods Lake and the Gods River and then finished on the Hayes River. Steve and Scott did the same, but started at Duluth rather than Grand Portage. They also took a detour through Quetico Provincial Park rather than following the Minnesota-Ontario Border. Kip, Kees, and Chris also detoured through Quetico. From there they paddled west through Atikaki Provincial Wilderness Park in Manitoba reaching Lake Winnipeg via the Bloodvein River. I do not include those who paddled to York Factory from Minneapolis. Although it is an equally challenging trip, it does begin at a different place.

would paddle. Jean was excited for me and wonderfully supportive. Moose, my Weimaraner, even gave me a look like he understood what was coming. He then walked off to whine at and scratch on the pantry door for that treat that would, for now, soothe his angst.

I read and reread Tom's and Dan's journals to develop a workable itinerary. Searching for helpful details, I also scoured the Internet for additional journals. Rereading Eric Sevareid's book, *Canoeing with the Cree*, was of some help. Sevareid started in Minneapolis. His was a different beginning, but the goal was the same. I mainly gained inspiration from his classic trek. Smart money says, "Don't go off into the bush without a plan." The plan need not be rigid; rather, it must be practical and flexible enough to fit a fluid journey.

As the summer waned I dove in to developing some trail recipes that used food from off the Piggly Wiggly grocery shelf. For those not from the South who have not yet seen *Driving Miss Daisy*, Piggly Wiggly is not only a place to shop, but also a small town social adventure.

One of our restrictions was that, at least in the Boundary Waters Canoe Area, we could not use cans or glass. Glass is just plain stupid on the trail, but tin cans are easily crushed and hauled out. The problem was that in the past, people did not take tin cans out, so American and Canadian Park Services banned both. But, when we could use cans, our menu expanded greatly.

In early fall, our crew size increased. Israel called saying that he wanted to be included. He had already talked to Charles and Jim. So now we were four. I felt smug that I had picked up the extra tents.

October hugely changed Jean's and my life. Sydney Rose, my granddaughter, came to live with us. Overnight I became a father again. Albeit a welcome role, it was life changing! On several occasions, I told Jean that she needed to let me know if she could handle being a single grandma over the summer. If not, then I would stay home. Sydney is a handful. Jean always said, "Go! You have thought of this trip for too long." I didn't know that she knew my private thoughts so well. So, the expedition was still on.

Charles and I occasionally e-mailed and phoned. He was busy with school and I was busy with my new fifth grader. I don't remember when Karl decided to join exactly, other that it was before the deadline we had given him. Karl called Charles, and Charles called me to say that Karl had decided to join us and ask if I had any objections? I did not. However, Karl's joining meant that we needed to find a sixth crew member. Equipment wise we were in good shape. Israel and Charles had already bought a second canoe. Karl had a third. We brainstormed and kept coming up blank. Almost at the last minute Jay Timmerman said that he was interested. Jay is an old hand. I knew him to be excellent on the trail. The rest concurred, so we completed the crew. The six of us would start at Lake Superior, cross Grand Portage, follow the border to Lake of the Woods, then follow the Winnipeg River, Lake Winnipeg, and the Hayes River to York Factory on Hudson Bay. We would also have one extra strong back on the first two legs; Clayton Hafernik wanted to paddle from Superior to International Falls. I was glad to have him along. Not only is he a congenial young man, but also excellent on the trail.

JAY WRITES:

About a decade ago I began guiding canoe trips at Charles L. Sommers Canoe Base. It was then that I found Scott Anderson's book, *Distant Fires*. In 1987, Scott and a friend, Steve Baker, canoed from Duluth to Hudson Bay. It started me thinking, "I want to do that." Then I read *One Incredible Journey*, Verlen Kruger's and Clayton Klein's chronology of a 1971 canoe trip from Montreal to the Bering Straits. I was hooked. These two adventures whet my wanderlust appetite and fanned the flames of desire to do the same.

With my experience guiding at Sommers Canoe Base I felt comfortable with canoe expedition planning and logistics. But difficulty in finding a partner caused me, at least for the time, to resign myself to a daydream rather than an actuality.

Out of the blue in December 2007, the possibility of canoeing to Hudson Bay came within reach. I was in Washington, DC, having a beer with Charles. We knew each other from Sommers. During that brief conversation in a tavern across the street from Union Station he told that he was part of a group that was planning to paddle to from Lake Superior to Hudson Bay.

"If there are openings, Charles, count me in! I already have several of the maps, and would love to take a trip like this!" I blurted out my thoughts rapidly and excitedly—almost as if they were one sentence. Charles, too, was as animated as I was, but commented that my going depended upon a vacancy. He would have to check with the other crew members. They wanted to limit the crew to six people, at the most seven people. In the meantime, if I was to go, I had to concentrate on writing and finishing my thesis for my master's degree at Saint Cloud.

My thesis studied Minnesota's freight and passenger rail volume decline during a period of increased railroad construction. I loved trains and frequently took the train from Saint Cloud to Florida to visit family. Washington, DC, was typically a layover and transfer stop. Love of trains was leading to my real love—canoeing.

Riding the rails back to Saint Cloud I was filled with anticipation. I could sense my decade-long dream culminating. I was going to be able to trek to where most canoeists only dream about! I would tour York Factory. This was a place that for centuries was central to the Canadian fur trade. In my mind's eye, I saw myself standing in front of York Factory's historic depot, a three-story white clapboard building that stands lonely sentinel over the Hayes River as it flows into Hudson Bay. As I stood there in my thoughts, the wind blew back the brim of my hat and cooled my face. In my mind I reveled in the satisfaction of completing such an epic trip.

Several weeks later Charles called to say there was room. "Do you still want to go?" he asked.

"Yes!" I was quite excited. "Yes! Yes I do!" I had no trace of doubt.

In my spare time that spring I began studying my maps and ordering additional maps. I read and reread my other canoeing references on the Winnipeg River and Hayes River. Some portages I marked on my maps. Others I committed to memory.

When I told my parents, they sent me an e-mail saying, "Go ahead and take the trip." They were encouraging. I held off mentioning it to the rest of my family until early May at graduation. When I announced my intentions, several people were dumbfounded by the trip's duration and distance. They asked inquisitively with a slight undercurrent of disbelief, "Has anyone else taken a trip like that before? How much planning has gone into the trip? Tell me again how long the trip will be!"

"Two and one half months. It is about thirteen hundred miles. We are taking some extra precautions. My contribution is some maps and getting us a satellite phone. The sat. phone will reduce our risk. It will give us communications no matter where we are."

I answered each question methodically. In the end they were all still amazed and still worried, but wished me the best of luck.

FRED WRITES:

With Jay on board we were set. We would admit no more crew members. I would buy and pack food for only six men—seven on the first two legs. Over the fall I had tested recipes and amounts on Jean and Sydney Rose. They loved them all. We had chili with cornbread dumplings, chicken spaghetti, chicken and dumplings, and curried lentils with chicken. The list goes on. For dessert I had come up with peach cobbler, banana pudding, and cinnamon rolls. Jean and Sydney Rose both applauded when I got it just right. Sydney Rose took the leftovers to school for lunch. Importantly, all of these recipes fit the Boundary Waters' rules—no cans. Now the real work began.

CHAPTER II

THE LOGISTICS

And the pleasant water courses,
You could trace them through the valley
By the rushing in the springtime,
By the alders in the summer,

"The Song of Hiawatha"
by Henry Wadsworth Longfellow

[SUMMER 2007–26 MAY 2008]

FRED WRITES:

Any old soldier will tell you, "Amateurs study tactics; professionals study logistics." Being a retired, professional, old soldier, I knew that our success would depend on the preparation. Charles was handling the entry point and entry date. He was also getting a GPS. Jay obtained hard copies of maps. Karl was making spray skirts for our canoes. Israel was coordinating transportation home.

My responsibility was food packing. First, however, I had to buy it. Before Christmas after sharing the recipes with the others and asking for their objections, comments, and suggestions, I decided on a menu. From that I knew what I needed to buy. Having packed hundreds of meals for the trail at Sommers gave me the knowledge of how much pasta, dried vegetables, rice, and meat we needed per supper. Lunch was always cold—trail mix, peanut butter and jelly, or sausage and cheese. I used flour tortillas and rye crackers for bread. They just don't spoil. Breakfast was usually dried fruit, granola bars, and coffee. Knowing what we needed per meal made it easy to do the math for sixty-five days. In addition to our planned meals, I packed an additional reserve of ten days plus some basic staples like bannock and grits. I would modify final food amounts as summer neared. If need be we could supplement supplies along the way at Kenora, Pine Falls, and Norway House. I now knew what we needed so I started buying our food. I would do an exact itinerary later.

I had become accustomed over the years at Sommers to packing each meal separately in its own plastic bag for trips. That way everything needed for the meal was in one place. I decided to use the same method. In that way we would not have to rummage nightly through food packs. Pull out one plastic bag and everything would be there.

—FOOD SUPPLIES—

3 lbs instant cheese sauce

13 lbs beef Jerky

20 boxes crackers

15 lbs processed cheese

23 lbs pepperoni sausage

maple flavoring for syrup

26 bottles strawberry and grape jelly

2 pkgs gumbo soup mix

12 lbs coffee

54 pkgs tomato soup mix

9 pouches tuna

15 lbs summer sausage

5 lbs freeze-dried vegetables

14 containers chili

26 jars peanut butter

2 bottles dehydrated bell
    peppers

9 lbs lentils

1 lb dried mushrooms
26 lbs dried fruit
7.5 lbs roasted peanuts
4 lbs Parmesan cheese
4 pkgs cobbler mix
2 lbs pancake mix
2 lbs dried potatoes
5 lbs canned peaches
12 lbs red or black beans and
   rice mix
4 pouches clams
3 pkgs three-bean chili mix
9 lbs canned chicken
14 boxes pudding
4 boxes sweet potatoes
150 pkgs pre-packed trail mix
1 qt soy sauce
9 lbs Bisquick mix
2 lbs brown sugar
6 lbs grits
9 oz dried garlic
spice kit

13 lbs gnocchi
472 granola bars
5 lbs raisins
72 ounces instant cream
6 pkgs bacon bits
12 pkgs cornbread mix
20 pkgs muffin or brownie
   mix
16 pkgs gravy mix
30 lbs pasta
36 pouches seasoning mixes
3 pkgs beef stew mix
6 canned hams
4 lbs canned corn beef
3 qts vegetable oil
1 pkg instant potato soup
5 pkgs instant cheese cake mix
9 lbs rice
½ lb diced dried onions
14 bags flour tortillas
3 lbs butter
3 bottles camp soap

In addition to the food we had crew equipment and personal equipment to gather. Knowing what we needed in crew gear was based on a Sommers' packing list. The big change was that I opted for a four-man tent. Normally we used two-man tents for two people. We, however, would be in it for two and one-half months so the extra room would be welcome. Besides, there were no free two-man tents. I also added a solar shower. A hot shower on a cold day is a real luxury.

It was a short list, but everything adds up—volume and

weight—especially when you pack enough for two and one-half months. More importantly it all had to fit into the canoe. I checked, double-checked, and even triple-checked the crew and personal gear. We were going to be as well-heeled in the bush as possible.

—CREW GEAR—

3 canoes with 3 paddles per canoe
2 sets of maps
satellite phone
GPS
tent vestibule
pot set
coffee pot
2 camp ovens, one large and
   one small
2 Coleman stoves
solar camp shower
2 Granite Gear personal
   equipment packs
2 guide packs
6 Kevlar food bags
2 Dromedary bags
filet board
water pump for water purification

3 bottles of Polar Pure for
   water purification
first-aid kit
bear ropes and pulley
folding shovel
3 four-man Eureka tents
dining fly
plastic pack liners
cooking utensil set
hatchet and saw
2 food packs
1 Kondos gear pack
ALICE pack
collapsible bucket
100 ft 3/8" line
fuel bottles
soap kit for washing pots and
   pans

—PERSONAL GEAR FOR EACH MAN—

stuff bags
sleeping bag liner
2 pairs of trousers

sleeping bag
ground pad
1 long-sleeve shirt

2 tee shirts	*knit cap*
3 pairs of underwear	*fleece vest*
long-sleeve fleece	*rain jacket and pants*
camp shoes	*boots*
belt	*toothbrush and toothpaste*
mess gear	*2 Nalgene water bottles*
insect repellent	*suntan lotion*
ChapStick	*foot powder*
camera	*flashlight*
fishing equipment	*mosquito head-net*
compass	*personal first-aid kit*
knife	

In the spring I finalized our itinerary and e-mailed it to Tom for him to review. He e-mailed back that it looked good to him. He also recommended that I pack plenty of extra food. "You even eat when you are wind bound," Tom wrote. It seemed obvious, but even the obvious needs verbalizing. I packed enough for at least an extra two weeks

I knew that we could supplement meals with fresh-caught fish. But we needed to continually monitor our rations. Once we left Pine Falls on the Winnipeg River, we would have no place to buy food on Lake Winnipeg until we reached Norway House. After Norway House the only place to resupply would be Oxford House. Keeping that in mind, I checked and double-checked amounts and portions, refined our menu, and then packed and labeled all our food. With my additional Mr. Mom jobs—picking up Sydney Rose from school every day, helping her with her homework, and all those time-consuming parental projects that have no name— food buying and packing took the remainder of my time. Five days before it was time to leave I was ready. I think that Jean was ready, too. Food and canoeing equipment occupied every vacant corner in the den, hallway, and our bedroom. Jean was really understanding of my temporary invasion.

Our cooking equipment was packed and ready. My personal gear was packed. I had put up all the tents and checked them with a garden hose to ensure that they didn't leak. Lastly I printed my cookbook. I was ready to go. Jean once again assured me that she was ready to be a single "mom." Sydney Rose reluctantly promised to behave. On May twenty-first, the day before I was to leave, I packed the truck. Gypsy, Sydney's Corgi, happily growled what sounded like an approval. My food packs would be in her way no more. Moose, looked as if he knew what was going to happen. He had seen me load the truck before. Turning his back to me, he opened the back door with his front paw and nose and walked inside as if to pout. I strapped the Champlain—an eighteen-foot kevlar canoe made by the We-no-nah Canoe Company—on top of my truck and then went back to make sure that nothing was left. The house seemed empty with all the food out of the den and the equipment out of the bedroom. One last time I went upstairs to rummage through my camping equipment boxes to see if there was anything that I might use. There wasn't.

The morning of May twenty-second came too quickly. The alarm rang all too early, but I didn't press the snooze button. There was one last morning to feed Moose and Gypsy before I left, and one last cup of coffee with Jean before I headed north. Six o'clock rolled around and it was time to go. Jean gave me one last forlorn, I'll-miss-you look. Then we kissed good-bye and I headed toward St. Louis. Looking back, our good-bye happened too quickly—almost in fast-forward.

The first day on the road, in my mind I traced and retraced

our route to Hudson Bay. The part from Lake Superior to Lac la Croix was familiar. In my thoughts I walked what I remembered of Grand Portage until I was exhausted. All of the lakes between Grand Portage and Lac la Croix I had traveled at least once. Most lakes I had paddled several times. Mentally, I paddled them again. By day's end I was just north of Kansas City. I was making good time. I had crossed at least thirty portages and paddled at least forty lakes. Tomorrow I would be in the North Woods.

The drive through Iowa was uneventful. I stopped at Cabela's in Minnesota. There wasn't anything that I needed except to stretch my legs. Cabela's is a camping and hunting Mecca—if it exists, Cabela's sells it.

I didn't stay long. I needed to get at least to Virginia, Minnesota. Driving through Minneapolis there were numerous detours from a 2007 bridge collapse. Finally I made it through. Just past Hinkley was my first birch tree. It always stands quietly as a welcoming sentry. Not much farther down the road would be Cloquet. From there I was truly off the beaten path. The roadside is rich with birch trees and glimpses of lakes and streams. The temperature always cools noticeably as you cross the Saint Louis River and come within reach of the Mesabi Range—the iron range.

Midmorning on the third day I was there. The familiar Ely water tower loomed over the horizon. I stopped at Piragis, an Ely outfitter and bookstore, to pick up a copy of *Song of Hiawatha*. I read it at least once a year and love to read it on the trail. My copy was back in Mississippi. Then I headed for Sommers. There was a slight chill in the air. The leaves on the birch trees along the Fernberg Trail were still that youthful, almost pastel, spring lime-green. In the past I had seen deer, moose, wolves, and fox along the road, but this time there was no wildlife. About fifteen miles from Ely I turned left onto Moose Lake Road. It twisted and wound around the terrain and then rose over some hills. At the end of the road was Sommers Canoe Base. The eight-foot wooden replica of the base patch was there to greet me. It was still early, rather pre-season, so few staff were present.

In the administration building, Kean-san, the base clerk, told me that all but Jay had arrived. Kean-san didn't know where they were, but said that Angela Stuart, the Chief Interpreter,[4] was around and that she probably knew where they were. Everybody affectionately, but respectfully, called her, "boss lady." I found Angela in her office. She told me to pick any staff cabin. The rest of our crew was in the First-aid Cabin. Rather than pick a cabin, I elected to use the two-man tent I had brought. I would be sharing space for the rest of the summer so a couple more nights without a roommate seemed like a good idea. After setting up I drove to the First-aid Cabin to unload. About the same time the rest of the crew, except for Jay, shuffled in.

That night we checked the food and gear for probably the fourth or fifth time. Then we settled up on the cost. Each of us had spent money on various trip aspects so it was time to reconcile the books.

The next day was a flurry of activities. I went to the bank to deposit money and tried to find one of the staff who would be willing to take us to Grand Portage. I came up blank on the last task. Everybody was busy. Our fall-back plan was to take two cars, leave them at Grand Portage, then retrieve them after the first leg. We had a three-day layover between the first and second leg, so there was ample time.

Angela told me that we could leave the rest of our food in the First-aid Cabin while we were paddling our first leg in from Grand Portage. We tagged our provisions and stacked them in

---

4 Years ago, to satisfy the Canadian Park Service the term "guide" was dropped and "interpreter" used in its place.

the closet. When we returned from Grand Portage we would take what we needed to get to International Falls. Angela or one of the other staff would bring us the next leg's supplies there. What we would do with the rest was still up in the air. Getting Jim Richards to take it to Bissett and bring it to us in Pine Falls was the optimum solution. If he could not, we would mail it general delivery to Norway House.

JAY WRITES:

After tying up all my lose ends in St. Cloud, I headed for Sommers. The miles seemed to drift by slowly. Finally, late on the afternoon of May twenty-fifth, Ely's water tower came into view. Thirty minutes later I pulled up next to the staff cabins. Having my pick of all the empty staff cabins, I decided to spend the night in one rather than try to crowd into the First-aid Cabin.

FRED WRITES:

The morning of May twenty-sixth we headed south down Highway 1 for Grand Portage. I carried my canoe along with most of the gear in my truck. Charles took the other two canoes on his station wagon. Highway 1 is more like a paved country road than a highway. Its two lanes coil like a huge lazy roller coaster through and under a canopy of birch trees. At Lake Superior it connects with Highway 61, which is a broader and straighter thoroughfare connecting Duluth to Minnesota's North Shore vacation getaways and Thunder Bay, Ontario.

Superior's water looked cold that day. It was a deep blue color, but it still looked cold. When the lake has a gray tint it looks even colder. Although the sun was shining and summer was around the corner, the temperature was below fifty degrees.

In the distance, scattered clouds floated above the Great Lake, eventually sinking below the far-off horizon.

JAY WRITES:

After taking care of some last-minute errands in town, we headed to Grand Portage National Monument. Fred had to go to the bank. Others needed some last minute supplies at Piragis. On Highway 1 leading to Lake Superior, a light rain fell. Even with the mist on the windshield our spirits were high. I took this as a good sign considering the hike—the test—that would take place the very next day. We arrived at about four o'clock that afternoon. There are no camping facilities at Grand Portage itself, so we set up our tents in the nearby RV trailer park.

Even though I had crossed Grand Portage several years earlier, I was still uneasy about the next day. This would be my first time crossing Grand Portage with a full kit. I resolved to shake off my nervousness and apprehension as merely pre-trip jitters—butterflies fluttering in my stomach.

I had acted in high school theater productions. Once, I even had a singing role as the Pharaoh in *Joseph and the Amazing Technicolor Dream Coat*. The butterflies I had now were the same ones that flapped their wings on opening night. As a teenager I kept them at bay by being over prepared.

In a sense this trip was the same as opening night. I was headed for a new experience. I tried to think of what I would do if plans went awry, and developed a contingency plan. Unlike a play, there would not be a teacher to whisper a line when somebody forgot the script.

I knew that the trail would have some hardships ahead, but told myself, "No matter what happens, we will work our way through the trials." I tempered the butterflies with the knowledge that I had done numerous wilderness canoe trips. This experience was going to test friendships. I trusted that our friendships would sustain me through any challenges that lay ahead. Mentally I steeled myself for the morning's trek. I would be ready to knock the audience dead.

FRED WRITES:

At the RV park, I first thought of using my tent for one last night of solitude, but then decided not to. After setting up camp and securing our food in the vehicles, we walked down to the Grand Portage stockade.

JAY WRITES:

Grand Portage, in addition to being an historic fur trade post, is an old trail that connects Lake Superior with the Pigeon River. The French used it, the Ojibwe used it, and the North West Company used it. It bypasses the river's un-navigable lower twenty-two miles. Once on the Pigeon River, eighteenth- and nineteenth-century fur traders pointed their canoes westward to a trading post network spread out as far as modern-day northern Alberta and Saskatchewan.

FRED WRITES:

Walking between the Indian village and a replica voyageur encampment I found Erik Simula. He was lacing birch bark shingles to a wigwam frame. I introduced myself to him again. He remembered me.

"I still have your card," he quietly offered.

I first met Erik a couple of years earlier when Jean flew up to meet me for a North Shore vacation. Erik is an old-time Charlie Guide[5] who literally lives in the 1800s—maybe even earlier. Summers, he works at Grand Portage as a reenactor, building birch bark canoes. Winters, he is a dog musher. His home is a one-room log cabin that he built himself. It stands on a plot of land deep in the woods. The only way to get there is by canoe, foot, or, in the winter, dog sled. I have never been there. I know nobody who has. I only know what Erik has shared with me about his cabin.

He was dressed in a voyageur costume. His long hair fell loosely to his shoulders from underneath his multicolored toque. His loose-fitting off-white shirt was untucked—as it should be. Around his waist he wore the voyageur sash, the ceinture. His buckskin-colored trousers broke loosely around some hand-made Indian moccasins. That is his normal wear while working at Grand Portage. I suspect that it may always be his normal wear. On colder days as that one was, he wears a period jacket. On warmer days he discards the jacket and the toque. Erik obviously loves what he does. He is peaceful to be around.

I introduced the rest of the crew and told Erik of our plans. He knew Dan Carter. During the conversation he asked if we had heard the weather report. I told him that we had not and asked, "Why?"

Erik softly commented that there was supposed to be a frost. For the most part he has disavowed the twenty-first century. With the exception of owning an old pickup truck, he lives in an enviable long-lost time. I took from his comment that he

---

5 Charlie Guide is a nickname for any of the trail staff and former trail staff at Northern Tier National High Adventure Base. The name itself is derived from Charles L. Sommers Canoe Base.

occasionally stepped forward in time to listen to the weather report—maybe in his pickup truck.

It was good to see Erik again. He had started to build a new northern canoe. The one he was working on when we first met was in a new display at the National Monument. The other crew members walked up to the depot leaving the two of us alone. I turned to Erik. "Did you go on the canoe trip you were talking about?" I asked. I didn't remember his exact route, but the last time we met he told me of a "slick little fourteen-foot birch bark canoe he had built that would be perfect for a long trip."

"No, but I am going to use that canoe this summer. My daughter is graduating from high school. I am going to paddle to Duluth for her graduation." He was still holding a three-foot-square piece of birch bark in his left hand.

I nodded, not in approval, but in admiration. "That will be a great trip."

"Yes, that is the way I need to go—by canoe."

We shook hands. I headed up to the depot where the others had gone to see Erik's new canoe. It was still in its early stages. He builds all his canoes by hand, splitting white cedar with a homemade froe. He has a special handmade knife to split the spruce roots for lacing the birch bark together. Unlike some canoe builders, Erik only uses bear fat to seal the seams. I walked over and stood under the thirty-nine-foot reproduction birch bark Montreal canoe that hangs from the ceiling. I had seen it several times before, but it was still an awesome feeling to look up at such an historic and massive canoe.

We then entered the fort. The day was chilly so I was glad to find a fire in the kitchen hearth, even though it was small. John Pelley, a retired Texas teacher, was a reenactor cook. He, too, wore moccasins, tan trousers, and a homespun-looking cloth shirt. Over it all he wore a tan apron. On his head was the obligatory toque. He gave us an informal tour describing the period foods and spices. The chill had permeated the kitchen, so I gradually edged back to the massive fireplace for warmth.

From there we went to the Great Hall. The Great Hall was where the trading partners and management—the company aristocrats—dined during their summer occupation. It could feed one hundred guests. Now, it is a living history. The tables are set with the china, silver, and crystal used for meals. At one end is a table with the finest china and crystal that the owners and their families would have used, while the more mundane pewter was used by the clerks and guides. There are also stacks of furs and trade goods. At each end is a massive stone fire place. Stone is never at a shortage in the North Woods. It is jokingly called the renewable natural resource.

Inside, nestled in among the furs, was a robust young man in a green and black kilt. I had met him before also. The last time I was at Grand Portage he portrayed a North West Company cook. This summer he was a trading partner. He warmly greeted us, "Welcome to the Great Hall!"

His black, wavy—almost curly—hair was parted in the middle, pulled back and plaited tightly into a single braid. In addition to his tartan kilt he wore an ornately patterned, glimmering gold vest. For the cold he wore a beige-lined azure great coat with eight large silver buttons. Around his waist were a black leather bag and a black powder pistol tucked into a red voyageur sash—a ceinture. I didn't see them, but I am sure that somewhere hidden in his garb was a powder horn and a knife. He looked as though he was just returning from one of the end-of-trading-season balls that were held annually in the Great Hall. In any other venue he would have been gaudily dressed, but here at Grand Portage his costume was purely proper and a readily understood sign of his high stature with the company and obvious close affiliation with the "Old Marquis," Simon McTavish.

I introduced myself, "We met in 2006. You were working in the kitchen that summer."

"Jeremy Kingsbury," he said, shaking my hand. "They move us around. I'm in the Great Hall this year."

Jeremy proceeded to give us a tour, talking of the trading goods and the stacks of pelts. He had a manner that engaged the visitor in a dialogue. I remembered him having the same approach while explaining Grand Portage history when we first met in the kitchen. I felt as though I had stopped in to have a conversation with an old friend.

While we were talking, the Texan came in with a wooden flute and said that he would like to play us an old Ojibwe tune, "Farewell to the Warriors." He knew where we were going. We had discussed it while touring the kitchen. His song was melodic and soothing. It was almost haunting. Although being an old Ojibwe tune, it was adopted by the War Department in World War I. When the Dough Boys departed for the future battlefields in France, the bands played "Farewell to the Warriors." My grandfather probably heard a much more martial version of the same song when he left Camp Jackson for "Over There."

Jeremy is also a piper. Not to be outdone by John, he took his bagpipes to the yard. In the cold clear May afternoon he marched slowly up and back in rhythm while he piped. The rasping notes of the pipes hung softly in the air.

"I enjoyed that. I love bagpipes," I said. The North West Company was owned by a group of Scots—McTavish, McGillevray, McLoughlin, Mackenzie, among the more notable partners—so a bagpiper being at Grand Portage that day added a wonderfully authentic touch.

Jeremy nodded that he appreciated my comment, adding, "I

hear that there is a bagpiper at Norway House. Would you carry him a letter? I don't know of any other way to find him."

"Sure. I'd be glad to." It seemed so little in payment for his piping. He later gave me his letter, written on parchment like paper, sealed with dark red wax, and addressed "Bagpiper of Norway House, by way of Canoe Carrier—from Jeremy Kingsbury, Piper N.W, co depot, Grand Portage, MN." I tucked it safely into the bottom of my dry bag. It would be a while before I would need it.

That night I took Erik's warning of frost to heart. I unrolled my liner; slid in, and then slid into by sleeping bag. I didn't lie there long before the next thing I heard was my alarm.

JAY WRITES:

Our tent was hard, cold, and rocky. I was glad that I had packed a small air mattress with me, as the temperature that night got down to the freezing point. Just a few yards to the east, North America's largest liquid icebox splashed against the shore. I slept in my clothes and fleece pullover to keep warm. The air mattress, called a Therm-A-Rest, proved its usefulness. It was three-quarters-length, supporting only my torso. My feet were chilled, but the mattress kept the rest of my body noticeably warmer. I thought it bulky, but found it heaven sent during other future cold trail nights.

CHAPTER III

THE GRAND PORTAGE

"I see de track of hees botte sau-vage
On many a hill an' long portage
Far far away from hees own vill-age
An' soun' of de parish bell—

"The Voyageur"
by William Henry Drummond

[27 MAY 2008–2 JUNE 2008]

FRED WRITES:

The night at Grand Portage was cold but there was no frost. I knew that our hike across Grand Portage would be a tough, dry trek. There is no potable water along the mostly uphill eight-and-a-half mile trail. We each carried two quart-sized Nalgene water bottles. In addition, we had seven liters of extra water in two dromedary bags. The day was cool. *Maybe it won't be as bad as I thought*, I mulled as we ate breakfast. Just before ten o'clock we started across. Each of us was carrying seventy-five to one hundred pounds in packs or canoes or both. My load was the equipment pack, stove gas and extra water.

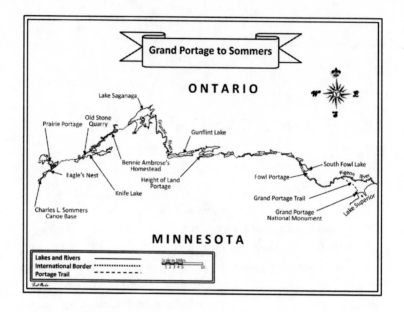

JAY WRITES:

Our hike was nine miles. The first leg was a half-mile hike to the Grand Portage entrance. Then we began our eight-and-one-half mile trek to the Pigeon River. In the background, bagpipes gave us an upbeat, musical send-off.

All of the crew were as heavily laden, if not more, than I was. We were all struggling, "feeling the burn," under the voyageur-sized packs. I took the second-heaviest pack, wanting to carry my share. They could have easily been filled with concrete. Those of us who carried in canoes sweated and ached under their unwieldy burden.

FRED WRITES:

Leaving, I could hear Jeremy back at the Great Hall piping "Lord Lovat's Lament." Even though it had a slower tempo, parts reminded me of "Garryowen," an old US Army, Seventh Cavalry tune. The tune seemed reminiscent of what the piping and fiddling must have sounded like wafting into the night air from the Great Hall during the annual summer balls. I don't know if the old voyageurs started trips with music playing, but it would have been a grand procession if the pipers piped. We each reveled in such a memorable send-off. We melted quickly into the boreal forest. As the bagpipe music faded away, we portaged back over 200 years in time.

Most of the way was shaded by the tall pines and leafy birches. The trees kept any breeze from stirring up the air. The cool day that I thought would be our friend was quickly erased by the still air. At first Grand Portage was just a gradual climb. In fact, most of the portage is only a gradual climb, but it is a seemingly unending ascent. I quickly began to tire. I think all of us did.

After about an hour—maybe less, I never looked at my watch—Clayton took on the responsibility of leading the group. He carried a Souris River canoe and small pack. Clayton walked for fifteen minutes and then paused. His fifteen-minute walk was probably one-half to three-quarters of a mile depending on the trail's incline. By lunchtime we crossed old Highway 61. Old Highway 61 is about four miles from the Great Hall. This left us only four and one-half miles to go. "Not bad for the first two hours," I thought. There, we stopped for lunch and a longer, much-needed break. Jay and I had crossed Grand Portage going east and downhill. The shared opinion was that it was exponentially harder going west.

Our peanut butter and jelly lunch ended all too soon. By now the sun had noticeably warmed the day. After lunch we grudgingly trekked on. Our full bellies noticeably slowed us down. It was still a tortuous uphill climb. The next landmark was the beaver dam. This meant that we still had a couple of miles to go, but also signaled that the trail's end was near. Finally, at about the seven-and-one-half mile point, was a brown stained sign with yellow letters, "Highest Point on Grand Portage." I don't know about the rest of the crew, but I breathed a sigh of relief knowing that the climb was over. Finally, we staggered to the end to our camp on the Pigeon River.

JAY WRITES:

At the last rest stop before arriving at the Pigeon River, I could see the river's water shimmer in the distance through the trees. "It seems high," I thought. "We won't be scraping the river bottom like we did on my first trip." To see the river at last was a rose amongst the trail's thorns of heavy packs, exertion, sweat, and exhaustion.

Four years earlier my crew and I took five and a half hours to cross Grand Portage. This trip took about eight hours. The deciding factors were that we had empty food packs and were hiking downhill. This trip we were fully loaded with fuel, food, and gear. Going west, we were climbing a tortuous, steady rise in the terrain. The first time across I was able to walk forty minutes before taking a rest stop. This time I found myself needing a break at least every twenty minutes or so.

Fred and I are now members of an elite group who have portaged this historic trail in both directions. It is an unofficial group. In fact, I don't think they know that they are a group. I can now say that I "did the Grand" both the "eastbound easy way," and the "grueling westbound way." Northern Tier trail staff, the Charlie Guides, speak of "doing the Grand." They always say, "The Grand," with admiration and awe, as it is one of the most challenging of all of the Boundary Waters Canoe Area trips.

FRED WRITES:

Every year over 200,000 people come to the Boundary Waters to canoe and fish. Of that number only 200 to 300 trek across Grand Portage. Among the Charlie Guides, to paddle to and cross it has always been ultimate test of canoeing skills. It is a classic and the definitive canoe trip.

At one time Fort Charlotte stood somewhere at Grand Portage's west end on the shores of the Pigeon River. Now heavily wooded, the area exhibits no visible trace of the old fort. In fact, there is no reliable record of what the fort actually looked like and how the buildings were arranged. But it was here every summer that voyageurs converged in their twenty-five-foot northern canoes laded with the previous winter's furs. It was here that they later reloaded with trade goods to be taken west to Rainy Lake. Up to 200 of these twenty-five-foot birch bark crafts, packed to the gunwales, paddled upriver to a place on the Canadian side called The Meadows, where they camped and staged for the trip west.

I walked down to the river. The last time I was there I had lain back in the sun on a flat rock on the river's shore. It occurred to me then that the rock was a good place to launch a canoe. It was a natural pier. This time the rock was under water a couple of feet or so. The river was high—extremely high—and swifter than I remembered.

Since all of the recipes were mine, I volunteered to cook. The curried lentils were at the top of the food pack. It is a hearty meal. I quickly decided that after a long hike it was exactly what we needed. I got the idea for curry back in 1985. I was attending a British Ministry of Defense school in Kent. Wednesdays in the officers' mess is always curry-for-lunch day. It dates back to when the British army was posted in India. My mess mate was Derrick. He commented, savoring the curry and reminiscing about his jungle survival training. "Curry is the neatest bit of kit," he said. "It makes anything from grubs to lizards to lamb taste good." So Derrick's neat bit of kit was the inspiration for my lentils.

As supper simmered and the aroma of curry filled the air, Clayton found the dried fruit. We all dug in. It was juicy. It was sweet. In short order, it was gone. About thirty minutes later supper was ready. Not long after being served it, too, was gone. We then finished off some banana pudding, washed the dishes, and settled in for the evening.

I guess that it was about nine o'clock when I got to bed. Crawling into my sleeping bag liner first, I then slid into the sleeping bag. The sun was down and temperature was dropping. I was sore from the hike, but felt good that we had finished. Tomorrow would be the Pigeon River. After Fowl Portage at the end of the river, the trip's—rather, expedition's—two hardest portages would be over.

I was glad Grand Portage was over. I hurt, but I wasn't as sore as I expected to be. In fact, except for being tired, I felt good. Like Grand Portage, Fowl Portage would be mostly uphill. In addition, Fowl Portage had numerous downed trees. Along the border trail some portages are on the American side and others are on the Canadian side. Fowl Portage is in Canada. Various treaties dating back to the 1842 Webster-Ashburton Treaty, The Treaty of Ghent, and the 1783 Treaty of Paris allow Canadians and Americans to freely use any border trail portage.

With only 200 to 300 people crossing Fowl Portage yearly, Canadian resources probably dictate a low priority for portage trail maintenance there. An American Forest Ranger told me in 2006 that they planned to try to obtain permission to clear it. As I lay there, I hoped that they had at least partially kept their promise. In 2006 it was not a portage as much as it was a bushwhack across. Trees blown down in storms littered the trail. In some places, the trail all but disappeared.

Morning again came too prematurely. It was chilly in the tent, but I still made myself get out of my sleeping bag, dress, pack, and crawl outside. I knew that if it was chilly inside, it would be even colder outside. It was. I dropped the bear bags from a large pine tree, woke the others, and put on coffee. The rest of the crew got up slowly. We ate and then packed. It took a while, but finally we were on the Pigeon River.

It was May twenty-eighth, our entry day for the Boundary Waters. This would be our first day to paddle.

JAY WRITES:

We paddled upstream on a flat, almost motionless stretch of the Pigeon River. Our first portage was Partridge Falls. It was nothing like the previous day. It was shorter but a steeper climb. Notwithstanding, we were across in short order. Everyone seemed to know what to do as we reloaded the canoes and headed upstream.

FRED WRITES:

Historically there were two additional portages on the river north of Partridge Falls: Big Rock and Caribou Portage. Both are gone today. With the demise of the fur trade and consequently the end of the voyageur canoe, the need to unload and portage around is gone. Smaller canoes can track, line, or shoot the rapids.

First were the rapids at Big Rock. The sun was still shining and the weather was warm. With high water there was no place to walk on or near the shore so we had to wade in the icy water.

Although mostly only knee-deep the swift current made me feel like I had fifty-pound weights wrapped around each ankle.

JAY WRITES:

Passing Big Rock Portage's approximate historic location, we occasionally waded in waist-deep water. While pulling a canoe upriver with a rope, Charles slipped on the slick algae-covered river rocks into the unpleasantly cold waters. He floated down river in the swift current. At the bottom of the rapids he somehow reached shore. Soaked and cold he casually walked back upstream.

At this same location, four years earlier, I had my most serious canoe mishap. It was early afternoon, just after lunch. Heading downriver, the water seemed low enough to be safe to paddle through the swift current. The first canoe made it through. The rest of us waited our turns. Next was my turn. I paddled about ten yards. We scraped bottom, so I slid out of the canoe to lighten the load. From behind me, I heard anxious voices in the third canoe saying, "Let's go! We can't allow them to get ahead," followed by their frantic instructions, "Turn! Turn!"

I twisted around in time to see the last canoe get pinned against a rock in the middle of the river. It struck with such force that one of the paddlers was thrown into the water. For an endless, slow-motion moment I watched helplessly as the canoe tilted and then began to fill with water. An empty canoe weighs seventy-five pounds. A canoe full of water caught in a current can weigh a ton. Our work was cut out for us. The current, even in that low water, was powerful enough to not only pin the canoe against the rock, but to also begin bending it around the rock.

Quickly we secured my canoe on the riverbank. I then slogged my way through the river and immediately began unloading the pinned canoe. All of us unsuccessfully pushed and rocked the canoe trying to dislodge it and avoid any further damage. We raised one end of the canoe to drain the water and hopefully relieve some of the stress. All the while, I could hear the canoe's ribs snapping, popping, and yielding to the Pigeon's power. I was convinced that I was going to have to piece back together that canoe from several jagged aluminum sheets. As we fought frantically to save the canoe, I could also see my future employment at Northern Tier fade before my eyes. I just knew that my tenure as a Charlie Guide would painfully skid to an abrupt end in the General Manager's Office.

After an endless twenty or thirty minutes, as one of the crew went for a rope, the rock lost its firm grip on the doomed canoe. It quietly floated downriver to the foot of the rapids where the first canoe was tied. It waited calmly while we gathered our scattered packs in disbelief and headed downstream.

The canoe had no leaks, but it was seriously bent. With brute force we punched the hull back into a workable shape. The thwarts, too, were bent. To add additional strength we wedged and tied in wooden cross pieces. Fortunately we were only a few miles from Grand Portage, and this would be our last full night on the trail. The afternoon's events deeply dissipated our happy feelings on reaching Grand Portage. Our trepidation of crossing Grand Portage the next day also weighed heavy. In the end the canoe was beyond repair, but I was forgiven.

FRED WRITES:

At Caribou Rapids, the next upstream obstacle, Karl and I tied a bear rope to our canoe thinking that it would be easier to track.[6] For twenty minutes it was. Then the current caught the bow and tipped the canoe toward us, partially filling it with water. As I shouted "No!" the current jerked the rope from Karl's hands. I held onto my end as the canoe dragged me into a deeper part of the river. Somehow, even with the water up to my armpits, I managed to dig in with my heels and keep the canoe from floating off. The equipment pack and Karl's map case floated downstream. Something floating by mid-river to my left caught my eye. It was Jim. The dark, coursing, murky water, made his dark complexion and black hair seemed to blend together. He hollered something as he passed. I shouted something in reply and pointed with my eyes and a nod to the equipment pack. Next Charles appeared, almost miraculously pausing briefly in the current. Like Jim, he too almost blended in with the river. "Where's Jimmy?" He shouted. "Is he okay?"

I nodded downstream and shouted, "Yeah!" By this time I had managed to get the canoe into shallower water and tie it to a small tree. Karl helped me unload the remaining packs. We turned the canoe over to dump the water out and reloaded the packs. Jim and Charles emerged through the bush more quickly than I expected with our equipment pack, but Karl's map case and rain jacket were gone. We quickly regrouped, walking the rest of the rapids. From there we paddled lazily to Fowl Portage.

---

6 Using a rope tied to the canoe you track upstream and line downstream.

JAY WRITES:

We were all exhausted, soaked, and sore by the time we reached mile-long Fowl Portage at six that evening. Hanging from a branch, faded and tattered red surveyors' tape marked the eastern end landing. The landing itself was narrow but grassy. This allowed us to unload two canoes at a time.

FRED WRITES:

At some point in our upstream paddle—I don't recall where—I had commented, maybe over lunch, that there were about fifty trees to climb over or crawl under throughout the entirety of Fowl Portage. It is the most challenging portage I have ever seen. A couple of the group thought that I was exaggerating. At the end they admitted that I had not inflated the number.

The maps say that Fowl Portage is 300 rods.[7] Having crossed twice, I thought both times that it seemed longer. It is not because of the dead trees littering the trail, it simply seems longer. I have even said, when asked, that it should be spelled "Foul Portage" instead "Fowl Portage."

I have always made it a personal goal to never put a canoe down on a portage once I start. It is simply more difficult to pick it back up than it is to continue on—even with aching shoulders. So it was with Fowl Portage. I hurt and I was tired, but I did not put the canoe down. Mainly I ached because of the rapids and high water on the Pigeon. I don't know how long it took—it was late—but looking down the hill and seeing the landing on

---

7 One rod equals sixteen and a half feet or five meters. There are 320 rods to a mile.

South Fowl Lake was a welcome sight. South Fowl is not a pretty lake. It is shallow. Algae and water grasses are prolific. But, after crossing the portage's obstacle course of trees, the lake looked absolutely inviting and beautiful that evening.

On the American side of Fowl Lake is a vacant campsite high on a rocky promontory. We took it. Knowing that we had weathered a hard day, I pulled out a chili with cornbread dumplings dinner.

JAY WRITES:

All of us had wet clothing from our Pigeon River trials. I was sunburned. Others were bruised or had strained muscles. We were on schedule, but on these first two days we had covered only sixteen grueling miles. The air cooled off quickly once the sun set. After a late supper we turned in about nine thirty.

FRED WRITES:

It was the twenty-ninth of May—day three. I was up early again. I have always been an early riser. I woke the rest of the crew and put on a pot of coffee. The sun was up. It remained sunny until after we portaged Long Portage into Rose Lake. Long Portage, although not hard, is long. For the most part it is flat, open, and well traveled, but it is two miles. Most of the other portage lengths are talked of in rods. Long and Grand Portage lengths are described in miles.

Coming to the portage's west end, into the lake, I heard a white-throated sparrow. Seldom seen, they perch high up, hidden in the leaves. You often hear their welcoming song signifying that the lake is near. I have always thought it appropriate, as it seems to mimic the melody of an old favorite spiritual, "Let's

Go Down to the River to Pray." The sparrow whistles, "Down to the river to pray." With that ever-present musical welcome I knew that we were almost at the portage's end.

JAY WRITES:

Part of Long Portage was at one time a branch of a narrow-gauge logging railroad line operated by the Northwest Paper Company. Completed between 1924 and 1925, it was part of a rail line that connected to the narrow-gauge Duluth and Northeastern Railroad, at Hornby, Minnesota. The rails were removed by 1940.[8]

I was the last one across the two-mile portage. I slogged through the mud and crushed gravel of the former railroad bed, while many of the others forged on ahead. I had to stop and rest. Israel came back, despite his own aches and pains from the first two days, and took the canoe from me for the last several hundred yards on the portage. The others had arrived ahead of me and had loaded the canoes with the exception of my canoe and pack.

The rain increased in intensity as we pulled into camp. This left us no choice but to hurriedly pitch the tents to keep them as dry as possible.

FRED WRITES:

Again I was cooking. The reward is that the cook always gets the most protected spot under the dining fly. I had brought a second

---

8 Richard Prosser, *Rails to the North Star* (Minneapolis: University of Minnesota Press, 2007), 90-91, 229. See also Hugh Bishop, *By Water and Rail: A History of Lake County Minnesota* (Duluth, MN: Lake County Historical Society, Lake Superior Port Cities Publishing, 2000), 106.

tarp as a spare. In this case it became an extra so the rest could stay dry. Periodically I left the safety of the tarp to get wet, but warm up by a roaring fire. Tonight was chicken and dumplings. It is not a hard dish, but it is peppery and filling. Jay took one bite and looked at me softly, uttering with a contented groan, "Thank you." The rest of us enjoyed it also, but Jay's comment was the most unforgettable and gratifying.

On and off through the night the rain fell. It was still raining when I got up at five thirty. As has always been my monotonous morning habit, I dressed, packed, and got out of the tent. My alarm also had a thermometer so I knew the temperature. It was forty-two degrees in the tent and noticeably colder outside. Israel got up next and made coffee that was heartedly welcome on such a cold, wet morning. After a breakfast of granola bars and fruit, we headed toward our day's goal, Gunflint Lake.

JAY WRITES:

On May thirty-first the weather remained overcast. We again got up later than I was used to. On bad weather mornings, canoeists must find the gumption and drive to get up and get going. Cloudy or overcast days can be depressing. I have personally found that to get through the day you have to make deliberate effort to be upbeat. We finally departed camp between eight thirty and nine in the morning.

Leaving camp late every now and then will happen. Sometimes you even need that extra hour of sleep. However, it was at this point that I became concerned that we might be getting into a bad habit of late departures. I thought, *If we fall into this routine at this point, it will be difficult if not impossible to break bad habits when we really need to launch early*. I thought of Lake Winnipeg in particular.

Our breakfasts were deliberately light, which translated into me feeling short of energy by the middle of the morning. Today our destination was Gunflint Lake.

FRED WRITES:

First we had to cross an historically unique portage from South Lake to North Lake. It is open and only one hundred rods. At both ends stand silver-painted conical border markers. But it is not the markers that make it a notable crossing. The French voyageurs, too, knew that they had crossed an important divide. They knew that they were leaving what, before the end of the French and Indian War in 1763, was called New France. This portage crossed an old unmarked border from New France into Rupert's Land. From here on west they were invaders in the Hudson Bay Company's domain. They called it *Portage du Hauteur des Terre*, and so we call it the same in English today— Height of Land Portage. Here is where you leave Lake Superior's drainage basin. On the north side of the portage all of the water eventually flows to Hudson Bay.

Crossing was always celebrated with the new voyageurs' baptisms. Each was made to kneel while old hands sprinkled them with water from a cedar bough. Once wetted, they had to promise, among other things, "to not kiss another voyageur's wife without her permission and to perform this ceremony on all new voyageurs." In honor of our predecessors, the three of us who had already crossed carried on the tradition. Jay, having been the first among us to have portaged *Portage Hauteur des Terre*, was given the honor of conducting the ceremony. It may seem rather puerile, but for those who paddle the border wilderness it is more of a sacrament. And tradition is important. In conclusion, as with the early voyageurs, the four were pronounced *hommes du nord*, "men of the north." In a neighboring tree the white-throated sparrow sang as it has sung for hundreds of years, "Down to the river to pray."

After crossing, the old voyageurs, the new men of the north, were then allowed to paint their paddle tips red or place a feather in their toques. In the culture of the Charlie Guides, we, too, paint our paddle tips red as a silent boast of our journeys.

Following the ceremony we paddled on. Customarily, the voyageurs fired several volleys and then goaded a clerk or other important traveler into opening their private cask of spirits for a celebration. Our celebration was to paddle in a cold mist and wind to Gunflint Lake in search of a campsite.

We approached Gunflint with some anxiety. In 2006 there had been a huge forest fire around the lake. In fact, in 2006 I had gone through just ahead of the fire, paddling east to Grand Portage. Canadian and American fire-fighting aircraft landed on Saganaga Lake to fill up with water. We were close enough in our canoes to recognize and wave to the pilots as they set down to take on more water.

That fire left us unsure of present campsite availability. We hoped that one of the island sites had survived the fire. One had and was vacant. A primitive table sat in the center surrounded by excellent spots for our tents. After supper we settled in for the night.

JAY WRITES:

Gunflint Lake was calm when we arrived. The campsite we stayed at was well used, but okay for a lake with motorboat traffic.

The west end of Gunflint Lake is not in the Boundary Waters and thus has private summer homes. Several are quite fancy.

One is a Swiss chalet. Instead of sitting on a mountainside, it occupies an entire island. The yard is carefully trimmed. The boathouse and chalet are both neatly painted. Although it is a beautiful home, it does seem out of place after canoeing through the backwoods. Its prim, colorful appearance stood in stark contrast to the previous year's forest-fire-charred trees surrounding the lake.

FRED WRITES:

The next morning we headed across Gunflint. It was windy, cold, and overcast. The clouds hung low in the sky. Waves were manageable, but even while wearing two fleeces and a rain jacket I was chilled. By lunch time we had crossed Gunflint and had partially paddled down the Granite River. Below Little Rock Falls, at the end of our day's first portage, we ate lunch.

JAY WRITES:

We paddled through the Granite River, which was also recovering from the Gunflint Lake forest fire. The sun broke through around Maraboeuf Lake. Maraboeuf is a name that is yet another reminder that this area was once part of New France. From Old French, its translation means "caribou."

FRED WRITES:

The 2006 fire's effects on the river were stark. With a monotonous, colorless sky, everything was a bleak gray or a desolate black shadow. Campsites were gone or closed. Portage trails crossed barren, fire-blistered necks of land. The dark water held no reflections. We turned south around Devil's Elbow and then headed back north. High above on a partially burned, lifeless, leaf-barren tree, a bald eagle watched with idle curiosity as we paddled by.

The last portage of the day would be Saganaga Falls just south of the Granite River's mouth. It is not difficult, but the last few rods wind arduously around, under, and over a narrow, tree-enclosed stretch covered with slippery logs. Carrying the canoe and a guide pack was at least mildly dicey. To cross you have to balance on logs while inching across, maneuvering the canoe under and around low-hanging white cedars. I kept focusing on getting across and finally was able to ease the canoe into the fast-moving water.

Now it was only a short paddle into Saganaga Lake where we had to find a camp. In the Boundary Waters Canoe Area, all of the campsites are designated and marked. On Saganaga the Park Service allows motorboats. This crowds the lake. In a busy week, campers traveling in motorboat can sometimes occupy available campsites by midafternoon. Since it was after six, all of us were anxious about finding a campsite. We knew it would be late when we started down the Granite River, but we also knew that we had to keep on schedule. Anyway, the earlier fire limited camping on the river. Our uneasiness quickly faded when we found a pleasant site just north of the Granite's mouth.

JAY WRITES:

From Saganaga an alternate route west exists in Quetico Provincial Park through Kawnipi Lake to Sturgeon Lake and the Maligne River. Senior North West Company clerks and administrators followed it to and from Grand Portage each summer. This gave them several days of peaceful travel unencumbered by the bawdy fur brigades.[9] Having to resupply at Sommers Canoe Base precluded us from using this course. We had always planned on staying on the border anyway.

FRED WRITES:

Canoeing Saganaga the next day was almost effortless. The day was pleasantly calm, so we glided gracefully across the water. Leaving Saganaga we paddled through a stream consisting of a series of wide lake-like areas and meandering narrows. Usually there is a short portage into Swamp Lake, but with the high water we were able to easily paddle through. At a Canadian campsite on Swamp Lake we ate lunch. Last fall's leaves and pine needles covered the ground. Underneath this mat, swarms of gnats and mosquitoes waited to be disturbed so they could find a blood feast. We ate quickly and then paddled to Monument Portage, which leads to Ottertrack Lake.

Ottertrack is where Benny Ambrose had his homestead. Benny was a trapper, prospector, and sometimes-guide. Not much is written about Benny. Some of the area old-timers may have stories about him. After a stint in the Army in World War I, Benny came to the border country. He first settled on McFarland Lake in 1919, moving to Ottertrack Lake in 1927. Some say that he resettled to Ottertrack because of rumors that Blackstone, a Lac La Croix Ojibwe chief of the late 1800s, had hidden his gold nearby. Benny never found the gold, or if he did he never let on, but he raised his family there and at one time had a cozy home-stead. Today, all that is left are stonework foundations, walls, paths, bits of metal, a landing, and a Forest Service sign inviting

---

9 I have not been able to locate a source for this information, but remember running across it in some of my reading.

visitors to stop and enjoy but not camp. In July the summer flowers, not originally wild, bloom profusely in the Ambrose's bygone garden. Benny died in 1982.[10] Across the lake, friends placed a plaque on the cliff-face in his memory. Any place else the view from his homestead looking southwest down the lake is a million dollar view, but, in the Boundary Waters, it is free for those willing to make the trek.

Paddling up to Benny's place, Jay asked where exactly the homestead was located. His query surprised me because Jay had guided in Quetico and the Boundary Waters for eleven years. I always thought that he knew all the points of interest. I pointed to the rocky point of land where Benny lived. His landing still sits in a shallow cove below. Later, Jay commented as an after-thought that there were other commemorative plaques, but that they were back in the woods. I made a mental note to ask him, the next time the two of us had time, where they were.

As we left Benny's place, two thunderstorms raged close behind us to the north. The wind remained calm until we got to the south end of Little Knife Lake. There we passed through rocky narrows into Knife Lake. Given that the wind was picking up, we stopped at a sheltered camp just east of Thunder Point. From there we were only eighteen miles and several easy por-tages from Sommers.

JAY WRITES:

It remained cloudy until we reached the west end of Ottertrack Lake. As we pulled into camp at Thunder Point on Knife Lake,

---

10 Shirley Peruniak, *Quetico Provincial Park: An Illustrated History* (Insert Location: Friends of Quetico Park, 2000).

the sun came out. It felt good to be warm, but the sun did irritate my Pigeon River sunburn.

This was the first night that we could enjoy sitting down and talking. It felt good to exchange canoeing stories, talk about some of our past crews, and enjoy a fire before needing to start the camp chores. We had divided up into pairs, meaning that each pair would take turns cooking, cleaning, or getting the evening's water.

Once the sun set, the temperatures dropped again. It would be a cold night. As I fell asleep I thought with great satisfaction, "We averaged twenty miles a day, so we covered one hundred twenty miles in six days."

FRED WRITES:

Knife Lake is mostly known as the lake where Dorothy Molter, the Root Beer Lady, lived. I have known of Dorothy since my first trip, back in 1962. Dorothy was a registered nurse, but forsook civilization to live in the Boundary Waters. Originally she helped run a fishing camp. Her home was eventually bought up under eminent domain by the U.S. Park Service. Dorothy still stayed. In fact, public support forced the Park Service to find a way to allow her to stay. The federal government made her a U.S. Forest Service volunteer. She also had friends and supporters in the Forest Service. This appointment satisfied the federal bureaucracy.

Dorothy made money selling homemade root beer. Actually, she gave the beverage away to paddlers for a nominal donation. She died at her place on Isle of the Pines in 1986. She was seventy-nine and the last person to live in the Boundary Waters.

My main interest in the lake was piqued by Bob Cary. Bob

was a local legend. He served in the Marine Corps in the Pacific in World War II. Then, after a career in the newspaper business in Illinois, he moved to Ely in the mid-1960s, opening an outfitting business. Among his numerous endeavors he wrote, painted, fished, and at one time ran for the presidency under the Bass Party ticket. A great supporter of scouting, Bob came to Sommers every summer to talk and tell stories to the staff as part of their training. The first summer that I was on staff he talked about Knife Lake. Being a curious man, Bob asked where lakes' names came from. His answer for Knife Lake came from the Ojibwe. According to Bob, the white man just didn't know.

On the portage from Knife Lake to Crawford Lake there is an old quarry where the Indians used to get the stone for their arrowheads, knives, and tools. The rock is a gray chert-like material. Chert resembles flint, but has a tighter grain. It consists essentially of a large amount of fibrous chalcedony with smaller amounts of cryptocrystalline quartz and amorphous silica. I know these esoteric facts from looking chert up in *Webster's*—not from any passing knowledge of geology. I have had people tell me that it had to be obsidian, but once they actually see it they come to the same opinion as me.

For years, especially prior to being contacted by the French, the Ojibwe went to Knife Lake to quarry the stone. Based on changes in the shapes of arrowheads and spearheads, archeologists know that somebody has quarried there for about 3,500 years. In campsites around the lake, you find chips that represent thousands of years of knapping. The Ojibwe have always called it Knife Lake—*Mookomaani-zaaga 'igan*.[11] The French voyageurs knew why they called it Knife Lake. In fact, the French called it *Lac des Couteaux*—"Knife Lake." Major Joseph Delafield even

---

11 All Ojibwe translations come from the *Freelang Dictionary*.

referred to it as Knife Stone Lake in his journal when he surveyed the border for the United States in 1823. At one time
the white man knew where the name came from. Institutional
knowledge does get lost.

Before the Ojibwe, the Dakota Indians made their weapons
and tools from the same stone and almost certainly called it
Knife Lake. Even before the Dakotas, the Laurel Indians made
their tools and weapons in the same place. We don't know their
language, but I bet that they, too, called it Knife Lake. So it
stands to reason that Knife Lake may be one of the oldest con-
tinuously used place names in North America. I would at least
like to think so.

The lake's quarries began to decline in use beginning in
the mid-seventeenth century. This was a result of the Indians'
access to iron tools. At that time the Ojibwe's main settlement
was La Pointe in the Apostle Islands off the coast of Wis-
consin. In a dream, one of their religious leaders proclaimed
that he had seen a white spirit and that he would find him.
He paddled east until he came to a cabin with smoke coming
from the chimney. When it came time for him to return, the
white spirits—the French—gave him an ax, a knife, beads, and
a scarlet cloth. They must have known that red was a sacred
color. That Indian was Ma-se-wa-pe-ga—"Whole Rib." The next
spring he returned with a number of Ojibwe. They took furs to
trade and returned with more steel and iron implements. They
also returned with guns. Ma-se-wa-pe-ga's first trip and these
subsequent trips caused the Ojibwe to vault dramatically from
the Stone Age to the Iron Age.[12]

---

12 William H. Warren, *History of the Ojibwe People* (Minnesota Historical
Society Press, 1984).

JAY WRITES:

All of the lakes, rivers, and portages along our route are centuries-old fur trade and Indian routes. As such, many names are old. Fowl Lake was simply translated from the French word *outard*. Watap Portage is from an Ojibwe word meaning "spruce root." (The Ojibwes lash the wood and sew the birchbark in their canoes together with the "watap.") Gunflint Lake in French was originally *Lac des Pierres à Fusil*. *Saganaga* is an old Ojibwe name that translates into "Lake with Many Islands."[13] Ottertrack came from the Ojibwe name, *Nigig-bimikawed-zaaga'lgan*—meaning "Ottertrack Lake."

And Knife Lake—be careful walking around camp on Knife Lake. There are numerous blade-like, sharp rock outcroppings.

FRED WRITES:

The last day on the trail to Sommers for our first resupply was beautiful. The sun warmed us. We made good time to Birch Lake where we had lunch. Because the water was high, we were able to shoot some of the rapids along the way. I had reservations since I always had portaged around, but Karl had whitewater experience so I decided that it was time to learn. As we went through our last rapids, a group was portaging upstream. We shot out like an arrow past them. Not expecting us, their jaws dropped as we almost scraped a rock and then casually paddled on.

---

13 Alexander Mackenzie, *Journals of Alexander Mackenzie: Voyages from Montreal. On the River Saint Lawrence, Through the Continent of North America, to the Frozen and Pacific Oceans: in the years 1789 & 1793, with a Preliminary Account of the Rise, Progress, & Present State of the Fur Trade of That Country* (Santa Barbara: The Narrative Press, 2001), 47.

After lunch we portaged into Sucker Lake. It was only a few rods. From there we headed the last six miles toward Sommers.

The eagles on Sucker had nested again. The only year they did not nest was in 2004. This year there were two eaglets. The adults perched nearby in separate trees. Nonchalantly, they quietly watched us as we passed. When I guide at Sommers, I paddle past this nest at least ten or twelve times each summer going to and coming from Prairie Portage, so I get to watch the young grow and eventually fledge. Eagles mate for life, using the same nest each year, so these two adults were old friends.

Less than one-half mile west of Sucker Lake nest is another nest on the eastern end of Horseshoe Island. It is hard to see, but if you know where it is, there is one vantage point. I headed to that spot. Again, there were a couple of young.

When I came to Quetico as a teenager, eagles were endangered. As part of our support to help an endangered species, we counted eagles and recorded where we saw them. I am not sure how it helped. I don't even remember how many we saw. Now, it is nice to know that these absolutely majestic birds have recovered. Each summer brings memorable encounters. On a previous trip on Crooked Lake, in 2002, an eagle swooped down and glided past about six yards off to my right. He was watching and I had this feeling that our eyes met.

JAY WRITES:

We had clear weather paddling into Sommers. Numerous times in the past, at the end of a trip, winds whipped violently up the lake. We struggled into the headwinds. I was always relieved to reach base. Today's weather allowed us to casually paddle the last seventeen miles to Sommers Canoe Base before early afternoon.

FRED WRITES:

About an hour past the eagles' nest we turned south around a point of land just east of Scout Island. Ahead lay the Sommers landing. The Bay Post and the Base Commissary nested in the trees high up the hill. On the lake were several aluminum canoes. My thought was that these were some first-year staff getting some extra practice on the water. They were. Helping them was an old friend, Jonathan Dyess. In fact, I had trained him. Jonathan was getting his master's degree in geology. After skipping a season he had come back for a third summer. It was good to see him again. He is a good man on the trail.

JAY WRITES:

The canoe landing felt like a homecoming of sorts. I worked there for ten summers. It brought back pleasant memories of leaving wakes down the length of Moose Lake both arriving and departing. I had guided several hundred scouts during my tenure. I have also known hundreds of staff members. Many are still friends today. There was always a welcome feeling at the end of each trip and the anticipation of the next adventure.

As I passed Twin Islands, Scout Island loomed closer. My first crew was from Dallas, Texas. I have lost track of them. In my mind, I flipped back to my earlier Grand Portage trip. At that time it was considered to be reserved for Charlie Guides for an end-of-season trip. Here I was finishing that same trip again. But, this time it was not a trip. It was only the first leg of a quest.

FRED WRITES:

We left the canoes in a grassy area near the landing and headed up the hill to find Angela. She assigned us a cabin where we dropped and sorted our gear and then headed to the sauna to get cleaned up.

—CHAPTER IV—

OFF THE TRAIL

Twas a balmy summer evening, and a goodly crowd
was there.

"The Face on the Barroom Floor"
by Hugh Antoine D'Arcy

[2 JUNE 2008-4 JUNE 2008]

FRED WRITES:

I always have mixed emotions coming off the trail. There is obviously the satisfaction of completing a trip. Getting a hot shower, warming up in a sauna, shaving, and putting on clean clothes gives me a very human feeling. But, by the time I open the aftershave and look into a mirror to comb my hair, I begin to long for the trail again.

At the Bay Post we separated our garbage and took it to the dumpster. We then headed for our cabin. It was still early in the season so there were no crews on base. The staff was going through the mandatory training in preparation for pre-season

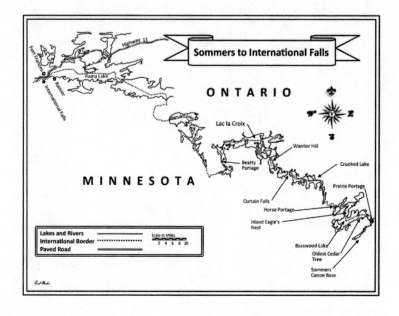

crews and a training trip—a swamper trip for the first-year trail staff.

Years ago, first-year trail staff in training were called swampers. The name "swamper" comes from the North Woods lumber-jacks. In a lumber camp the men lowest in the camp hierarchy were the swampers. They were the entry-level ax men, there to learn a trade and tackle numerous menial tasks. At Sommers Canoe Base, our swampers worked for free and had to cheer-fully endure a similar initiation period. At some point they were deemed ready for the trail and went out on a training trip with an experienced guide. If they passed, they became a Charlie Guide. Today the only part of the tradition that remains is the training and the name, swamper.

After claiming a bunk I headed for the sauna building. The hot water in the shower felt good. There were times on this first leg of our trip that I just could not get warm, so the drumming of hot shower spray on my aching back was something that I was looking forward to.

JAY WRITES:

When we were on the Pigeon River and Fred's canoe was partially swamped, the satellite phone got wet. This in turn damaged some of the phone's circuitry. Charles and I called the satellite phone rental company to inquire what to do next. Although very helpful, they told us that if it was not repairable, we would to have to pay for its replacement. We were going to have one rather expensive strike against us very early in the trip. The phone was a necessity so I arranged to send the bad one back and have them send a replacement to Sommers. A week later and one hundred sixty miles farther along, somebody would bring it to us at International Falls, our next layover and resupply stop.

FRED WRITES:

After cleaning up, we headed into Ely to the Ely Steak House to celebrate. We had talked about a steak dinner, but I opted for a hamburger. They call it the Bucky Burger. They serve it on a platter, not a plate. It is one-half pound of juicy ground round on a huge bun topped with mushrooms, several types of cheese, onions, bacon, lettuce, and tomato. It comes with homemade fries and coleslaw. I always add a side of jalapeños and extra mayonnaise. The mayonnaise is something that I gained a taste for in Berlin. Instead of catsup, I love mayonnaise with my French fries.

The Bucky Burger is my personal reward at least two or three times a summer. Their Kick Butt steak would be my reward after returning from Hudson Bay.

The Ely Steak House is a friendly place. Even though most of the customers are tourists, not locals, it still seems as if they are all more than just casual acquaintances. The ambience is warm, with walls covered with wood and primitive wooden stools shoved up against the bar. The ceiling is held up with rugged, barkless tree trunks. The corners have large-screen televisions, each showing a different sporting event. Every few minutes the bell in the kitchen service window rings, breaking any lull and alerting the server to pick up an order.

It was a Bucky Burger happy meal. We had already accomplished what few achieve. Jay and I had done it twice. The server asked if we were coming in or going out. That is the standard question from any local. Of course, we answered, "Both," bragging of what lay ahead. She acted politely interested.

JAY WRITES:

I could taste my porterhouse from just reading the menu. It was as mouthwatering as I anticipated. On the side were mushrooms sautéed in butter and a hot, tender baked potato stuffed with sour cream, cheese, and chives. The steak steamed and sizzled on my plate. It was just what the doctor ordered after completion of our trip's Grand Portage first segment. A few cold, bubbling beers hit the spot, too.

FRED WRITES:

The next morning I got up early and headed for Sommers' dining hall. It is one of those comfortable buildings crammed full of scouting memorabilia from people and crews who have visited the base. Above the windows running the length and breadth of the dining room is a shelf neatly lined with scout council coffee cups from all over the United States. On one of the back walls are cases filled with Order of the Arrow[14] patches. Between the windows are framed prints of the old French voyageurs.

I grabbed a cup of coffee and a comfortable seat. About halfway through my coffee, Dick Shank walked in. Dick is an internist in Minneapolis. I first met him in 2002. He is a great friend of Sommers Canoe Base. He helps every year for a couple of weeks with staff training. I always look forward to seeing him. We always have a pleasant conversation. I asked facetiously, "Are you sure you don't want to go?"

Dick very seriously affirmed, "I do want to go!" I have never been on the trail with him, but he is known to be very serious about canoeing. His personal canoe is a forest green wood and canvas, the classic of the North Woods. It is the only canoe for the serious paddler. There is nothing better on the water.

About that time Charles and Israel came in and joined us. Breakfast was ready so we got in line, ate quickly, and headed for Grand Portage in Israel's car. It was a quiet drive. Charles crawled into the back seat and slept most of the way. We stopped a couple of times along the way for coffee and arrived at Grand Portage just before lunch. We got our vehicles and headed up the hill.

There is a new heritage center across the road from the stockade. For lack of time we had not seen it a week earlier. We took a short tour. I wanted to see the new exhibits. Upstairs was the completed birch bark canoe Erik was building when I first met him. I also wanted to sign the visitors' register for having portaged across Grand Portage and obtain the seven slips of paper with the National Parks seal that state, "Crossed Grand

---

14 Order of the Arrow is the national honor society of scouting.

Portage on (fill in the date)." They were out, but gave me seven voyageur contracts that I passed around when we returned. I also asked about Jeremy, the bag piper, and Erik. They were both off, so I left my card with a note.

The drive back was uneventful. Again, I hoped to see some wild life. I didn't. The next day would be busy. I had clothes to wash and some trip logistics to resolve. The only way to make sure there is enough time is to start early.

After breakfast we took our food for the leg from International Falls to Pine Falls to the commissary. I then found Angela to show her what food was ours. In the commissary everything is packed in green packs. Ours were no different so we tagged them to eliminate confusion.

I later found Jim Richards. He was glad to take the last of our food to Bissett and bring it to us at Pine Falls. After thinking about it, I decided that with no portages on Lake Winnipeg, we would be better off picking up all of our food in Pine Falls. The rest of the crew agreed. Future events proved it to be a good decision. We would load it on Jim's trailer first thing in the morning. Minnesota has numerous black bears. If you don't want to share your food with them, don't leave it outside overnight!

The rest of the day was relaxing. I checked my e-mail, called home, and had a leisurely supper. I also checked the long-term weather forecast. Rain was in our future.

CHAPTER V

FOUR PIPE LAKE

Ax heem de nort' win' w'at he see
Of de Voyageur long ago,
An' he'll say to you w'at he say to me,
So lissen hees story well—

"The Voyageur"
by William Henry Drummond

[5 JUNE 2008–9 JUNE 2008]

FRED WRITES:

The sun comes up early in the North Woods. It woke me before
my alarm went off. I immediately packed my personal gear. Then
I woke the others. We all met at the dining hall for breakfast.
After eating I got my truck and met Charles at the First-aid
Cabin where we loaded the remaining supplies that Jim Richards was taking to Bissett. In the parking lot we tucked it neatly
in Jim's trailer underneath the canoes to keep it dry. Rain was
predicted. I found Jim to give him the packing list for Canadian
Customs and to tell him where our food was packed.

We all wanted to get on the water. Training trips—with the
swampers—were starting this morning along with a couple of

pre-season trips. The landing would be congested and we wanted to stay out of their way. Besides, we knew that we would probably overtake them on the way to Prairie Portage.

By nine thirty we were on the water, which wasn't bad with all that had to be done. Prairie Portage was only six miles off. For us, that was at most a ninety-minute paddle.

It was a typically cool June morning with negligible wind and a clear sky. We glided through the narrows from Moose Lake into Newfoundland Lake. We regrouped and paddled past Horseshoe Island and the eagles' nest on Sucker Lake. My old friends perched near their nest watching our canoes skim across the water toward the northeast. The route to Prairie Portage was empty except for a couple of Sommers groups. I think that all of us felt relieved to be back on the water.

At Prairie Portage we crossed to Inlet Bay and reloaded the canoes. Since there was no line of people at the Canadian ranger cabin waiting their turn for Quetico permits, I headed that way. Over the years I had gotten to know many of the park rangers and wanted to say hello.

Kathy was on duty. She has always been a very pleasant woman. Often she simply tells my crews, "Fred knows what the rules are, so just listen to him." It was nice to see her again. I told her of our plans. She physically winced with envy. In fact, she said as much. About that time the rest of the crew came in. Not knowing who she did or did not know, I introduced them. She wished us luck and watched as we paddled to the narrows leading to the main part of Basswood Lake.

Basswood is one of the larger border lakes. The voyageurs called it *Lac Bois Blanc* or Four Pipe Lake. The first name comes from all of the white cedars that line the shores. The other name comes from the voyageurs' habit of stopping every fifty minutes or so for a smoke break. It took four pipes of tobacco to cross. The Ojibwe called it Dried Berry Lake—*Baase-miinan-ni-kok-zaaga-igan*—because every year they would go to United States Point to pick and dry blueberries for winter. Nobody knows where the Basswood name came from, as there is no basswood anywhere around. Longfellow writes of basswood bowls at Hiawatha and Minneha'ha's[15] wedding feast. I don't know where old Noko'mis[16] got the wood, but it didn't come from this lake. My feeling is that Basswood is somehow derived from the Indian name.

Basswood was unusually calm on this day with only a light wind blowing. It remained the same for the rest of the day. So often after lunch, the wind picks up and the lake becomes treacherous. So far we were fortunate.

We stopped on Beaver Island for a fresh sandwich, trail mix, and fruit lunch. It was chilly, fifty degrees. Clayton had a thermometer on his watch and would periodically announce the temperature to the rest of us. A quite tenacious red squirrel kept sneaking up searching for a meal of dropped trail mix. He, too, ate well.

A couple of hundred yards south of Beaver Island is the oldest white cedar tree in Minnesota—1,100 years old. I usually stop when I pass by. It is an interesting sight. The tree is not any taller that the rest of the trees encircling it. In fact, you don't see it until you are about twenty or thirty yards away. It is gnarled. It is twisted. Its fourteen foot girth is impressive. This summer, however, I would miss it. We needed to get to Basswood Falls and take advantage of the calm water.

---

15 A Dakota woman who became Hiawatha's wife.

16 Hiawatha's grandmother.

JAY WRITES:

Paddling across Basswood was like shaking hands with an old friend. This historic lake served as the starting and ending point for over two dozen of my trips into the backcountry. This was a lake that tested a crew's skills with wind and waves. As we passed some of my favorite campsites I almost expected past years' staff to appear over the horizon and shout the camp greeting, "Hol-ry!"[17]

Being a large and long lake, Basswood is susceptible to strong wind and large waves. Rounding United States Point I expected the wind to increase and chap my face. It usually does, but today my friend remained calm.

FRED WRITES:

After lunch we headed for our goal for the day, Horse Portage. Basswood is a Z-shaped lake. From Prairie Portage you paddle southwest about six miles. Then you turn due north for five miles. That takes you to United States Point. On the way, in the middle of the channel a couple of miles south of United States Point, there is another eagles' nest. It is a rather classic-looking symmetrical nest overlooking the lake. No young were visible, but there was one adult perched on the nest. This early in the year the young were probably snuggled deep in the nest out of the wind The other adult was certainly nearby. At United States Point you turn southwest toward a bay that leads to Horse Portage.

We rounded the point and headed for the bay across the lake

---

17 Hol-ry comes from the name of a rye cracker that was used for years by Sommers Canoe Base for peanut butter and jelly lunches. The staff adopted it as a hail to distant canoeists so scout crews could recognize each other. The comeback, Red Eye, sprang from a nickname of a red fruit punch flavored Kool Aid.

where we found a comfortable camp near the Horse Portage landing. Supper was fajita stew. It is the traditional first-night meal for Sommers crews. It is filling and it is rich with flavor. The heavy Mexican spice aromas usually permeate the camp with an enticingly warm supper promise. I often fix it at home. It started when my wife asked what we ate on the trail. I made it that night for supper. Jean said, "This is a keeper." Fajita stew would be our last fresh trail meal for a great while.

For some reason I had been sleepy all day. It could have been the cold air. So, when all the camp chores were done, I was glad to be able to get in my tent and stretch out. It rained hard all night. Strong winds blew. Karl got up to check the canoes. They were alright, but to make sure he tied them down. When I woke in the morning it was still raining and the wind was blowing. I packed and then woke Charles. On the trail, no matter what, you have to get ready to go. Often the weather will break as fast as it comes in. Finally, the rain and wind let up enough for us to get on the water. We headed the short distance to Horse Portage. Floating in the water near the portage was a bloated moose carcass.

Horse Portage is a little over 320 rods long—a mile. It winds around Upper Basswood Falls. For the most part it is well traveled. All of us had crossed it numerous times, so we saddled up with our packs and canoes and headed across. About thirty minutes later we dropped our canoes into the Basswood River and paddled downriver to Wheelbarrow Falls.

There are two portages around Wheelbarrow Falls. Canoeing west, the first is called Wheelbarrow Portage. The second one is unnamed. Neither is particularly difficult. The difference is where you come out. The first trail ends between two falls. The second comes out downriver below both falls.

The water was extremely high, so we opted to portage below both of the falls. Taking the first portage even with lower water levels can be tricky. Water rushing in from two directions creates dangerous eddies. I have seen people paddling through it with disregard for the power of the water, or simple lack of knowledge that it is dodgy. In the blink of an eye, as if an invisible hand magically twisted their canoe 180 degrees, they are in the river struggling to get their canoe to shore. Any bad decision could ruin our trip. None of us wanted that to happen. We crossed in fine shape and headed for Lower Basswood Falls. After portaging into Crooked Lake, we stopped for lunch at a campsite just north of the Lower Falls. It was a wonderful view with the roar of the water, but it was still chilly and the wind was still blowing. The sky was still a cold gray.

Over peanut butter and jelly and trail mix, Charles and I checked the maps to identify a campsite on Crooked Lake. I pointed out a couple of campsites several miles down the lake. I had been to both and knew them to be large enough to hold the seven of us. It would also put us reasonably close to Curtain Falls. Jay and I had both portaged Curtain Falls, however, this would be new territory for the rest.

On cliffs spotted throughout the rivers and lakes from Lake Superior to Manitoba are Ojibwe pictographs. Over the years many have faded from the weather. It is hard to date the drawings, but the consensus is that they are between 300 to 500 years old. All are red, a sacred color to the Indians. Some Ojibwe say that all of the Quetico and Boundary Water pictographs were painted by a powerful medicine man named Aamoo-Bee. The Ojibwe believe that the pictographs draw strength from the power of the rocks. They are sacred to the Indians, but many of their meanings have been lost.

In 1955, two Canadian college acquaintances, Selwyn

Dewdney and Kenneth Kidd, laid the foundations to locate and record the Quetico pictographs. Kidd was a curator in the Royal Ontario Museum. Dewdney, at the time, was a book illustrator. Together with the help of the Quetico Foundation they began their research. Before these two began, we knew where some pictographs were. Many others were just waiting to be found.

In 1957, Dewdney set out to find the rest of the pictographs in Quetico. Over the years he expanded his search west and north into Manitoba, east into Lake Superior and south into parts of Minnesota. He asked questions. The Ojibwe were excellent sources for locations. Trappers, fishermen, rangers, or anybody else who had occasion to travel through Quetico were all questioned. He checked maps and flew over lakes to find likely sites. Once he had done his research he paddled through Quetico with his son to locate and copy the primitive artwork. Dewdney and Kidd published their first findings in 1962. It was updated in 1967.

The drawings are important to me because, although sketchy, they are a primitive pictorial record of Ojibwe events. The Ojibwe scratched pictographs as mnemonics. In addition to drawing on the rock cliffs, they drew on birch bark. This helped them, among other things, to remember religious incantations or the story of an important event. Most likely, these primitive cliff drawings fall between a story-telling aid and a pictorial commemoration of a long-forgotten event.

Traveling west along the border from Grand Portage, the first pictographs a paddler finds are on Crooked Lake. Many know the place as Picture Rock. Among other drawings on the Crooked Lake cliff is a pelican, a moose smoking a calumet, and a large canoe with a tall pole in the stern. First guess might be that it is a *canot du nord* with the North West Company flag flying, or maybe a canoe with French explorers. But, because it was likely painted prior to the advent of the voyageur and certainly prior to the formation of the North West Company,[18] I think it is not. Jay said that he thought that it was a banner that signified that an important medicine woman was on board. He might be right. I interpret it as a war canoe returning from a fight with the Dakotas. What looks like a banner is a scalp pole with enemy scalps. If the pictograph is a true image of native history, there are four scalps and eight victorious Ojibwe warriors.

The pictographs and cliffs are and have been landmarks for hundreds of years. Alexander Mackenzie and others commented on these cliffs in their journals. Prior to the western incursion, the Dakotas shot arrows into the rocks' cracks to frighten their enemies. The Ojibwe continued this practice replacing Dakota arrows with their own arrows. It is a must-stop spot every time I pass. The arrow shafts are all gone, but I suspect that if you could climb the cliff and look closer, the stone arrowheads from the quarry on Knife Lake are still wedged tightly in the cracks.

Crooked Lake, as its name would indicate, twists and winds north, with vast bays creating its western border. Each bay is named for a day of the week. The story is that if you get lost on Crooked Lake, it will take a week to find your way out.

We easily reached our first-choice campsite only to find it full. The alternate was a mile or so across the bay. Just then the wind picked up, creating significant whitecaps. It was obvious that crossing Thursday Bay would not be advisable. In fact, I don't think that we could have safely crossed. The wind was as

---

18 *Indian Rock Paintings of the Great Lakes* [Hardcover] Selwyn Dewdney and Kenneth Kidd, University of Toronto Press, 1962.

strong as I have ever seen it. The breakers were at least a couple of feet. Fortunately, there was a camp on the Canadian side of the narrows. We found a protected landing and paddled over. Even though we had no permits, we had no other choice. It was getting late and we had to set up.

JAY WRITES:

Out on Crooked Lake the wind was blowing so abnormally strong from the southwest that any further attempt to continue westbound would have been futile. It looked as though a front had blasted through and the sky was still roiling from the storm.

The wind continued unabated into the evening. It was strong enough that in order to cook we had to erect some makeshift windscreens from some of our dining flies.

FRED WRITES:

After unloading, getting water for supper, and securing the canoes, we managed to get the tents up. The wind kept trying to blow away my and Jay's tent. The stakes simply would not hold it, so we had to anchor it with some large stones in each corner and then get our gear in to add some extra weight. The wind continued to blow, causing the rain-fly to billow like a taut spinnaker. But, the tent easily held and we slept comfortably.

The next morning we left camp at about nine. The wind was still strong and the water was rough, but we had to go. Along the way we found a dead black bear floating in the lake. I suspect that the bear and the dead moose were simply victims of the winter. Coming across Crooked Lake we had found some protection from the wind behind islands, but for the most part we had to fight Crooked's wind and waves.

JAY WRITES:

We continued westbound toward Sunday Bay, following the border. The past several days we were paddling lakes that I was so familiar with that I did not need a map, but once we got west of Sunday Bay and Iron Lake, that was to change.

Sunday Bay was plastered with whitecaps. It is wide enough that the wind howled across unimpeded. The water was rough enough that we had to follow Sunday's southern shoreline to Curtain Falls. It was not calm, but it was calmer. I had the feeling that the wind was testing us. Maybe we had to earn the privilege to a smoother Lac la Croix crossing.

Crossing Curtain Falls Portage we encountered a fawn. It apparently had come to the falls to either graze or have a drink. We watched quietly until it scampered off into the woods.

Each of our crew had several years of experience, but since Fred and I were the only two who had been this far west. I felt a strong sense of satisfaction putting Crooked Lake behind us and beginning to paddle new territory.

FRED WRITES:

The falls drop about thirty five feet from Crooked into Iron Lake. They are loud and they are violent. After portaging and reloading the canoes, we pulled them off to the side up on a muddy bank and walked back up the portage for a better view of the falls and to take a group picture.

Paddling out from the landing, eddies swirled around our

canoes. They were not exceedingly perilous but didn't need to be ignored. By this time the sun came out warming the day. I thought, *It's about time*. It didn't take long before we had crossed Iron Lake and were throwing packs and canoes onto our shoulders to cross Bottle Portage into Lac la Croix.

At almost every point it was obvious how high the water was. Bottle Portage was extremely wet. Even though the portage rose slightly over a hill, we waded through muddy water most of the way. At the end were the remains of an old pickup truck bed that had been converted into a trailer. Earlier, on Crooked, there was the rusting carcass of an old 1928 Buick. Both of these were remains from times when there were fishing camps in Quetico and the Boundary Waters, or from the era of the lumberjack.

JAY WRITES:

The man in the fur trade era who knew the boundary country best was David Thompson.[19] Thompson was born to a poor family, but showed enough intellectual promise that he was enrolled at London's Gray Coat School. The school, now a school for girls, was founded in 1698 to provide an education to the poor of St. Margaret's Parish so that they might become, "loyal citizens, useful workers and solid Christians." After graduation he became a Hudson Bay Company apprentice. He remained with the company for the next fourteen years. He then left to join its competitor, the North West Company. When heading east to Grand Portage to join the North West Company, he passed Curtain Falls. Thompson describes the lower landing of Curtains

---

19 Grace Lee Nute, *The Voyageur Highway* (St. Paul: Minnesota Historical Society, 1969), 26.

Falls portage as "very bad," with a steep bank.[20]

I had only been across Bottle Portage once before. This time was much muddier than the first. We trudged and slipped and slopped our ways across the trail. When we reached Lac la Croix, we were rewarded with sunshine. It must have been dry when Thompson had to traverse Bottle Portage, as he only described it as an uneven 300-yards-long portage.[21]

FRED WRITES:

Now we were on Lac la Croix. The Indians called it, "Lake Surrounded by Pines—*Zhingwaako-zaaga'iganiing*. The French renamed it after de la Croix, a French Missionary who died there.[22] It is a huge lake. I had been on it once when even the motorboats were wind bound. We decided to paddle to Fish Steak Narrows to look for a camp. On the way we passed Warrior Hill. Warrior Hill is a huge, bald rock rising several hundred feet from the water. Being the highest rock around, the Ojibwe used it as a lookout point for their enemies, the Dakotas. Additionally, the hill was used as a test for the young men. In order to be accepted as a warrior, one of a candidate's challenges was to run to the top.[23]

Not far away to the west of Warrior Hill is Fish Steak Narrows. Paddling through the Narrows not only provided us with a good island campsite, it also gave us a way to avoid the main part of la Croix and any potentially bad wind. As we settled in to camp,

---

20 Nute, *The Voyageur Highway*, 27.

21 Nute, *The Voyageur Highway*, 26.

22 *Lake Names of Quetico Provincial Park*, Friends of Quetico 1992, Atikokan, Ontario, Canada.

23 Peruniak, *Quetico Provincial Park: An Illustrated History*.

I realized that I had no idea what day of the week it was. I knew the date because I had written it every time I made an entry in my journal. But I had no clue as to what day it was. I decided to rectify that by always writing day and date in my journal entries.

Back in the woods from our camp, while looking for a tree to hang our food in, a crow cawed loudly and frantically at me from above. Two years previous on another trip, camped on Argo Lake, I had helped save a crow that was tangled in fishing line. As the crow flies, Argo Lake is only a few miles from Fish Steak Narrows. The poor bird had somehow gotten fishing line wrapped around its feet. It then landed in a tree. The line became entwined around a limb. The harder the crow tried to get loose, the more entangled he became. We found him hanging upside down, frantically flapping and twisting in an hysterical effort to escape. Cutting the line, we freed the bird and then cut the remaining line away from his feet. He lay calmly in my hands while we untangled him. Above, his mate circled and called out from time to time. He finally looked at me and squawked as if to say, "Okay. Thanks, but I am ready to go now." After we turned the crow loose, the pair circled a couple of times and then flew off. I knew that it couldn't be the same bird, but thought that it would be nice if it was and if it maybe remembered me.

Every group seems to have a pyromaniac. Ours was Clayton. He loved large fires. A small fire even on the warmest of days is nice. The smoke seems to keep the mosquitoes and black flies down. So, when I came back from my search for a tree, there was a roaring fire. Clayton stood over it with a self-satisfied look.

Again, I was the cook. One of my trail recipe innovations was gnocchi.[24] It is easy to cook and it's filling. It is a good comfort food. Charles and Jim had eaten it before this trip. The rest had only had it once on our first leg. They liked it then, so I figured that they would enjoy it now. They did.

In the morning, the rest of the crew were up when I went to wake them. I was glad, since we really needed to get an early start across la Croix. We got the food bags down, made coffee, ate, and got on the water. It was seven thirty. We had never started paddling that early.

JAY WRITES:

The next day we were rewarded again with sunshine, so we hurried to cover as much distance as possible before the weather changed. On large lakes, canoeists are more vulnerable to inclement weather and wind. Experience on the larger Boundary Waters and Quetico lakes had taught us that morning waters are calmer. The wind usually does not pick up until early afternoon. Although we left before eight a.m., it still seemed rather late to me.

FRED WRITES:

La Croix was calm. The Boundary Waters dictum to leave early for calm water held. As we headed toward Beatty Portage we paddled past cottages along the Canadian side. The lake was extremely high. At non-floating boathouses, water levels almost reached the entrances' tops.

By two thirty we had safely reached Beatty Portage. In the middle next to the path across the portage were two houses, a generator, and a couple of sheds. One house was for the portage

---

24 An Italian potato and ricotta dumpling

owner and the second smaller house—more like a cabin—was for the caretaker. As we approached, the caretaker was just finishing mowing the grass. A neatly trimmed yard in the middle of the woods with no road around seemed out of place to me.

Beatty was a railroad portage for power boats. Narrow-gauge tracks run across from Lac la Croix to Loon Lake. Hooked by cable to a gasoline-powered winch in the center of the portage is an old narrow-gauge railroad car that looks like a leftover from the logging days. The car's bed has a platform shaped to nestle a motorboat in. It works by letting the car roll down the rails into the water. When the rail car is deep enough, the power boat scoots forward with a burst of its engine onto the car. Next, the operator simply winches driver and boat across to slide off the rail car into the next lake.

This portage, along with several others on the border, allows motor travel from International Falls to Lac la Croix. It is used mostly by the big motorboats and jetboats that ferry guests back and forth to the resorts on Lac la Croix.

The thought crossed my mind that the old border route is still heavily traveled in the summer by modern-day voyageurs. They don't trade in furs—they trade in vacations. Each portage has a kiosk selling Cokes, candy bars, tee shirts, and gas, making them also vestiges of the old trading posts.

We walked across the yard, feeling uncomfortable trekking through somebody's space. It is much the same as portaging through a campsite. You try to avoid it. But if the campsite is in the middle of a portage, there is no choice. The owner, his wife, his daughter, and his father were there along with their caretaker.

"Do you live here all summer?" I asked the younger man.

"No. I wish that I did. I used to when I was their age." He pointed spontaneously to his daughters. "But, I spend some time here early in the summer. The snow and ice do a lot of damage to the rail ties. Excuse me." He walked up to the house looking preoccupied.

I took it from what he said that the portage had been in the family for a couple of generations—possibly since Teddy Roosevelt made Superior our first national forest.

Our maps showed no campsites on Little Vermilion Lake, our goal for the day. I went to ask the older man if he knew of any sites. He pointed out several on the map and asked where we were going. Proudly I said, "York Factory." Before I could add, "on Hudson Bay," he told me that he had a friend from Duluth who had done that. His friend was a pilot who had died several years ago. I told him that I knew exactly who he was talking about: Scott Anderson.

"Did you know him?" the older man asked.

"No, but I am familiar with his book, *Distant Fires*," I said. I had not yet read it, but was going to after the trip.

"Scott loved to canoe," he added. "Good luck." I thanked him and headed back to the canoes. Over my shoulder I heard Charles and Jim holler—actually, it was more like a scream. I turned and caught a glimpse of them as they leaped off of the pier into Lac la Croix to celebrate the crossing.

As we were loading up our canoes, the rail car clanked over the hill. On it was the younger Beatty standing in his boat. He looked like he was surveying what he had done on this trip and what needed to be done the next time he came. Behind him, his wife and children ambled down the hill. The older Beatty stood on the dock, intensely watching the operation. The rail car rolled into the water. The boat slid off. By this time as if on cue the rest of the family lined up on the pier. They climbed in and took their seats. The children gave us a wave. Then the younger Beatty lit a cigar, started the engine, turned his baseball cap backwards, pulling it tight on his head, and nodded good-bye to us. In a few minutes they were gone. The boat's wake briefly jostled our canoes, causing them to slap at the shore. About the same time, Charles and Jim got back and we headed for Little Vermilion Lake.

First we had to cross Loon Portage, another motorized portage. It, too, operated with a winch and cable. As we approached, a large launch passed us. Some of the people waved. They all looked surprised to see our canoes. At the Portage all the passengers got out to walk over while the boat was taken over by another small rail car. It all seemed very orderly and happened quickly.

As we were getting ready to portage, the operator told us that we were going the wrong way, saying that we needed to go back to Loon Lake as the Loon River didn't go to Little Vermilion, it went to Crane Lake. It does eventually get you to Crane Lake by going through Little Vermilion Lake. He was confused. "I'll show you my map," he mumbled. "Now where is my map? I must have lent it to somebody. Eh? It's waterproof."

I just couldn't follow his logic. Who would he have lent his map to? After all, it was waterproof. The only western exit from Loon Lake would bring us here and the Loon River empties into Little Vermilion Lake. He wanted to argue for a brief minute, then said that he understood what we were doing and misunderstood where we were going. I am not sure which. It's hard to understand how he could be where he was supposed to be and still be lost. We all got a chuckle from his disorientation. I guess you had to be there. He did warn us of the powerboats. There, he was not disoriented, as it was a warning worth heeding.

We headed on down the river. We ran through some fast water named Rapids 56. Several boats came past. They go full speed up and down the river. Normally there are no canoes in this area so there is nothing for them to look out for. Some tried to or did slow down. Others just sped by leaving us to slosh around in their wake.

About five thirty we reached Little Vermilion and found the campsite that the elder Beatty recommended. He had said that the first site was good but that it was probably wet because of the high water. The second one was probably our best bet. He was right on both accounts.

JAY WRITES:

Charles turned on the GPS. We had paddled in excess of thirty miles. I paddled with Clayton that day, which meant that I was one of the lead canoes. My arms and back ached from the distance and working to hold the lead, but we had to stay on schedule so Clayton could return to Sommers in time to meet his crew.

Although dry, the campsite was infested with mosquitoes and tiny black flies. The bug shirt I had was getting its workout. After supper we did not delay in getting into our tents. I resolved to learn to be more conscientious in getting the tent's vestibule, screens, and door flaps more quickly shut in order to prevent the little bastards from entering the tent. Fred seemed much better at keeping the bugs out than I was. Two people sharing a tent simply doubled the bugs' chances to join us inside.

—CHAPTER VI—

RAINY LAKE

Above us on de sky dere, de summer cloud may float
Aroun' us on de water de ripple never show,
But somet'ing down below us can rock de stronges' boat,
"W'en we're comin' near de islan' of de spirit
    Windigo!"[25]

"The Windigo"
by William Henry Drummond

[10 JUNE 2008–12 JUNE 2008]

FRED WRITES:

We left camp on Little Vermilion for a short paddle north to
Namakan Lake. Namakan is a form of the Ojibwe word for "sturgeon," *nahme*. Minnesota and Canada have numerous lakes with
names relating to sturgeons. Atakaki Provincial Wilderness Park
in Manitoba has a lake named, "No Name." Actually, in Ojibwe
it is pronounced, "na nahme," meaning "five sturgeons." Quetico

---

25 The Windigo in Ojibwe mythology is a cannibalistic winter monster. It is
also simply a cannibal. Some Windigos are described as ice monsters. Humans
at times have turned into Windigos.

Provincial Wilderness Park has Sturgeon Lake. Sturgeon was an important fish for the Indians, being a source of food and oil. You can go back to Longfellow's *Song of Hiawatha* and find Mishe-Nah'ma, the great sturgeon. Hiawatha did battle with him on Lake Superior, Gitche-Gu'mee.[26] He then fed the carcass to his friends, the gulls.

We had decided that we would portage around rather than paddle through the Namakan Narrows. After all, the portage was only 180 rods. We had tackled much longer trails.

The voyageurs always went through the narrows. They avoided portages where they could. Alexander Mackenzie paddled through the narrows on his way west to the Pacific Ocean in 1792. He was the first man to cross North America north of Mexico. Mackenzie noted in his journal that the Indians were spearfishing for sturgeon. His observation reflects the lake name's more exact meaning—"where the sturgeons are plentiful."

We found the portage exactly where it was supposed to be. It was wide and open. But, it was knee-deep in mud. I had the canoe and a pack. Over the first half I was okay. Then the pack started to slip and the portage seemed to get deeper in mud, so I decided to drop the pack, take the canoe across, and return for what I'd left behind. I had already seen Charles sink in up to his waist in slimy cold muck with a gear pack. He laughed when it happened. I wasn't going to have it happen to me. As I went back for the pack, I kept thinking that I should have sucked it up and continued. The trail seemed muddier as I returned with my second load. But my hands were free to grab limbs and trees to steady myself, although I think that I easily found the deepest part of every puddle of water and mud.

---

26 These are Longfellow's spellings.

JAY WRITES:

The following day, we departed Little Lake Vermilion and entered the eastern portion of Voyageurs National Park at Sand Point Lake. We made it to a campsite in the Wolf Pack Islands archipelago.

Namakan Lake was enormous. I found it awe-inspiring to round that easternmost corner of the lake and look out across the bay and see the water stretch to the horizon. The first Europeans to see the lake only knew how far it was to the other end from what the Indian guides told them. Our experience was only different from the first explorers and voyageurs in that we had detailed maps. I also felt a tightening feeling in my guts— maybe the butterflies were flapping again. Looking across that wide-open expanse of water, I knew what mountainous waves lay ahead if the wind increased. Fortunately, the wind remained only a slight breeze, allowing us to easily make our distance for the day.

FRED WRITES:

Basically, Voyageurs National Park is Namakan Lake, Kabeto-gammi Lake, and Rainy Lake, with some surrounding acreage. The Indians fished there. The voyageurs paddled through. The last commercial use was for lumber. At lunchtime I found a heavy iron ring driven into a rock. It was probably used to tie off log rafts. There is a similar one near Prairie Portage on Sucker Lake and on Jean Lake in Quetico. If you look, there is sometimes a relic. Voyageurs National Park was established in 1975. Now its sole use is recreation.

After lunch we paddled north through some narrows into

Namakan's main body. Not far to my right, imbedded into a rock almost under the water, was a metal, obelisk-shaped gnomon. These gnomons line the border. They are there because in 1823 a U.S. Army Major, Joseph Delafield, and a Canadian, Dr. John Bigsby, surveyed the border. After nineteen years of discussion, in 1842, the United States and Great Britain signed the Webster-Ashburton Treaty recognizing the two men's surveys. These gnomons were not placed there by Johnson and Delafield, but they do represent the points that they surveyed. I thought as we paddled by that I was glad that the water was clear so we could see this hazard. An unseen border marker could rip a titanic gash in a canoe.

Namakan Lake is big and beautiful. Occasionally a houseboat or motor launch enters the view and spoils the quiet with the sputter of its motor. The park has designated campsites. We knew this, but our maps did not show their locations. Finally, Israel spied a brown sign far on the shore to the southwest in the Wolf Pack Islands. We headed there. Sure enough it was a wonderful camp. There was a great fire ring and metal boxes to protect your food against bears.

As we were unloading Karl quipped, "I never liked bear boxes."

Clayton, never being at a loss for words, retorted loudly and sarcastically, "No, a steel box is not as good as putting your food under a Kevlar canoe. That's where it's really safe." We already had a discussion about putting food bags under the canoes. There is a philosophy among some that the best way to protect your food is to put it under a canoe with pots and pans on top. If a bear invades your camp, you hear him and can scare him off. It may sound good, but in practice it is dangerously wide of the mark. I insisted on putting our food high up in a tree where a bear could not reach it. Clayton's cynicism gratified me, as I'd had a similar thought.

Not long after we got the tents up, the rain set in. It rained hard for about an hour and a half. Once the rain stopped, I cooked supper. Then we turned in. From then on it rained on and off until morning. Sometimes I woke during the night, but the patter of the rain on our fly lulled me back to sleep.

JAY WRITES:

We had a fire to warm ourselves. However, once the sun set, I had to put on my fleece jacket and rain pants on to keep warm. Even then, as the evening progressed, I was still uncomfortable from a persistent, permeating chill. It made the ground feel harder, too. I continued having to wear a fleece even in my sleeping bag.

FRED WRITES:

When I got up, the wind was still blowing hard, but it had stopped raining. Initially I just put on one fleece and my rain jacket. They were not enough. I could still feel a chill, so I added a fleece vest. Clayton got up, stared at his watch for a moment, and then announced that it was forty-two degrees. I was thankful for his watch. After the rest got up, we ate, packed, and headed for Kettle Falls.

JAY WRITES:

Kettle Falls was the only portage of the day. Even though I was riding duff—in the middle seat—it was cold enough that I, too, had to paddle to stay warm. Cabins peeking out from behind the trees lining the shoreline reminded us that we were no longer in the Boundary Waters.

FRED WRITES:

Kettle Falls is the last motor portage leading to Rainy Lake. Rather than a rail portage, there is a road that winds around the dam. A truck backs a trailer onto a sandy lake bottom. The boat slides on and is towed to the other side where the process is reversed.

A short walk from the falls is the red-roofed, white clapboard Kettle Falls Hotel—somewhat reminiscent of a New England bed and breakfast. It was built in 1913 and has accommodated travelers ever since. We crossed on a gravel road and then went up to the observation deck to see the dam and the falls. It probably would have been beautiful on a warm day. On that cold day the falls' mist was not refreshing. I was already wet and cold. We all regrouped by the canoes where we had another quick peanut butter and jelly sandwich lunch.

It had been cold and windy all day, but the temperature seemed to rise and the water seemed to calm as we headed onto Rainy Lake. This was the largest lake to date that any of us had paddled. It was quite overwhelming. We found a great campsite on aptly named Big Island. Again, we had curried lentils with chicken and rice. On a cold day when you are tired and wet the aroma alone partially warms you. Then the meal finishes the job.

From the long-range weather reports I had read earlier, I knew it was supposed to be stormy over the next four days. I thought, *We'll see.*

JAY WRITES:

Today Kettle Falls is a place for a family getaway. It is situated in a quiet area, close enough to the falls to be able to walk, yet far enough away that the roar of the floodgates is muffled. Being located in a remote Canadian border area, it was a popular location for smugglers during Prohibition.

A group of young girls were sightseeing with their parents. While we were on the viewing platform overlooking the falls, the girls were also there. Despite the presence of adults around, including us, they saw fit to carve their initials and leave graffiti in the wooden railing. While there was nothing historic about the viewing platform, it certainly was not a blackboard. I found it irritating, as the adults either were oblivious or did not care what their young charges did.

Several summers ago, a Northern Tier Order of the Arrow crew paddled to International Falls. They were taking a trip after performing a work project in the Boundary Waters Canoe Area. They were the first crew from Sommers to paddle this part of the border. From just west of Kettle Falls, they paddled to International Falls in one day. It was quite a feat.

FRED WRITES:

In the morning it was still raining and the wind was blowing. Finally about eight thirty a.m. it calmed enough for us to load up and go. At first it was only choppy, but as we headed west the wind speed increased and the temperature seemed to drop. Waves had to be at least three to four feet. I was paddling bow with Jay in the stern. He kept taking the waves head on. As we came over the peak, the bow slapped down in the trough soaking me. I would then shout back for him to come across at an angle. It is almost counterintuitive to come across big waves at an angle. It would seem that they would capsize you, but if you get it right, the canoe slips across and the bowman—me, in this case—stays dry. As it was cold, staying dry was my sole objective. Jay finally learned to keep me dry, or at least drier.

JAY WRITES:

Weekend cabins lined the U.S. side of Rainy Lake. Motorboats raced east and west. One motorboat blasted heavy metal music. I found it humorous and incongruous to have paddled all this way to be welcomed by the screaming guitars of "Paradise City."

FRED WRITES:

It was not a long distance, but because we had to zigzag across big waves through a headwind it took us four hours to get around Soldier Point and into the largest part of Rainy Lake. On the horizon was sky. No land—only sky. I had only seen a view like that on the ocean or at the Gulf of Mexico—never on a lake. I wondered how long we would have to paddle to find land.

Charles found a protected place to stop for lunch. Then we headed west. The wind switched to a tailwind. The waves were still big, but they seemed to propel us forward. We were almost able to surf them. Jay did a great job keeping us going. Being on a large lake in a small canoe with four-foot waves was both disconcerting and exhilarating. As we crossed, trees came into view on the horizon. The waves also got bigger. It was impossible to stay together. As we got into the narrows heading to the Rainy River channel, Charles and Karl's canoe seemed to drift farther to the north. Because of the wind and waves, Jay and I had trouble moving in that direction. Eventually they pulled up to an island and started to unload. Jay and I both figured that they had found a campsite. Rainy Lake, on both sides at this point, is private property, so campsites in this area are at a premium. We were right. There was a small campsite only barely big enough for the seven of us.

JAY WRITES:

The winds rose throughout the afternoon. Prior to making camp we found ourselves in waves so high that only our friends' heads in the other canoes were visible bobbing just above the waves' crests. I became concerned what water on Lake of the Woods and Lake Winnipeg would be like if Rainy Lake was this threatening.

FRED WRITES:

Jay guided us to the island's leeward side. Right behind us was Clayton, Israel, and Jim. Tents went up and then Clayton got an enormous fire started. I was glad that he had the dubious pyromania avocation, as we were all wet and cold.

During supper, the stoves started to sputter. At first I thought that it might be the wind. Then I figured that they might be dirty. I would clean them at International Falls. I have fixed hundreds of stoves over the past few years. In fact, this trip started almost a year earlier while Charles and I were repairing stoves. After supper, Charles and I secured the canoes and took down the dining fly. Then we headed for bed.

The second big leg of our trip was ending tomorrow. We were only a morning's paddle from International Falls.

The wind blew all night. Although it was still blowing too strong to get on the lake when I got up, I went ahead and woke the rest. They seemed sluggish. I guess that we were all tired from the wind and waves. Jay and I were packed, but it was worth getting back into the tent to get out of the wind. I had already tried to find a tree or a rock to use as a windbreak, but there just weren't any. In my mind it seemed like we had been in the wind forever and would be in it again today.

When the others started to stir, I got some coffee going. We ate our extra granola bars. I said a short, desperate prayer for good weather. Not long after I did, the wind miraculously stopped and Rainy Lake became smooth.

Today Karl and I would paddle together. Each day we changed partners. Because of the previous days' waves, we put spray skirts on the canoes. I had never paddled with a spray skirt so was a little hesitant. The skirt fit wonderfully. We headed to Rainier, a small community just east of International Falls. In the distance, the Boise Cascade Paper Mill smoke stacks and buildings rose. The day cleared up. The mills were a great sign that we had reached International Falls.

JAY WRITES:

Today Clayton would be leaving us to return to Ely for a last trip before his Air Force ROTC summer camp. Most importantly, our replacement satellite phone would be there. Once we were in the remote Canadian bush, it would be our only means of communication.

We were now near the location where the North West Company met their Athabasca Brigades. Here is where they would exchange goods for furs coming from the Canadian far northwest. International Falls is present-day Portage de la Chaudière. The Ojibwe called it Koochiching Falls, meaning "mist over the waters." The portage is gone now. Before the power station it was 320 paces long around the twenty-foot-tall falls.[27] A North West Company trading post was located

---

27 Barbara Huck, *Exploring the Fur Trade Routes of North America* (Winnipeg: Heartland Publications, 2000), 145-146.

two miles downriver past the falls on a high bank on the Canadian side of the Rainy River.[28]

We were looking for someplace to land, prior to our entering International Falls and the Rainy River proper, when we met Joanne Finstad, one of the local citizens. Charles' canoe was in the lead. He was looking for a way around a double set of rapids where Rainy Lake enters the Rainy River, just upriver from International Falls. Joanne came out to give us her advice.

FRED WRITES:

Ahead, the other canoes had stopped at a pier. Although we could not hear them, we could see that they were talking to somebody in a red sweater. This turned out to be Joanne Finstad, owner of some lakeside cabins. In the winters, Joanne lives in New York City, but she returns home to Minnesota in the summer to run an old family lakeside resort business. She doesn't advertise and is happy with her word-of-mouth guests. Joanne is absolutely charming and proved to be extremely helpful. She called her friend at International Paper to arrange for us to be truck-portaged around the Rainy River hydro station.

When International Paper built their paper mill they also built a small hydroelectric dam to run the paper mill. Because this obstructed river traffic, they agreed to provide a vehicle to portage boats and canoes around the dam. I knew that International Paper was responsible for portaging to and from the Rainy River. I just wasn't sure how it was supposed to happen. Joanne

---

28 Mackenzie, *Journals of Alexander Mackenzie: Voyages From Montreal. On the River Saint Lawrence, Through the Continent of North America, To the Frozen and Pacific Oceans: In the years 1789 and 1793, With a preliminary Account of the Rise, Progress, and Present State of the Fur Trade of That Country*, 50.

solved that problem for us. She then called the local paper to write an article on us and checked out hotels to find a vacancy. All the time, she apologized hoping that we didn't think she was too pushy. I wish that more people were so pushy in her helpful way. She is a lovely lady.

Joanne's help continued. She asked her friend, Burk, to take us to Border Bobs to meet whoever was bringing us the rest of our food. We stashed our gear behind one of her sheds while Charles and I went to Border Bob's. Border Bob's is a souvenir shop, ice cream parlor, and candy store located a couple of blocks south of the border crossing. It has always been a Charles L. Sommers meeting place. Anytime we need to pick up or drop off something for our Atikokan canoe base, we meet at Border Bob's. The rest of what remained of the day was a whirlwind of activity.

Doug Hirdler brought us our food. Doug, now retired, was the Northern Tier general manager. The best way to describe Doug is that you always know he is there. He is a wonderfully boisterous basso with bright mischievous eyes and an ever-present, infectious smile. When he shakes your hand, it is a firm grip you remember. Doug drove us to drop the food off at the hotel. He then took us back to Rainier to get our other packs. From there, Charles, Jay, Israel, and Karl went to Canadian Customs to get Remote Area Border Crossing Passes.[29] Jim, Clayton, and I went to get a hamburger and then headed to the hotel. On the way Doug picked us up. We said quick good-byes so Clayton could get back to Ely to guide a crew that was coming in. The others staggered in and went to get dinner.

---

29 The Remote Area Border Crossing Pass allows you to skip customs and emigration and enter Canada anywhere between Lake Superior and Lake of the Woods.

JAY WRITES:

Entering and leaving Canada was an experience. I had done it so many times, but this time seemed more difficult. Actually, entering Canada and renewing our Remote Area Border Crossing Permits was simple, but slightly time-consuming. Returning to the United States was something of an ordeal. Customs had difficulty believing that we would walk across, leaving our gear in the United States, and why we were having our gear trucked past the dam. Our group ranged in age. The four youngest were in their twenties. I was thirty-eight and Fred was sixty-two. We all came from different parts of the country. This made us even more unusual in the eyes of the U.S. Customs officials. I was tempted to be flippant but realized that doing so would only result in a longer delay. So we answered their questions and went on our way. Actually, we had walked across the bridge at the border thinking that it would be easier to do so.

Once we had cleared Customs, we set off to meet our rides to the motel. Once there and settled in, some of us walked across the highway to a grocery store for more bread, jam, and hot chocolate. Along with the rest who did not go to the grocery store, I walked to downtown International Falls for burgers and beer. It tasted good and went down fast. The first meal a trail guide has once he is "in town" is usually something that he seriously looks forward to. It can range from the sublime bacon cheeseburger to the outlandish mushroom-and onion-smothered steak.

CHAPTER VII

INTERNATIONAL FALLS

Gone is he now, an' de beeg canoe
No more you'll see wit' de red-shirt crew,
But long as he leev' he was always true,
So we'll drink to hees memory.

> "The Voyageur"
> by William Henry Drummond

[12 JUNE 2008]

JAY WRITES:

International Falls has no campsites, so we stayed in a motel. It was reasonably priced and convenient. Primarily, the hotel survives on fishermen who come to International Falls for an inexpensive weekend on Rainy Lake. For us it worked out better than camping since we were able to make phone calls home, shower, and pick up some additional personal supplies. I had to locate some sort of new durable eyeglass case and some vitamins.

FRED WRITES:

The last thing that Joanne did was introduce us to Bob Hilke. "Bob used to paddle with a fellow named Oberholtzer. Do you know who he is?" she asked.

"I certainly do. He and an Ojibwe guide, Billy Magee, paddled to Hudson Bay and back," I answered. Oberholtzer and Billy's trip was in part my inspiration for this trip. Billy was somewhat of a hero to me because he had been in his late forties—maybe ancient—when he accompanied Oberholtzer to the Bay. He was my Ojibwe Freckles Brown. I hoped Bob could tell me more.

Bob is a long-time International Falls resident. He is either in his late sixties or early seventies. As a young man he canoed routinely with Ernest Oberholtzer. Joanne wasn't introducing us to Hilke so he could regale us with stories of Oberholtzer. She wanted us to meet because Bob, too, had a great love of canoeing. We had something in common.

Bob's friend, "Ober" as he was known by his friends and also the public, had explored much of the Rainy Lake basin and parts of Canada by canoe. He had a great talent for finding and photographing moose. He sold many of his photos to National Geographic. However, his real contribution was his active involvement in conservation and consequent preservation of some of the North Woods wilderness.

Ober and Billy first met back in 1909 when Billy guided for him in Quetico. In 1912, Ober and Billy went on a paddle to Hudson Bay. For much of their route they either had partial maps or no map at all. The two found their way by compass and Billy's skills. Along the way, Ober chronicled their trip with his journal and by drawing maps.

I have to believe that part of what helped them succeed was Billy's spirit name. Billy's mother named him Tay-tah-pah-sway-we-tong,

"Far Distant Echo." "He seemed to be able to sense where the trail should be," Ober once said.

In that one 1912 adventure, Billy lived up to his spirit name, paddling with Ober to Hudson Bay. He is a fascinating man.

Ober was a Harvard graduate from Iowa. Billy had grown up in the woods, trapping, guiding, hunting, fishing, and working for the Hudson Bay Company. Together, in 1912, they paddled through Reindeer Lake to Nueltin Lake down the Thlewiaza River to Hudson Bay. They came back up the Hayes River and down Lake Winnipeg. Ober had left a note in a tin can on Nueltin Lake under a cairn. In 1962 he returned, taking Hilke with him. The can was still there. The note had earlier been retrieved by some prospectors.

I was anxious to meet Bob, so I called. He was not there, but I left a voice message.

In the meantime I called Jean. It was her birthday. I have bragged many times how lucky I am to have her as a wife. She so profusely has encouraged me in everything.

After a wonderful and welcome conversation with Jean, Bob called. I told him to please come over even though it was getting late. He arrived just before nine. In *Toward Magnetic North*, Bob had written an essay on Ober. My sole knowledge of Ober was from Shirley Peruniac's book, *Quetico Provincial Park: An Illustrated History*, and from rather extensive print interviews by the Minnesota Historical Society, so I was anxious to meet somebody who knew him personally and who had paddled with him.

Bob is a delightful man. He had just finished building a rowboat and was planning to row solo across Rainey Lake to Kettle Falls and back. The North Woods is full of men and women like Bob who enjoy the outdoors and never let age get in their way.

I think that he was somewhat surprised that a southerner even knew of Ober. As we talked he asked several rhetorical questions. To some, I had the answer, but I wanted to know what he knew.

"Tell me about your trip to Nueltin Lake," I suggested. Bob went back with Ober fifty years after Ober had first been there.

"I had just moved back from International Falls. Ober found me and said, 'We are going to Nueltin Lake. I have a plane ready.' I used to paddle with him every summer. Sometimes we would go for thirty days. You know I have the tin can that Ober left his note in a cairn on Hawkes Summit. Two prospectors took the note to York Factory in 1937 where they inquired about who Ober and Billy were."

"You do! That is a piece of North Woods history! It is a true treasure." I was excited.

"It is on a shelf at home. You know that Ober and Billy came close to freezing. Had he not found the entrance to the Thlewiaza River when they did, they would have died. Finding the river without a map was quite a feat."

We talked for a while about how Ober got up the Hayes River using a sail. Bob commented that it was only because of the sail that Ober and Billy made it up the river. I knew of Ober's solution to get up the swift current. Billy's self-confidence and faith in Ober and himself was clear-cut and quaint. Knowing the difficulty of getting to their destination, Billy merely said, "Maybe find portage," meaning, "We'll find a way."

"Did you know Billy Magee?" I asked. Billy died in 1938. I guessed that Bob was enough older than me that he might have met Billy or maybe Ober had stories that only he knew.

"No, I never knew Billy. Ober talked about him some. You know Billy was an expert at shooting rapids. Many times he paddled the canoe down by himself while Ober portaged the packs around." Like all of the North Woods people, he had the French pronunciation of portaged. It was distinctly "portáged."

About this time Charles and Jay came in. I introduced them. We talked on for a short while, but it was getting late and Bob commented that he had to leave.

"Bob, the only Ojibwe legend that I have been able to find is *The Legend of the Black Sturgeon*. Where are the rest that Ober collected?" Ober was known by the Ojibwe as Atisokan, "The Story Teller" or, more literally, "The Teller of Legends."

"I think that the Minnesota Historical Society has them all. You know, every time he told the black sturgeon story, he told it the exactly the same way. I always found him to be delightfully animated when speaking with his Ojibwe friends. I don't speak Ojibwe, but I loved to watch and listen to him."

I had heard of *The Legend of the Black Sturgeon* and finally found it in an interview with the Minnesota Historical Society. I find it to be particularly poignant because all the places Billy speaks of exist. Some I have been to. By Ober's description, Billy spoke very poor English. From the Minnesota Historical Society interview, Ober speaks:

We had a fire, and then [Billy] said, rather solemnly, "Guess got something say." Well, what he meant was, "You've been asking me to tell you something, and now I'm going to try to do that." "Just got something to say." But I didn't know that he was referring to that at all, and I thought, *Oh, heavens, is he going to say to me now that this is the worst trip he ever took, and I was a hell of a man, and he was anxious to get home?* He was very friendly in his appearance, but he was so solemn that I thought it was something pretty serious."

And the thing was, it was solemn for him to screw up his

courage to the point of telling the story like this in his broken English to an outsider. He didn't know whether I had any respect for Indian mythology, you see. Well, I have a tremendous respect for it. The others have since learned, just through experience, that I never dismiss anything that they tell me as worthless or untrue. Anything of that sort, if it's a decent Indian, is true to me to the degree that it ought to be. I think it ought to be true in these sacred old stories.

So it made such an impression on me that I remembered it almost word for word, the manner and everything, and I tell it that way, even though it may be difficult for people to understand. He [Billy] speaks:

Long time ago—maybe thousand year, maybe ten thousand, dunno—long, long time ago, big Injun village, go up TChi-ma-og-i-nay River (that's the Seine River) springtime. By and by come big steep rock, lake, lots sand beach, lots pine tree. Pretty soon come big sand beach just like bow. All big pine trees stand all round. Injun get 'em out canoe maybe ten canoe Injuns—lots of Injun men, Injun squaw—want come, fish for sturgeon. Injun squaw, she build wigwam.

Injun man, he go fish in lake. All day long Injun squaw she build wigwam—fifty white wigwam stand all new. (I said fifty; I guess it was more than this, the number of men.) But, fifty white wigwam stand all new on sand beach at night, just like bow, lots pine trees stand all around. Oldest Injun never remember so many sturgeon. They catch 'em lots sturgeon—only not just the same sturgeon black on back, white underneath. Some sturgeon was hang from wiggywam pole to dry. Lots sturgeon, cook on fire. Injun have big feast, dance, sing. Everybody happy. Only one young squaw—she no build a wiggywam. She go way back on hill, just sit and watch other Injun—comb long black hair, all night. By and by, Injun get tired, dance, sin—lie down and go sleep, fire go down. Injun squaw on hill, she sit just the same and comb long black hair. Next morning, Injun squaw go down— young squaw. She call father. Father no answer. She call mother. Mother no answer. Little brother—just the same. She go in the wiggywam everybody lie still. Next wiggywam—just the same— all wiggywam's just the same. I don't know, guess true. Oldest Injun say so. Every Injun, dead. Young squaw, she jump quick in canoe—want go down river and get other Injun, come back, bury dead Injun. Last thing see fifty white wiggywam in sun—all white—lots sturgeon hang from wiggywam pole to dry—pine trees stand all round—great big pine trees.

Three days Injun squaw come back—ten Injun men (that's where the ten comes in)—want bury dead Injun. Come close— big sand beach just the same lots of pine trees, stand all around. Fifty white wiggywam—all just the same. Only no sturgeon hang from wiggywam pole to dry—all sturgeon gone. Injun get 'em out canoe, go look in father's wiggywam. Father gone. Mother gone. Little brother gone. Next wiggywam just the same—every wiggywam—all Injun gone. Only little lines in sand—just as many as dead Injun—go down into the water. I don't know— oldest Injun say so. Every dead. Injun turned into black sturgeon. Maybe white man he eated black sturgeon—no poison. Injun never eat black sturgeon—sure poison."[30]

I thought to myself, *The legend must have happened after 1792 when Mackenzie saw the Indians spearfishing in Namakan Narrows.* Today, the black sturgeon is protected. Nobody eats them.

---

30 Oral history interviews with Ernest C. Oberholtzer. Minnesota Historical Society.

CHAPTER VIII

ALONG THE RAINY RIVER

I'm proud of de sam' blood in my vein,
I'm son of de Nort' Win' wance again—
"The Voyageur"
by William Henry Drummond

[13 JUNE 2008–16 JUNE 2008]

FRED WRITES:

As much as we all hated to leave the comfort of a warm hotel room, it was time to get back on the trail. Two men from International Paper picked us up at the hotel at eight. Behind a new truck, they were towing an old weather-beaten trailer with a wooden bed. Since the others were not ready, Jay and I went with them to retrieve our canoes and the crew gear we left in Rainier. Our stoves were there, so I did not get a chance to work on them. In fact, I forgot all about it. Once we had the canoes and gear we headed back to the hotel to check out and pick up the rest of the crew. They were up but still packing. I apologized to the two International Paper men for them.

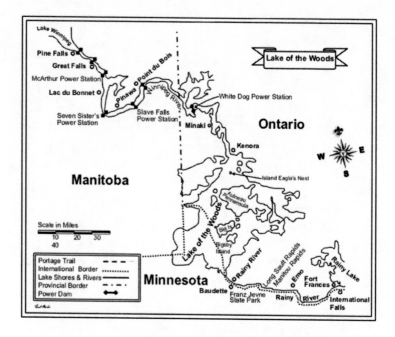

"It's okay. We're on the clock. We can stay all day. So take your time," one of them replied as he took a puff on his cigarette. The smoke lingered in the air and then slowly dissipated in the cold morning mist.

Finally the others finished packing and loaded their packs onto the trailer with the canoes. We then headed for the landing on the Rainy River. On the way we stopped at K Mart for a few last supplies.

JAY WRITES:

The Rainy River is so named because it drains from Rainy Lake. Rainy Lake takes its name from the French, *Lac la Pluie.* We fortunately encountered heavy rain only once, though, on either waterway. Our Rainy River paddle started from a public boat ramp about two miles downstream from the International Falls hydroelectric dam. The river water was high because the lake was high. All of the dam's floodgates were completely open. This gave us a noticeable push from the current.

FRED WRITES:

I paddled with Jim. It drizzled on and off all day with a strong wind in our faces. In addition, there were waves that sometimes seemed to push us back upstream. Somehow it seemed wrong that we had to struggle to get downriver. We ate lunch on a grassy hill, then paddled farther. All of us knew that there were few campsites on the river. With the water as high as it was, there were even fewer sites. Joanne and the International Paper men had said that Rainy Lake was several feet higher than normal. It told on the river. With the water overflowing the banks, it looked more like a tropical mangrove swamp than North Woods.

JAY WRITES:

Wind blew into our faces the entire day, countering the current's help, but the heavy rain held off. We reached the closed Grand Mound Historical Site, where we camped. This only came after we landed on the Canadian side, going to a farmhouse to ask permission to camp on their property. Finding nobody home, we paddled downriver less than a mile to the confluence of the Rainy and Big Fork Rivers to the Grand Mound site. This was also a junction to a route south. From the Big Fork River via a three-mile portage you can reach the Mississippi River.[31]

---

31 Michael Budak, "Grand Mound," no. 23 of *Minnesota Historic Sites Pamphlet Series* (Saint Paul: Minnesota Historical Society Press, 1995), 8.

FRED WRITES:

Israel and Karl walked up to the house to ask if we could camp. Unfortunately, nobody was home. We all agreed that we did not want to camp without permission. Less than fifteen minutes down the river Charles pulled up beside my canoe and said emphatically, "We have to find a campsite now!" There was a sense of desperation or maybe urgency in his voice and in his demeanor that I had never before seen. We paddled to the American side of the river to a place that looked level. After checking it out, we discovered that it was the old Indian burial ground. The signs only said, "Do Not Disturb the Mounds."

At first we thought, "Let's leave." Then we thought, "We should be able to camp as long as we don't disturb the mounds, otherwise there would have been a sign posted that said 'No Camping,' 'No Trespassing,' or 'Keep Out.'" By this time it was getting late with a storm approaching, so there were few choices. We stayed.

I tried, without any success, to light the stoves for supper. They would not even sputter. I could not hear the hiss of gas when I turned them on. There was no choice but to disassemble them to find the problem. Charles and I then took them apart and tried to clean them. They still would not light, so we decided to have a cold supper. The only solution seemed to be that we needed new generators. We retrieved a lunch of pepperoni, cheese, and crackers for dinner and then went to bed.

JAY WRITES:

I made the observation that the flying insects were approaching legendary mass, if not Alfred Hitchcock proportions. This was also one of the few times during the trip when I considered the bugs to be truly bad.

In the morning we had to launch and eat our breakfast of granola bars out on the Rainy River to avoid the mosquitoes.

FRED WRITES:

The first town was Emo. On a high bluff, Tomkins Hardware Store faced the river. We landed and headed in. It was already eleven. I knew from living in a small town that stores often close early on Saturdays. I expected the same in Canada. They did not have any generators, although they knew what I was talking about. In the back of the hardware store was an auto repair shop. Tom, the parts manager, knew what our problem was and offered his air hose and sonic carburetor cleaner. Having no other options, we gladly took him up on his offer.

Charles and I retrieved the stoves from the pack, stripped off the generators, and threw them into the sonic carburetor cleaner. It did the trick on one of them. The other remained clogged. The working stove burned fairly dirty but it burned. I thanked Tom profusely.

A couple of hundred yards up river was Emo's city park. It was another place where we could tell how high the water was. The sidewalk along the river was partially underwater. The park had some faucets for water and some covered picnic tables. With clouds in the distance, we decided that here was a good place to cook a hot lunch. Israel went to the bakery and bought fresh cinnamon rolls for desert. Afterwards we cleaned up and repacked.

Before we could get on the water, the temperature dropped and a cold rain fell. It did not last long. As soon as it stopped we headed toward Manitou Rapids. Not being able to see the end of the rapids, Karl climbed up on a hill to read the water. It turned out it was a relatively easy shoot with no hidden surprises. We went down to the left then paddled through some moderate eddies. All three canoes made it in fine shape.

JAY WRITES:

Paddling with Charles gave me confidence when running Manitou Rapids, since he had more whitewater experience than I did. After scouting and finding no portage, we ran the rapids on the American side. Charles seemed ebullient when we hit the fast water. He obviously enjoyed the rapids.

FRED WRITES:

The next rapids, Long Sault and Little Sault (pronounced "soo"), were at Franz Jevne State Park. On the way we found an eagles' nest in large birch tree. It was almost hidden until you were right on it.

At Franz Jevne, we reconned the park. The campsites we wanted were below the rapids so we decided to run them and then get a campsite. Charles and Jay went through first. They made it with what seemed like little difficulty. Jim and I saw what looked like a good channel to run through toward the left shore. After we both agreed on the run, down we went.

I did not see it, but a crowd of a dozen or so had gathered near the boat landing to watch as Jim and I went down. We handled the first part with ease and then, as was our plan, we crossed a wave to head into some still water. On the other side of the wave was an unseen eddy that quickly turned the canoe and threw both of us into the river. As we went in, the crowd groaned then craned to watch our rescue.

I easily grabbed the canoe. Turning, I saw Jim hanging on o the stern. "Are you okay?" I gasped. He nodded that he was. I then turned to see Charles and Jay heading our way.

JAY WRITES:

Charles and I had just run the rapids and turned to watch the following canoes. Jim and Fred proceeded down and were almost completely through the rapids, when the current turned the canoe broadside and then flipped it. Charles and I paddled back toward them. We were both worried because the water temperatures at this time of the year were lower than sixty degrees Fahrenheit. This meant that anytime spent in the water could be dangerous. Hypothermia from the chilly waters was a real danger.

FRED WRITES:

Charles shouted, "Are you okay?"

"No! I am cold and wet," I replied with a sarcastic chuckle. The water was no warmer than sixty-five degrees. Its chill stung. Just then I turned to see that Jim had lost his hold on the stern. Later I learned that the eddy had pulled him away and down to the river bottom. Jim kept his wits and pushed his way back up. A motorboat came to our aid and gave us a tow to shore. Putting my feet on the sandy bottom was one of the most satisfying feelings I have ever had. I was back in control.

As I stood up, the man in the motorboat asked if I was alright. I told him that I was and asked if Little Sault was as easy as Long Sault. He said in a very matter of fact tone that it was easier. I don't think that he understood my self-deprecating disdain for being wet and cold.

By now I was only soaked, but not chilled. I think that having my rain jacket on helped to keep me comfortable. I had a dry bag hooked to the canoe with a long-sleeve fleece. After we had carried everything up the hill, I hung my wet shirt and rain jacket up to dry and put the fleece on.

JAY WRITES:

Karl and Israel followed through without mishap. In camp we built a large fire in order warm and dry Jim and Fred.

FRED WRITES:

We set up tents. In the meantime, we also checked the food. It was dry. We cooked, ate, cleaned up, and went to bed. I don't think a hot meal and a warm sleeping bag have ever felt so good.

JAY WRITES:

Departing the following morning, we paddled through Long Sault Rapids. The name comes from the French meaning "long jump rapids." The high water flooded and almost hid the rapids. We paddled through them with little effort. I'm certain the high water greatly assisted our downriver trip and added to our speed.

FRED WRITES:

The next day was cold and windy, although starting out with a fresh cup of coffee eased the weather's effects. I was personally apprehensive about Long Sault Rapids from my previous day's experience. As it turned out, my worry was unwarranted. Little Sault, except for a noticeably faster current, was almost indiscernible from the rest of the river.

Even with the sun out, the cold wind stung. We stopped for lunch, managing to get some relief behind trees bordering a farmer's field. After lunch we headed downriver again. On the way, several eagles and one goshawk soared overhead.

Our maps showed a campground on the river near the Canadian village of Rainy River. It was not readily visible, but we found it atop some high bluffs. We muscled our gear up the steep bluffs and secured the canoes on a high riverbank.

For a change, Jim and Jay cooked while Charles and I washed. The other two got water for dinner. At this point in the trip I felt great but was tired. I think that mostly I was ready for something different than the river. Tomorrow we would be on Lake of the Woods.

JAY WRITES:

Late that night we were awakened by a car driven by some of the locals. They apparently used the closed campground to carouse. We were in the way of their drinking. This was our only negative encounter with locals. We soon discovered an abundance of Northern hospitality and good wishes.

FRED WRITES:

At two in the morning the noise woke me. At first it sounded like a boat. It turned out that it was a beat-up old car, with a bad muffler, rumbling slowly around the camp ground. A voice from the vehicle said, "We've got your canoes. Watch out for bears." We had hung our food high in a Norway Pine. I peeked out the tent. The food was still in the tree. Karl and Charles also got up to check. I could hear one of them say that it was okay. We had obviously been visited by some locals with nothing better to do.

The next morning's weather was still windy and cold. I was beginning to wonder if we would ever have good weather. After about an hour's paddle we stopped at a campground for a water break. An older couple from Fort Frances sitting outside their camper asked where we were headed. We told them. They took our picture and wished us well. After talking for a while longer we said our good-byes and headed downriver. The wind was still blowing, but the sun was out. We found what looked like a vacant lot for lunch. While we were eating, a whitetail wandered into a nearby clearing, grazed while we ate, then casually left. As we packed up the wind seemed to let up some. I was glad, because we were almost to Lake of the Woods.

Blocking the mouth of the Rainy River are two islands. Pine Island on the American side of the lake is a scenic nature preserve, so stopping is prohibited except in designated areas. Sable Island lies, on the Canadian side, close by to the north. After checking out several marshy areas on the mainland we decided to check Sable Island. Both islands are long, narrow, and nothing but sand. As we paddled toward Sable Island, the wind calmed. The sun came out. I felt relieved. Maybe the weather would be good to us. Lake of the Woods is over seventy-five miles across by canoe, so bad weather can make it kind of dicey. Even a mild wind can cause a choppy lake.

We found a protected flat area on Sable Island. Jay and I chose a grassy spot protected on each side by sand dunes and set up our tent.

JAY WRITES:

Parts of Sable Island were littered with trash, but our site was clean. Surrounding us were white sand beaches resulting from several millennia of wave and wind action.

FRED WRITES:

I've camped in sand before. It can be fun, but you have to work extra hard to keep the sand out of your clothes, food, and tent. It can get into even the smallest of places.

On the windward side looking north, surf lapped on the shore. Clouds slowly dipped down to dance on a water horizon. Except for the lack of a salt air, it seemed like the Mississippi or Florida Gulf Coast. I felt good that day. We had paddled almost 400 miles. We were about one-third of the way there.

—CHAPTER IX—

ACROSS LAKE OF THE WOODS

Ev'ryt'ing so nice an' quiet on de shore as we pass by it,
All de tree got fine new spring suit, ev'ry wan she's
   dress on green.

"'Poleon Doré"
by William Henry Drummond

[17 JUNE 2008–21 JUNE 2008]

JAY WRITES:

We began our way northward toward Kenora, Ontario across
the vast, shallow Lake of the Woods. This would be the only day
that we would encounter strong winds. It happened while paddling from Sable Island across the Grand Traverse to Black Point
on Bigsby Island. There was no other choice. The Grand Traverse
was actually the shortest way across.

Since I had the maps, Charles asked me to pick a point. I
pointed to a small group of trees that, being taller, stood out
against the blue sky. "I suspect that those trees are on Black
Point," I told Charles. The rest of the group easily saw where I

was pointing. It turned out that they were on Black Point. I felt good about being spot on.

It started out calm, but we knew that if even a slight breeze began to blow, we would be vulnerable to the wind and the waves. To the west the lake fell over the horizon. About three-quarters of the way to Black Point the wind increased enough that we paddled through whitecaps.

As the wind increased the canoes became separated. We were close enough that we could see each other, but were too far apart to either hear the other canoes or render assistance if there was a problem. Fortunately, the waves did not build up any more than they did. Being too far apart became part of our travel pattern. I felt it was flawed.

FRED WRITES:

Like paddling the six miles from Sommers to Prairie Portage, it took about an hour and a half to cross the Grand Traverse.

We ate lunch on a beach on Bigsby Island. There were two fresh sets of tracks in the sand. One was a set of whitetail tracks. The second was a set of fist-sized wolf tracks. I don't think that the wolf was stalking the deer. They were probably both just at the water's edge at different times. Possibly it was something like the idyllic African watering hole where truces are sometimes drawn between predators and prey for a common need.

I had seen fresh wolf prints numerous times. Once on Sturgeon Lake in Quetico Provincial Park we camped on a sandy peninsula. The peninsula is known as the best camp site in Quetico. Its beach is excellent. That night a storm blew in. Large waves roared loudly as they lapped onto the shore. Winds were strong enough that I feared my tent would rip. Mentally I made plans to crawl under my canoe if that happened. The rainfall was almost torrential. Finally it let up enough that I was able to doze off. The next morning I got up and went to check the bear bags. They still hung securely in the tree. The canoes were fine and the other tents had survived the night. I walked down to the beach to get a better look at the weather off to the west. The morning was cold and the sky was cloudy. In the sand by the lake were two sizes of wolf tracks. The smaller tracks were probably a female. They were in our camp that morning, drank their lake water, and left. They could have still been watching from the woods, but probably had come and gone before I woke. The tracks on Bigsby Island were just as fresh.

JAY WRITES:

From Bigsby Island we stayed east and leeward of smaller islands as we worked our way north. These islands were numerous enough to be confusing. I now understand why many of the early voyageurs and explorers became lost or fell behind schedule on this lake. Even with a good map and compass, orienteering on Lake of the Woods is quite daunting. So much looks the same.

FRED WRITES:

After lunch we headed north. The sun was out, but the wind was starting to pick up. Karl wanted to stop and wait for calm air. We each had our chance to argue our opinion. Mine was that we had each paddled through worse wind and waves. If we let this stop us, then we would never get to Hudson Bay. We then voted. Karl voted to stay. Israel abstained. The rest said go.

At the north end of Bigsby I checked out a campsite. There was fresh wolf scat there. Bigsby is a huge island. Surprisingly, it is big enough to be a home for a wolf pack. Even without the wolf scat it was not a suitable site. From Bigsby we headed toward Dawson Island where we found a better campsite.

JAY WRITES:

We covered considerable distance each day despite launching no earlier than seven thirty. I was dismayed by this. Experience taught me to start early in the morning when crossing large lakes. This allows you to take advantage of the long summer days. More importantly, you can cover significant distance before the winds increase each afternoon.

Our GPS had its first considerable workout. It was an appreciated supplement to my map navigation. Lake of the Woods, with its numerous islands, bays, and channels, offered countless opportunities to become lost. Navigational tricks we had each learned in the Boundary Waters and Quetico Provincial Park were almost useless in a lake with such large vistas. I cannot imagine dead-reckoning with a poor map or no map at all.

While crossing Lake of the Woods, we continued to see pelicans, eagles, and geese. We paddled through the Aulneau Peninsula Park, which meant that we could camp where we pleased so long as we kept ourselves separate from other groups. This was simple to do, as we saw nobody else until our last day on the lake as we neared Kenora.

FRED WRITES:

The next day was gorgeous. There was no wind and not a single cloud in the sky. On our way to Painted Island, Jay and I came upon a woodland caribou bull. He was big and brown with knobby knees and mossy new-growth antlers. He was grazing in a small clearing. We came up unexpectedly but quietly. There was no noise but the gurgle of our paddles. It was enough, however, to startle him. He glanced casually at our canoe and then silently vanished into the woods.

That afternoon we stopped numerous times to check our location on the GPS. Our goal for the day was Tug Channel. We got there about five o'clock.

Charles said, "Let's look for a camp."

I immediately came back with, "How about this one?" pointing to a fire ring on a narrow rock ledge just over my right shoulder. It turned out to be an excellent site. We were all tired and were all glad it was there.

Being an early riser periodically gives me a chance to see some wildlife. There was a cold light rain the next morning, but I dressed and packed in spite of it. Down by the water I heard a commotion. It was a family of five otters. They stopped in the water, turned, watched me for a moment, then scrambled up on shore. Again they turned to see what I was doing, barked in their high-pitched soft voices, and bolted into the woods.

Jay was the next up. We had been tent-mates since the first night and had gotten our routine down. I would get up and pack. Once I was done, Jay began packing while I pulled on my boots. Sometimes he read another page or two in his book or wrote additional notes in his journal. Once out of the tent Jay got serious with his packing. In short order we were done and ready to take down the tent.

The two of us made coffee. Our one stove still burned extremely dirty. It sputtered with an alternately blue then red flame. I privately thought that we only needed one more night. The stove's flame looked like it would make it to Kenora. There, we hoped to find the needed spare parts.

JAY WRITES:

The stove's clogged generators continued to challenge us. They would light, but the flame sputtered and continued to be red and sooty. Periodically we scraped the generator tube with an internal thin wire in an effort to clean it. This was marginally successful. I found it disappointing that dual-fuel stoves, supposedly capable of burning either camp gas or white gas, become fouled if too much white gas is used.

FRED WRITES:

When we left camp the clouds had begun to dissipate. As the morning wore on they completely disappeared. Our next goal was French Portage. Actually it is not a portage. At some point it was excavated so boats could motor through. As we approached the narrows, a small pronghorn buck came out to drink and then swam casually across. Once we passed through the narrows at French Portage we were in the lake's northern section. High overhead the sun relentlessly beat down on us. The lake was glassy calm. Even without the salt smell it reminded me of some wonderful hot afternoons lying on the beach in the Aegean. It was the absolute quiet along with the still hot air and beautifully blue water that gave me that sensation of déjà vu. I dipped my hat into the water and put it back on. The icy cold water felt good as it dribbled down my back.

The flat water and still air was a godsend. We still had significant stretches of open water to cross. On such a large lake even a light breeze creates large waves. We paddled three or four miles then stopped for lunch on a small island's rocky outcrop. Behind us, high up in the fork of a tree, was another eagles' nest. It appeared empty, although any eaglets could have been hunkered down in the nest.

Periodically we stopped to match up our map position with the GPS position just to make sure. We were exactly where Jay thought we were. Late in the afternoon, Jim commented indifferently that an open spot on an island to our north looked like a campsite. I agreed. Since we were headed that direction anyway, I said, "Let's check it out." It was a great place with several grassy areas for our tents. In this part of the lake, the presence of Canadian weekend cottages increases noticeably. The farther north we would paddle, the more cottages we would find. Rather than take a chance on islands being occupied by homes, we decided to take this campsite. Anyway, we were only eight miles from Kenora and even with a late start would easily get there by lunch the next day.

After the tents were up, it started to rain. I crawled in partially to stay dry and partially to lie down, read, and enjoy the rain's gentle tapping. My job that day was to get water and I was done for the evening. The only thing I had to do was eat dinner when called. After supper Charles played with the GPS figuring that we had paddled twenty-four miles. I thought quietly, *Today's my birthday. I am sixty-two. Twenty-four miles is respectable.*

We thought that we had camped on Whisky Island, but, as we paddled out in the morning it turned out that we had camped on an unnamed island just south of Whisky Island. The water remained calm. We headed north again past Wolf Island. Eventually we entered a channel that led us to Devil's Gap. Through Devil's Gap to the right was a marina. Across from the marina to the north was Anicinabe[32] Campground. We paddled over to eat.

---

32 Pronounced "Ah nee she nah be." This is what the Ojibwe call themselves. It means "original people," with a similar sense of creation as found in Genesis.

JAY WRITES:

Approaching Kenora, navigation became easier. The five radio towers along the horizon marked Kenora's location. The name Kenora is an amalgamation of *keewatin*, Ojibwe for "north wind," and a nearby portage, Rat Portage. It was here that the fur traders and Indians portaged into the Winnipeg River. Now we, too, would cross the portage.

We had made it. We were in Kenora. It took us three and one-half days. That meant that we had covered at least twenty to twenty four miles per day. I thought, *Around seventy-five miles! In that time with a crew from Sommers, I would have thought that distance in the same time impossible. Not so with a crew of Charlie Guides. We covered the distance, in spite of later-than-customary daily launch times.* I felt a real sense of historical accomplishment. We were all now among the small group of paddlers who had paddled the entire length of the Minnesota–Ontario border. I felt a sense of satisfaction of having seen locations that I had only previously read of or talked about.

FRED WRITES:

While the others started lunch, Jay and I walked up the hill to inquire about camping there. We had earlier decided to take a down day in Kenora. In addition to needing parts and gas for the stoves, we simply needed a rest. We found the office. It was seven dollars per person per night. With a shower, laundry, and a nearby Walmart, we were set. I filled out the registration and paid. We then returned to the dock to eat. After lunch we unloaded and set up our tents.

While unloading, we struck up a conversation with two Canadians from Winnipeg. They asked where we were going. I replied that we were headed to Hudson Bay.

"We read about you," they said.

"Are you sure that wasn't the David Thompson Brigade?"

"No, it was you," they insisted. I figured that the Winnipeg paper must have picked up the article from the International Falls paper. It was nice to know that we had gained some notoriety.

JAY WRITES:

In Kenora I noticed some tensions begin to surface. Some individual trail habits were beginning to irritate other crew members. The tensions manifested mostly around the food. It varied from something as simple as taking too-generous portions to becoming annoyed with someone's asking to use another crew members' sunscreen. Something was causing tempers to flare a bit more quickly than earlier.

The campground had pay phones so we all called home to let our families know how our trip was going. It also had laundry facilities, so we took time to wash our clothes.

When we checked in, a young girl at the desk told us that we had made the Winnipeg newspaper. This was a pleasant surprise. Our one interview in International Falls preceded us.

FRED WRITES:

After showering, Charles and I headed for Walmart to find stove generators. They had none. We then walked across the parking lot to Canadian Tire. They, too, had no generators. Marley, the young girl at the campground office, had also recommended a third place. We would try there in the morning. In the Walmart McDonald's we had supper. It wasn't as good as a Bucky Burger, but it was warm and filling. Jay showed up next. After talking for a short while, he and Charles walked to downtown Kenora while I went back to call home and lie down. After all, this was supposed to be a rest time.

Earlier, when we checked in, Marley asked if we were part of the David Thompson Brigade. David Thompson is a revered and celebrated Canadian explorer, fur trader, and cartographer. Periodically his trips are either reenacted or commemorated. This particular trip commemorated an 1808 trip. In this tribute the brigade paddled twenty-five-foot fiberglass and Kevlar northern-style canoes from Rocky Mountain House to the annual rendezvous at Old Fort William on Thunder Bay. I knew from an earlier correspondence with Bill Erikson, one of the participants, that we might run across them.

JAY WRITES:

The brigade had planned stops in towns where they were involved in programs to celebrate Thompson's accomplishments. The stops were planned in order to celebrate the accomplishments through various programs about David Thompson and increase public awareness of his contributions to Canadian history.

FRED WRITES:

In the spring, Bill Erickson had e-mailed me about the paddle. Between the two of us we decided that we would probably cross paths somewhere on Lake of the Woods. It would be Kenora. Today was Friday. They would be arriving Saturday. I was anxious to see Bill again. Like me, he was retired and spent his summers exploring and enjoying the North Woods.

Saturday morning I got up and took another shower. The hot water felt so good. Charles was up so we strolled leisurely to McDonald's for breakfast. Afterwards, I returned to wash clothes. Then Israel and I headed downtown to search for stove parts. Israel had already called the place Marley suggested. They didn't have what we needed. We came up blank in our downtown Kenora search. After lunch we went to meet Karl for coffee. I stopped at a lumber yard on the way back. There were no spare parts but there was one lone butane stove. I bought it along with more than enough butane cans to get us to Pine Falls. It would be our backup. I knew that Jim Richards would have the generators in Bissett if we could not find them along the way.

Back at the campground office I met two of the men handling the David Thompson Brigade logistics. The brigade was scheduled to arrive at four. It apparently had been a rough trip trying to meld about 160 diverse personalities into a team. Down by our tents Israel was working on the stoves. They didn't work any better, but they also didn't get worse. I was glad I had bought the butane stove.

Waiting on the David Thompson Brigade, Jay and I met two couples from Winnipeg: Jim and Mary Ann, and Chris and Cheryl. They, too, said that they had seen our picture in the Winnipeg Paper. Again I was privately pleased with the press.

Thinking that the phones would be tied up once the Brigade arrived, I decided to call home again. Both Sydney and Jean sounded great. We talked about nothing in particular. It was just good to hear both of their voices. Saying our good-byes, I promised to call again in Pine Falls.

It was now about six. I had already eaten. Some of the Thompson Brigade members were enjoying drinks on a covered patio behind the campground office. Many were paddling for the first time. They were spending a down day in Kenora and then were taking two days to cross Lake of the Woods. From there they were following our earlier route to Lac la Croix. Once on la Croix they were headed through Quetico to French Lake. I have paddled that route to French Lake and did not envy them having to portage those big canoes across Doré Portage. It twists, it's narrow, it's wet, and it's all uphill.

Finally I glimpsed a lanky, gray-haired, shaggy-bearded man behind a large pillar. He was deep in conversation with a fellow paddler. "Bill!" I hollered. He saw me right away. We shook hands. He introduced us to his canoe crew. They seemed to be having a great adventure. Bill had some good intelligence on the Winnipeg River. In turn, I shared our experience on the Rainy River. The Thompson Brigade's entire trip was pre-planned with massive logistics. At major stops like Kenora, food was provided for them. Vehicles were there to portage them around the power stations. This in no way minimizes the human effort of pushing back water to propel the canoe forward. They paddled hard for long hours. We, on the other hand, were left mostly to our own devices. I think I like it better our way.

Bill and I talked late into the evening. I finally said good night and went to bed. I dozed on and off. I was anxious to get going.

JAY WRITES:

Bill told us that his group was hoping to cross Lake of the Woods in one day. I thought this would be biting off more than a group could chew, but Bill assured us that it could be done. In fact, the early voyageurs had crossed Lake of the Woods in one day—if they didn't get lost.[33]

---

33 Huck, *Exploring the Fur Trade Routes of North America*, 150.

CHAPTER X

DOWN THE WINNIPEG RIVER

De carcajou may breed dere, an' otter sweem de pool
De moosh-rat mak de mud house, an' beaver buil' hees
   dam

"The Windigo"
by William Henry Drummond

[22 JUNE 2008 – 29 JUNE 2008]

FRED WRITES:

Time had come to leave Kenora. It was early Sunday morning.
Israel was up. I woke Charles and Karl. Jay was already stirring as
I packed. The six of us seemed to head in several uncoordinated
directions. Israel went to get gas for the stoves. Karl and Jay went
for breakfast. Charles ambled up the hill to the shower. Jim and
I figured that we would walk to McDonald's for breakfast. It was
closed. Jay and Karl were nowhere to be seen. Standing outside
we saw Israel approaching.

"The A&W around the corner is open," he said.

It was worth the walk. *There is a place for breakfast and
coffee!* I thought. It was even better than I thought. They had

fresh eggs over easy fried in real butter—an excellent civilized treat.

Back at our camp we packed up. Bill Erickson came to wish us well, say good-bye and take a group photo. We then headed off to search for the Winnipeg River. I knew from talking with Tom Copeland that Rat Portage was not easy to find—I guess that several of us knew that it would be difficult. By canoe it is a winding, convoluted waterway with numerous chances for wrong turns.

JAY WRITES:

We resumed our trip, having been refreshed with a respite in civilization. Rat Portage was a little farther west than I first thought. Many of the channels leading to the Winnipeg River were rife with fast, dangerous water or were closed-off by log booms. We finally located the portage after going through a channel and a narrow underpass. Finding Rat Portage without diligent attention to both a GPS and a map is daunting for those unfamiliar with the area. Rat Portage is located in an out-of-the-way channel. Being less than one hundred yards long, it was one of the shorter and the easiest portages on the Winnipeg River. The landings and the portage were wide open. We then set our course northwest to Minaki, and beyond. The river travels unimpeded for thirty-three miles between Kenora and Minaki.

FRED WRITES:

After Rat Portage, our paddle was straightforward. Downriver our choice was to shoot the Dalles[34] or portage across Pine

---

34 Pronounced "dolls"

Portage. Bill said that with the high water that the Dalles current was fast and filled with eddies. Because of that, we opted to portage. Besides, Bill told us that the Thompson Brigade had done significant work on Pine Portage to get their canoes across.

As we paddled to where the route to Pine Portage split to the left, a couple sitting on their house deck stood and cheered us. The only reason I can think that they did so was our photo in the Winnipeg paper. Canoeing is part of the Canadian psyche. It is a national pastime. The canoe and the paddler are central figures in their history. In fact, the Canadian silver dollar is decorated with a canoe paddled by a voyageur and an Indian. Even if they were just cheering us because we were canoeing, it felt good.

About an hour later we landed at Pine Portage. It is marked, since it doubles as a snow mobile trail in the winter. We crossed quickly and found a campsite. While Jim and Jay cooked, Israel fished, catching a small pike. Pike is good eating, but it has a "Y" bone, making it a little difficult to fillet. Because the fish was too small to fillet, Israel let it go. Earlier we had seen a huge pike, about three feet, in the river. That one would have been a keeper.

The next town on the river was Minaki. I was still anxious about the stove. We decided that if there were any promising businesses close to the river, we would stop on the off-chance that we might find some stove parts. The sun was high and hot. In the river several motorboats were anchored. Each had a couple of fishermen lazily casting their lines. Next to the marina was a bait shop. We pulled in and grounded the canoes. Talking on a cell phone by the front door, a young, petite, black-haired, dark-complexioned young woman waved to us. On anybody else the jet-black hair color would have obviously come from a bottle. On her you knew that it was natural. Her bare shoulders each sported a tribal-genré butterfly tattoo. I generally don't care for tattoos, but those butterflies seemed to belong on her. As I approached, she hung up her phone. "We need some help," I said.

"What do you need?" She had a big, cheerful, pleasant smile. Wrap-around dark glasses hid her eyes, but you could guess by her ebullient smile that her eyes had to sparkle.

"Our stove generators are clogged. They didn't have any in Kenora. I was hoping that you might have some."

Without speaking another word she immediately started dialing and then asked us to come in the bait shop. She motioned to the corner where a fresh pot of coffee brewed and offered us some. The number she called was busy so, with a frustrating comment, she hung up. "Where are you going?"

"Hudson Bay, York Factory. My name is Fred."

"I'm Nicki. That's a ballsy trip. Where did you start from?" she lit another cigarette, inhaling deeply.

"Lake Superior," I answered. Nicki started to dial the phone again. It was still busy. She then called somebody else. Shortly after, a young man drove up in a pickup truck. Nicki explained what we were doing and what our problem was. He knew exactly what we needed, but didn't have the supplies to help us, although he offered to give us his two-burner stove. It was exceptionally generous and I was tempted to accept, but didn't. Thanking him, I said that we would continue to check as we went down the river.

"I've been to Hudson Bay. Used to live in Nunavut, ran a Northern for a year. Used to mush to work in the winter." Nicki said. She seemed to blurt out her autobiographical bullets. "Have done some crazy things, too."

"Like what?" I asked.

Even with the dark glasses you knew that she was looking straight at you when she spoke. "Went narwhal hunting with the Inuit once. I'm half Cree and half Black Irish." She never elaborated on her other crazy adventures. Nicki had returned home to care for an ailing parent. She was envious of our trip and wanted to help. Charles picked up some supplies. She gave him his money back, putting money from her tip jar into the register.

We hated to leave, but needed to get downriver. We especially needed to take advantage of the good weather. White Dog Falls was our goal for the day. After lunch on Rough Rock Lake, we ran into some unmarked rapids. Charles and I got out to recon them. Then we came back to describe them to the others. We went down the right side and then slid to the left. From there we found a channel to the end marked with that familiar "V" formed by water rushing through the deepest part of a channel.

Not much farther downriver were some Class III rapids. With the high water, we had seen all along the river that they were even more powerful than normal.

Rapids have six different classification levels. Basically a Class III has larger waves, faster currents, tighter passages, and stronger eddies. They usually require some scouting prior to shooting. With full canoes, there was no way that we were going to attempt them. On the right side we found and took a portage. From the portage landing we paddled through some fast water and waves to a calm cove.

The last set of rapids was hardly a Class I. However, it was bracing going through the swift current. I was beginning to feel like a pro.

At the end we could see White Dog Hydroelectric Power Station. On the right side of the dam we found a portage. It was mostly gravel and probably 160 to 180 rods long. Several of us got out to make sure that we could in fact get below the dam. We could. Along the route were brown and white signs pointing the way.

We single-portaged. This is always a point of pride with any Charlie Guide. I guess we had about one hundred pounds each except for Karl and Israel. They each had considerably more.

JAY WRITES:

The Winnipeg River eroded a course through bedrock. Prior to hydroelectric dam construction, the river sported spectacular rapids and waterfalls. Within Manitoba borders, hydroelectric dams have utilized 267 feet of the river's 272-foot drop to Lake Winnipeg. Historically, there were twenty-six sets of rapids along the way to Lake Winnipeg.[35] Not anymore.

Approximately ten miles below Minaki, the Winnipeg River once divided into two channels around an island. These days, the White Dog Hydroelectric Dam floods the south channel, while the north channel has been blocked off. The historic route was through the north channel. We took the south channel where we encountered an unmarked set of angry rapids. Our topographic maps were not always perfect. The rapids were certainly were not on my map, but they were in the river. We portaged around on the north shore. These rapids had a six- to eight-foot drop. Several standing waves in the middle were over four feet. The trail was several dozen yards long. The rapids' lower landing was in fast water with waves periodically splashing from below my knees to almost my waist. It made launching rather interesting.

Getting through the Winnipeg River rapids went along quite well. I welcomed the chance to gain some whitewater experience.

35 Eric Morse, *Fur Trade Canoe Routes of Canada: Then and Now* (Toronto: University of Toronto Press, 1979), 84.

FRED WRITES:

Once back in the river we paddled on for a couple of miles. On an island we found a great campsite. Charles and I cooked while Israel methodically worked on the other stove. I don't know what he did but he managed to get it to light. Even with the butane stove I was much relieved to see the second gas stove working.

Karl worked on a deer-antler knife from a piece of antler I had found on our campsite just south of Whisky Island on Lake of the Woods. He is talented with carving and was planning on a figural handle.

We had not yet had a hot breakfast and needed to. I volunteered to get up early to fix cheese grits with gravy. Charles said that he would help. Grits is not hard to make, but four hands are better than two. The next morning we ate, cleaned up, and got on the water by eight thirty. The wind picked up a little causing some small waves. It wasn't bad, though. In fact, the wind made the hot day more pleasant. By lunch we had paddled fifteen miles. I was pleased. We all were. When guiding trips with crews through Sommers, fifteen miles is a good full day's paddle.

JAY WRITES:

Paddling the river was a new experience. Whitewater does not exist in the Boundary Waters Area to the degree that it did here. I reveled in the experience of paddling through swift-moving water. I learned how to break through eddy lines, read the rapids, and paddle and work my way through turbulence with accompanying whirlpools.

As we shot through the middle of Boundary Rapids, a whirlpool suddenly appeared mere inches away from the canoe.

It opened to a nine-foot diameter. We were close enough that the whirlpool tilted us far enough to allow some water to pour in. Somehow we forced our way out of trouble. The whirlpools we encountered were temporary, but were large and powerful enough so as to be unlike anything I had ever encountered.

After Boundary Rapids, a large sign on the river announced that we had entered Manitoba. We paddled downriver to Eagles' Nest Lake, which was actually part of the Winnipeg River. We were now just upriver from Point du Bois Hydroelectric Dam.

FRED WRITES:

It only took a moment to see where we needed to go down Boundary Rapids. In no time we were at the other end. There was a nice campsite just past the rapids, but it was too early to stop. Paddling on, we crossed into Manitoba. Reaching Manitoba was a milestone, although the billboard-sized welcome sign seemed out of place. Paddling on several more miles, we found a comfortable place for the night.

I thought that we had found the right lie for the tent. But all night long I twisted and contorted my body around a large lump under my sleeping pad. For some reason I kept rolling back on top of the lump. It turned out that it was a dead root that I should have removed.

There was no wind the next morning. The current moved but was not that swift. By eleven we heard our first rapids of the day. They were an average Class I. We easily paddled down and headed toward Lamprey Falls. Karl wanted to run Lamprey Falls, but we decided to first eat, and then recon them. I thought that they were beyond our ability. With the high water, they had to be a Class IV. Class IVs are intense but predictable. In this case, the waves in the rapids were just too big. We finally all agreed to portage.

JAY WRITES:

Lamprey Falls was not marked on the 1:250,000 scale maps, but we had no trouble hearing it as we approached from upriver. I thought the high water increased the falls' difficulty to something approaching a Class IV.

Two hundred years ago Lamprey Falls was known as Jacob's Falls. The name came from an old eighteenth-century legend. A young man, Jacob, ran the falls on a dare from his fellow canoeists. The young man was killed in the attempt. His body was never found.

Prior to the hydroelectric dam construction, the falls were some twelve to fifteen feet in height. The dam has drowned out all but the uppermost bits of the falls, but they are still fifty to seventy-five yards wide, and over fifty yards long.[36]

FRED WRITES:

Another camper at the portage shared his map with us, pointing out some good campsites. We were now in White Shell Provincial Park. That meant designated campsites. We decided to go to the campsite closest to Point du Bois Hydroelectric Power Station. It turned out to be a great site with lots of grass and a heavy, metal fire ring. After the previous night's lump of tree root, I found this site to be magnificent.

36 Mackenzie, *Journals of Alexander Mackenzie: Voyages from Montreal. On the River Saint Lawrence, Through the Continent of North America, To the Frozen & Pacific Oceans: In the years 1789 and 1793, With a preliminary Account of the Rise, Progress, & Present State of the Fur Trade of That Country*, 53.

JAY WRITES:

We camped just upriver of the Point Du Bois Hydroelectic Dam, having yet again confronted our old trip companion, the Strong Head Wind of the West. Even on the sunniest of days since the beginning of the trip, our companion joined us. Sometimes he provided welcome cool breezes. Other times he was a cantankerous complication forcing us to dig deeper into our energy reserves in order to move onward. There were no big waves on Eagles' Nest Lake, though. What we had to deal with while nearing the Point Du Bois Hydroelectric Dam was the geese guano. It seemed to be all over the place. I would rather have wind. In addition, the ticks were as numerous as they had ever been. Now was the time of the year for the mayflies, or midges, to mate.

Our camp that evening had considerable quantities of goose guano. Fred and I had to take care so as to keep our tent goose-guano- and insect-free. Nonetheless, the campsite was comfortable. With the amount of waterfowl that we were seeing each day, it should come as no surprise that we should encounter the byproducts of their presence all along our route.

FRED WRITES:

We had settled in early in the afternoon, about two thirty. With the sun shining, that meant that it was time to swim. We all jumped into the water with all our clothes on. Might as well get them clean, also. The water was the coldest yet and actually stung my face as I went under. All the same, it felt good to get wet and a little clean. My trail rule has always been, "When it is warm and you are dirty, go swimming."

After swimming I just left my wet trousers on so the sun

would dry them. My shirt I hung up. Jim and Charles threw a line in but didn't get even a decent nibble.

JAY WRITES:

We had the chance to swim in the Point du Bois impoundment. I declined, thinking the water too chilly.

FRED WRITES:

The next power station to maneuver around would be Point du Bois. Jay's research indicated that we should portage on the right side. There was a landing there. Point du Bois is not only a power station, but also a small town. One of the things we needed to do there was purchase Manitoba fishing licenses. Jay had also been burning bad from the sun and needed some sunscreen.

A couple of us strolled up the hill to find the portage. It turned out to be a good idea. I passed a motor-pool building. Inside, several hydro workers were taking a morning break. One of them, Tim, described the portage route, then said, "Hop in the truck, I'll show you." We had a delightful conversation. Tim grew up at, and lives in, Point du Bois. There are four distinct seasons in that area. For Tim, every season is an opportunity for an outdoor adventure.

When we got back to the motor pool, I thanked him. Tim asked if we were going to portage around Eight Foot Falls. I said, "Probably."

Then Tim said, "Let me check with our supervisor. Maybe we can drive you around."

As if on cue, Scott, the supervisor, came through a chain-link gate. He turned to fasten it shut.

"Scott," Tim called out. Scott walked over to meet Tim. Tim explained the situation—who we were and where we were going.

Scott said, "Sure, we're always glad to help." I was really happy about this turn of events because it was going to be a long portage.

Earlier, Tim gave me a cup of coffee. I finished it and threw away the Styrofoam cup. We then headed to the maintenance office. On the way, I saw Karl and told him what we were doing. Inside, several men were still eating breakfast. They offered me some. I thanked them, assuring them that I was full from my own breakfast.

While they were eating, Adam came in. He pulled up some winter pictures of the Power Station, asking me if I was interested. In fact, I was. It was an amazing operation. They had a huge wheel-mounted chainsaw that they used to cut ice away from the dam to relieve the pressure. Underneath two or three feet of ice, the water moved fast enough to not freeze, but, without a relief cut, the ice put potentially destructive pressure on the dam. He also showed me a photo where the water-spray caked the railings with inches of ice. At forty degrees below, none of these men looked the same in their layers of winter clothing. Tim, a short, thin man looked much more robust in his winter orange work uniform.

They were all very proud that they worked at the oldest Canadian hydro station. It dates back to 1910. Other employees came and went while I was there. Tim introduced me to all of them and told them where we were going and where we had come from.

By this time, Scott had finished his breakfast, so we headed back to the motor pool to get the truck. In short order we loaded all our gear on an old trailer and dump truck and headed up to the store. We purchased our fishing licenses. Jay got his sunscreen.

Everybody bought a candy bar or two. Then we headed to just below Eight Foot Falls.

When we unloaded, Tim told me where the portage was around Slave Falls Hydroelectric Station. Point du Bois employees also service Slave Falls. They commute back and forth by rail in a yellow school bus fitted with train-car wheels for rail travel. We shook hands, thanked them again, said our good-byes, and headed downriver.

JAY WRITES:

We learned that Eight Foot Falls had been dynamited and made gentler. This dynamiting was done as a part of the original Point du Bois construction and helped to save us two portages in less than two miles. It also gave us a break in time to stop at the Point du Bois general store. I took the opportunity to purchase replacement sunscreen. Slave Falls Hydroelectric Dam was just a few miles downriver. We were there within an hour.

FRED WRITES:

Even though Tim had pointed out where the Slave Falls Portage was, it still took a little searching. It was left of the power station, but not to the far left.

JAY WRITES:

The Slave Falls Portage actually runs through an island just to the left of the power station. This was one of the longer portages of the entire trip. A triangular sign marked the upstream landing. It was a little close to the penstocks and floodgates, but we were never in any real danger. The downriver landing was next to a concrete dock. Not many canoes portage through, so it was in horrible shape. If the river had been higher or the current any stronger, launching and landing would have been difficult.

The portage trail was not much fun. It was cleared and had an obvious path, but my food packs and supplies were overly cumbersome. Charles was upset that I had set down one of my smaller bags. It didn't make any difference in time, as Charles had to slowly hand his canoe down the steep, slippery bank. In the meantime, I went back to get the green bag, slung it over my shoulder, and returned while the others loaded the canoes.

Slave Falls got its name from a local legend. Centuries earlier, a female Indian slave, in order to escape a cruel master, committed suicide by going over the falls in a canoe.[37]

FRED WRITES:

I was the first across the portage. With nobody in sight behind me, I headed back to see if I could help. Going back up the hill I spied an eighteen-inch garter snake. They are the only snakes in this part of Canada. The snake had a half swallowed field mouse in its mouth. It coiled up and struck at me. It seemed comical that it would do so. With a mouse in his mouth he was completely harmless and defenseless. Garter snakes are harmless anyway, but in that predicament he was even more so. Besides, I did not want his mouse.

Reaching the hill's crest I saw the rest of the crew. The best way down was not well-marked so I pointed it out. We loaded. Down the river a short distance was what looked like a good spot for a late lunch. We ate, rested a while, and then paddled on.

---

37 See Real Berard's illustrated map, "Winnipeg River Routes."

JAY WRITES:

An hour past Slave Falls Portage we came to Sturgeon Falls. We scouted the rapids on the right. There was no way down. We then paddled several hundred yards to the far left side to reconnoiter the cataract. The high water put Sturgeon Falls beyond any of our capabilities to run, but on the left side we found a fifty- to sixty-rod-long flat portage. We easily crossed and continued down river. I thought, *This is June twenty-seventh. We have already been on the trail a month.*

FRED WRITES:

Putting on my pack at the portage I broke my watchband. It was irritating because my alarm had a dead battery. Now my watch was broken. I always woke up before my alarm went off and I could easily put my watch in my pocket, but I had this feeling that something was missing. Tim had told us that Lac du Bonnet[38] was a good place to stop for supplies because the town was right on the river. It was not that much farther on so I thought to myself that I would get both the band and the alarm fixed there.

That night we stayed on Barrier Bay at a campsite that was marked on our maps. It looked like a campground that charged per night. Karl and Israel went to find out how much and where to pay. When they returned, Israel pointed downstream past some more rapids to the campsites. The park rangers would meet us there and collect the money.

Not long after we unloaded our canoes, the rangers came to

---

38 The Canadians all pronounced the town name, "Lac de Bonnie."

collect our money. They told us that a sow and two cubs had gone through our camping neighbor's food. They were car-camping. For the life of me I can't figure out why they didn't put their food in their car instead of an ice chest. I told Melissa, the park ranger, that any food not in Kevlar bags would be hung in a tree. Pleased, she gave us an approving nod.

We left Barrier Bay after a pleasant night and headed toward Seven Sisters Hydro Station. The wind was calm. The day started out cloudy, but cleared by early afternoon. Except for a few high-water swifts, the paddle through Dorothy, then Eleanor, and then into Natalie Lake was uneventful.

JAY WRITES:

The next day it rained lightly as we packed our gear and began the paddle through Dorothy Lake and Eleanor Lake to Natalie Lake. The colossal Seven Sisters Dam with its levees form Natalie Lake. Approaching, the four-story powerhouse loomed ahead as soon as we entered Natalie. I kept alert for any increase in wind or waves. If either happened, I was going to head for the closest shore.

The name, Seven Sisters, comes from the eighteenth and nine-teenth centuries. Seven portages and seven rapids were known as the Seven Sisters. At that time, the rapids and portages could all be seen from the either top or bottom of the stretch of river.[39] They are gone now. Natalie Lake has flooded them.

We landed on the dike just before noon. Jim and Israel went

---

39 Mackenzie, *Journals of Alexander Mackenzie: Voyages From Montreal, on the River Saint Lawrence, Through the Continent of North America, To the Frozen and Pacific Oceans: In the years 1789 & 1793, With a preliminary Account of the Rise, Progress, & Present State of the Fur Trade of That Country*, 53.

to the dam powerhouse to inquire about the portage location. The rest of the group waited next to the dike.

FRED WRITES:

Ed Johnson, a Manitoba Power employee, was on his way to lunch when he ran into Jim and Israel. He told them that the portage route was so drawn-out that he would take us around in his truck. It took three trips. Charles and I went on the last haul. As we crossed the dam heading to the east side, there was a sign on the yellow-brick power-station building with the name and construction date—"Seven Sisters, 1931."

The portage was long and it was convoluted. There were no signs. We would have spent a great deal of time scouting for a trail. Fortunately we met Ed. Just downriver from the dam we had lunch and then paddled to Lac du Bonnet.

Lac du Bonnet is a pleasant and vibrant village. The business district borders the river. When we got there, the village was beginning preparations for Canada Day coming up on July first. Just like the the United States' Fourth of July, Canada Day is a big event with fireworks and barbeques. Unfortunately we would miss it.

I found a jewelry store, but they did not have the right size watchband piece. Then I went to a trading company and found a band that would fit. They also had batteries that worked in my alarm. I felt whole again. It only took about an hour and we were gone. Some of the others bought some homemade candy.

Quickly we were back on our way to the north end of the lake. With all of the weekend cottages built in that area, there were, once again, fewer campsites.

JAY WRITES:

Continuing on under the Highway 314 Bridge, we met a group of motorboaters. One of the men offered to allow us to stay at his yard on the lakeshore. We declined his offer and took up his other suggestion to made camp on Lac du Bonnet's west side dike. We had covered thirty miles that day. I, for one, was ready to stop.

The cloudy weather and storms surrounded us all day. That evening the rain and wind found us as I drifted off to sleep.

FRED WRITES:

That night the wind blew hard and it rained steadily. In fact, it was still raining when I got up. I lay there for a while before my alarm buzzed, and hoped that maybe the rain would let up. Finally realizing that waiting would not stop the rain, I dressed and packed. The wind was blowing hard. As I looked out on the lake, it was obvious to me that we were going nowhere. A strong wind drove big waves—at least two or three feet—against the rock dike. There was just no way we could load without potentially damaging the canoes. I woke the rest of the crew, apprising them of the situation. All of them easily rolled over and dozed back off.

Me, I went back to our tent to get out of the rain. About nine it finally let up. The rest were up by now and making coffee. We were having trouble again with the stoves. I pumped the best one up enough to get the coffee going.

Two four-wheelers came through a gate on the south end of the dyke. With the drivers dressed in dark clothes and helmets, I thought that they might be local police coming to see who we were. It wasn't the police, but a local farmer, Blair, his friend, Darryl, and Darryl's wife. We introduced ourselves and I told them what we were doing, where we were going, and why we were stranded. They understood. Blair told me that he had heard of us on the radio. I asked if he was confusing us with two brothers from Minneapolis who were following Sevareid's old route. They would not be coming this way but had much more press than we did. Their route was down the Red River into southern Lake Winnipeg.

Blair said, "No. But, I know about them, too." We talked for a while longer. Then they moved on.

The wind persisted. With lunchtime approaching I suggested that we fix a hot meal. As we ate, the wind continued to blow. I was beginning to think that we would be stuck there for a second night. It was not a bad place to be, but all of us were anxious to continue. The good feature of the wind was that it dried our tents, which were soaked from the previous night's rain.

JAY WRITES:

On the lake, pelicans bobbed casually among the whitecaps. A down-covered lone gosling desperately fought the wind trying to reach a distant island. It eventually disappeared, hidden by large waves and whitecaps. Off to the north, I watched a storm brewing. The clouds swirled violently across the sky. I hoped it would miss us. We launched about four that afternoon. Within twenty minutes we became widely separated. I thought, "We need to close ranks. This can be bad. How will we be able to help each other?"

FRED WRITES:

We paddled for about an hour watching a storm off to the north. Ahead was shelter behind an island so we headed there. The wind began again to increase its speed. With the wind, the waves became fierce and difficult to maneuver. We simply would not reach the island.

Large breakers pounded the riprap dike. Charles and Israel managed to land. Farther north, Jim and Jay were out of my sight. Karl and I tried to paddle back into the lake. I rather preferred to fight the three- to four-foot waves than risk injury or damage on the sharp rocks. It finally became evident that we could not avoid the shore and that we had to land. The wind was just too strong or we weren't strong enough. We looked for a good spot, hoping for a brief lull in the waves. Then, with a dull crunch that sounded like a breaking bone, the bow lost its fight with the water and the shore. Now, it could not have been my fault. A *Mishi-bizhiw*[40] had gored it. Yes, it must have been the long-tailed water lynx with massive horns and large, boney scutes on his back and tail. He viciously slashed his tail, stirring up massive waves. Then with a fury he came after us individually with his horns, leaving his mark in my bow. That is what the Ojibwe believe, and I have no reason to doubt them. If it is not true, it should be. I didn't know that they, the *Mishi-bizhiw*, lived this far west. I have never seen one, but I have seen their pictographs on cliffs, so somebody must have seen one. Ojibwe legends and beliefs so often ring true.

JAY WRITES:

Before we reached the levee the storm enveloped us. Jim and I shouted back and forth as how to best maneuver the canoe in the growing waves. At first I was turning the canoe too hard into the

---

40 *Mishi-bizhiw* is an Ojibwe creature. The word has a couple of translations. One is "the great panther." Another is "the great lynx." *Bizhiw* means "lynx." *Mishi* has the connotation of "great." I prefer to not translate it. It is pronounced "mee shee bee shoo."

waves. As the stern paddler, I felt responsible, and in retrospect I probably should have paddled much closer to shore instead of allowing my canoe to get as far into the lake as it did.

The storm clouds raced across the lake as we paddled first north and then west in hopes of landing prior to the arrival of the storm. Jim and I were shipping water over the bow as the wind and waves increased in intensity. Three- to four-foot waves danced menacingly around us. As we crossed the waves, the bow broke deep beneath several of them. Jim frenetically bailed out over thirty quarts of water. We were too far away from shore for the conditions. The others were not faring any better.

The storm enveloped us before we reached the dike. It was difficult to maneuver our canoe that far out in the lake. The waves pounded and crashed sadistically on the riprap lining the dike. I was worried that we were in serious danger of swamping or foundering on the dike's rocks. Jim was equally concerned if not more so. Moreover he was angry with our predicament and with the choices being made. Lac du Bonnet is large and was wickedly sensitive to the wind. The waves were higher than anything I had encountered in the Boundary Waters or Quetico lakes.

After a tricky landing in driving rain and pounding three-foot waves, we rapidly unloaded. I slung the packs from the canoe to the dike. Then we drained our canoe and walked it up to the dike's top.

Once our gear was safe, we set off to assist the others. Israel and Charles landed to the south. Fred and Carl were even farther south of them. Fred and Carl overturned their canoe and found a puncture under the front seat. Karl patched it with duct tape. We waited for the front to pass and then set off for MacArthur Hydroelectric Station.

FRED WRITES:

We both got out trying to protect the canoe. Out of the corner of my eye I caught Charles and Israel running down the dike toward us. They had landed safely and were coming to help. We unloaded, tossing heavy packs to the two of them who in turn pulled them up onto the rocks. Then we got the canoe out. Although it all happened quickly, it seemed like it took forever. "How is Jimmy?" I asked.

"Don't worry about Jimmy. He can take care of himself. Stay here!" Charles abruptly shouted as the three of them raced off.

That's rather cavalier, I thought. *If Jim is okay and can take care of himself, why does he need all their help?* I was irritated and worried. I could not see Jim and Jay. Charles's terse comeback was not an answer. We would talk. I stayed back mainly to better secure our gear and partially because I didn't think that all of us were needed.

A couple hundred yards away I saw Israel lethargically walking my way. I turned to check out the canoe. There was a fist-sized hole in left side of the bow from the *Mishi-bizhiw's* horn. By now the rest of the crew were heading my way. Karl got some black duct tape out. We waited for the canoe to dry and then taped the hole. I had already had to do a field repair on a strut holding up the back seat. My battered canoe had certainly seen better days. I bought it knowing that this might be its last trip, but it was taking a bigger beating that I had expected.

By five, the waves and wind subsided enough for us to continue to McArthur Hydroelectric Station. It was an easy three-hour crossing. As we paddled into the evening, the wind subsided even more. Blair's earlier description of how to portage around was spot-on. We grabbed our gear and walked down the dike and then down some concrete steps with a metal railing to the landing. It was short and it was easy.

JAY WRITES:

We portaged along the west side of the powerhouse and paddled across a small cove where we made camp. It was mosquito infested. We made dinner with one of the lunches. It was an eventful day!

FRED WRITES:

Across a small cove was an old quarry. Being that it was eight thirty, we elected to camp there.

Sitting with my feet hanging over a chiseled, lichen-covered cliff, I called Jim Richards on the satellite phone. Troy Martin answered. "Troy, this is Fred. Is Jim there?"

"He is," Troy answered. "How's the trip?"

"Good. It has been good." Troy and I had started at Sommers the same summer. Troy handed the phone to Jim. "Jim, how are you! We will be in Pine Falls tomorrow. Can you meet us there?"

"Sure, I can meet you tomorrow afternoon," Jim answered with his usual friendly, but serious, tone.

"I need a couple of things. Two or three generators and three gallons of camp fuel. Can you help me?" I knew that at the very least Jim would have the generators or know where to get them.

"Sure, I can get both of those. See you tomorrow." We hung up. I felt satisfied that our stove problem was solved.

Supper was peanut butter and jelly and trail mix. We then put up the tents and anxiously crawled in away from the gathering clouds of mosquitoes and gnats.

In the morning I woke the rest of the crew and then immediately got coffee going. One of the stoves still worked, but burned repulsively dirty. We ate and then headed for Great Falls Hydroelectric Station. The weather was perfect. We easily made it well before lunch. The portage was on the right over a ten- to fifteen-foot-high stone and dirt dike and then down a gravel road to the water below. While we were putting in, two couples out for a walk asked where we were headed. Charles told them. The older of the two couples said that they had a place down the river and would wave when they saw us.

Leaving Great Falls, we first had to maneuver around a violent discharge. The outflow caused some three- and four-foot waves even at a reasonable distance from the dam. Jimmy and Karl decided to cut through closer to the dam than the rest of us did. As a result, they took on water and had to maneuver out to bail. When Charles and I didn't see them, we headed back. They were okay although aggravated that we had not heard them holler.

JAY WRITES:

Below the power dam, turbulent water from the open flood-gates raged. The standing waves were between two and four feet high. This gave us some more practice in paddling in turbulent waters, with eddies and whirlpools and waves. The more navigable water was close to shore. The turbulence produced waves rough enough for Karl and Jim to have to bail out their canoe.

FRED WRITES:

The first fast water past Great Falls was White Mud Rapids. We easily ran the initial stretch left of an island. The second part was much more turbulent. We looked for and found a rocky portage on the right. From there we headed to Silver Falls to find a place to eat.

The east shore was nothing but high grass and bugs. The west shore was all weekend cottages. With no other choice, we decided to paddle on. Just then a ski boat headed toward us. It was the couple we had met at Great Falls. They understood our predicament and offered their backyard and picnic table. We gratefully accepted. After weeks on the trail, a table is always a luxury.

Once we landed we introduced ourselves. George and Charlene Junkin lived not far from Winnipeg and on weekends cottaged on the river. We would call it a weekend place or cabin. The Canadians have made "to cottage" a most useful verb. We opened our lunch. George offered something cold. He had soft drinks and beer. Now, I do not often drink beer, but once or twice a year it fits. The day was hot and the sun was shining so I accepted. The rest also chimed in with, "Sure" or, "Yes." Then Charlene asked if we would like a steak wrap. I accepted for myself and the rest. In short order, Charlene and her daughter Heather came out of the "cottage" with a plate of steak wraps and another plate of fresh apples and strawberries. It was a feast. It was gone quickly and Charlene went inside to bring us seconds.

After lunch all but Jay and I went knee-boarding. Even though my rule is, "When the sun is out go swimming," I just wasn't up to it. Besides, we needed to get to Pine Falls to meet Jim Richards. I had called him on the satellite phone the night before. Jim said that he would meet us in Pine Falls at five today. He had our food and would bring stove repair parts, camp gas, and some other minor supplies. After much deliberation, we had decided that even though the stoves would work with white gas or lead-free gas, that this type of gas caused them to clog. We would switch to the special Coleman-brand gas to see if that would solve the problem.

At three, we got ready to leave. George took Karl and me across the river to look at Silver Rapids. He figured that we could shoot them on the right side. Karl and I decided quickly that we could run them. After returning and regrouping we paddled over. We went down the main channel and then turned a hard right and then a quick left back into the current and subsequently into some still water. The Junkins came over in their boat to watch. With an audience, I was glad we made it through successfully.

Farther down the river several bikini-clad girls were sunning on an inflatable raft. Their boyfriends were playing with some kind of ball and drinking beer. One of the girls asked where we were going. Charles and I had already passed by, but I heard over my shoulder one from our group say, "Hudson Bay."

The girls answered in disbelief, "No way!" If it was spoken, I didn't hear any reassurance from our side that we were actually going.

Around four o'clock we reached the reservoir created by Pine Falls Hydroelectric Dam. Jay's research had the portage on the left. George Junkin, though, said that he thought that it was easier on the right, but that we needed to be careful of the current leading up to the spillways. "Just stay right of an old sunken barge. You'll see it," he said.

We hugged the shore, finding a muddy landing. Immediately to our left was the dam. At the top of a low hill was a two-lane highway. Israel and I walked across it looking for a campground or information. We met a local, Paul, weed-whacking his driveway ditch. Paul pointed to the portage. Our maps had a campsite on the downriver side of the power station. Paul said that there used to be one, but now the only camp was next to where we had landed. We thanked him and headed back.

In the meantime Charles, Karl, and Jim had walked across the dam. Jim Richards along with two other friends, Troy and Andrew, were waiting for us on the other side. Aside from our food, he had our much-needed stove generators and gas. We loaded what we could into Jim's SUV and portaged the rest ourselves. Being close to dinner we set up camp and then by way of thanks took Jim to dinner.

JAY WRITES:

At Pine Falls, the campground we had originally planned on was closed, so we camped at the only other available campground close to the hydroelectric dam. Pine Falls was the last resupply for the entire trip. We chose to do camp and resupply there because we wanted to avoid running short of food while on Lake Winnipeg. Scott Anderson recorded having to layover on Lake Winnipeg for four days due to the temperamental weather. Tom Copeland was forced to layover for four days. Between Pine Falls and Norway House, there is virtually no place to resupply.

Lake Winnipeg sits in a channel of strong prairie winds. It is 280 miles at its greatest length and 65 miles at its widest point. For such a large lake it is remarkably shallow with an average depth of forty feet. Many wide areas are only twelve feet deep. This makes for steep-sided, choppy waves, different than the long swells of other lakes such as Lake Superior. Its size and depth also means that Winnipeg is capable of giving birth to rough waters after only a few minutes of wind, and because of numerous hidden shoals, rogue waves appear with little to no warning. It is the most dangerous lake in Canada for small watercraft.[41]

Reverend Egerton Young traveled in the 1890's on Lake Winnipeg by boat and canoe. In the winter he traveled with a dog sled. Young wrote that Lake Winnipeg was so mercurial and capricious that, "You might make the trip in four days, or even a few hours less, and you might be thirty days, and a few hours over." He told of one instance when inclement weather detained him for six days on a small spit of land on Lake Winnipeg's

41 Morse, *Fur Trade Canoe Routes of Canada: Then and Now*, 90.

shore. He was soaked to the skin in a driving rainstorm. There was insufficient soil to hold a tent stake and the wind blew so hard that he was not able to put up his tent. He reflected on how people of that time became upset when their railroad train was late while he had experienced longer delays under far worse conditions.[42]

Alexander Henry the Younger was delayed for eight days in August of 1808 because of Lake Winnipeg's inclement weather. He was with North West Company voyageurs—all expert canoeists![43]

FRED WRITES:

Being Sunday night, Pine Falls had only a couple of open restaurants. It is a pleasant-enough small town with an economy that primarily exists on a small paper mill and the power station. Even with a respite at the Junkins earlier that day, it was nice to sit down at a table again and lean back in a chair. I was beginning to gain an appreciation for how the earlier explorers felt when they chanced on an Indian village or returned to a European outpost.

---

42 Reverend Egerton Ryerson Young, *By Canoe and Dog Train Among the Cree and Saulteaux Indians* (Prince Albert, Saskatchewan: Northern Canada Evangelical Mission, 1992), 53.

43 Morse, *Fur Trade Canoe Routes of Canada: Then and Now*, 52 – 53, 88 – 90.

The Great Hall at Grand Portage.

Fred at Grand Portage on the Pigeon River.

TOP LEFT: Thirty-nine-foot long Montreal Canoe at the Depot.   TOP RIGHT: Grand Portage Indian Village.   BOTTOM: Kitchen behind The Great Hall.

ABOVE: Eagle's nest on Sucker lake.

TOP LEFT: Jay and Jeremy Kingsbury in front of the Great Hall, Grand Portage National Monument.

BOTTOM LEFT: Fred at Height of Land Portage.

Fred on Long Portage with an eagle watching in background just over canoe stern.

Gunflint Lake.

Warrior Hill on Lac la Croix.

Rail car on Beatty Portage.

ABOVE: Fred at Curtain Falls on Crooked Lake.

RIGHT: The oldest cedar tree in Minnessota on Basswood Lake.

LEFT: Rescuing the crow in July 2006.

BELOW: Jay, Fred, Charlotte and Ed Campbell, Norway House, Manitoba.

Fred at Robinson Portage on the Hayes River.

Hayes River eagle's nest with two fledglings in a tree destroyed by a forest fire.

LEFT: Fred and Jay in front of Depot at York Factory.

BELOW: York Factory Cemetery.

CHAPTER XI

PINE FALLS

But w'erever he sail an' w'erever he ride,
De trail is long an' de trail is wide,
An' city an' town on ev'ry side
Can tell of hees campin' groun'.

"The Voyageur"
by William Henry Drummond

[30 JUNE 2008]

FRED WRITES:

Leaving the restaurant (it was really more like a diner with
respect to the menu) I found a piece of metal tubing on the floor
of Jim's SUV. It had to be shortened, but was the right diameter
to repair my stern seat. It was a welcome find. One afternoon
on the Winnipeg River the stern seat broke when I sat on it. I
had it propped up with a small log, but that made the canoe
unbalanced for portaging. The aluminum strut would solve the
problem. That left only the hole gouged in the bow to patch.

Back at our campsite the mosquitoes and gnats were
swarming. It was a warm night. Our camping neighbor, Ed,
loaned us his fogger. More appropriately, he insisted that we use

it. It helped some. Then we got a fire started, which drove more bugs away.

Ed was one of those amazing, rugged individualists who can fix anything and not need a fancy shop to perform his magic. Ed's older truck, although not yet finished, had a paint job reminiscent of one from a specialty auto body shop. The boot contained an unorganized but seemingly complete collection of tools for emergency and roadside work. Various-sized nuts and bolts lay scattered among his tools, on his truck seat, and in his ashtray. Ed had already asked what the metal tube was for. Once he knew, he rummaged through his unruly hardware inventory finding several suitably sized nuts and bolts.

I had originally planned on using my multitool's metal cutting blade to shorten the tube, my hatchet to flatten the ends, and a large nail to punch a hole for the bolt. It was not necessary. Ed would not hear of it. He had a hacksaw, a large ball-peen hammer, a drill, and a socket wrench. Since it was getting late, we agreed to fix it in the morning.

Not long after the sun set, George and Charlene drove up. They had called Canadian Broadcasting Company (CBC) news, which was interested in a story on us. George gave me the number for us to call the next day.

As it grew darker the mosquitoes worsened. George and Charlene left. Ed meandered off to his trailer. The fire died. I threw some extra water on it, checked for embers, and then crawled into my tent.

I was up early. First priority was to fix the stoves. In short order I replaced the generators, then filled them both with Coleman gas. They lit immediately and burned beautifully. About that time Charles, Israel, and Jim were up and headed for a small store just east of us to get some fresh eggs for breakfast.

Ed was up next . As I worked on my canoe, Ed kept handing me tools from his truck and trailer. In quick order, the canoe was again whole.

JAY WRITES:

Our layover day in Pine Falls, June thirtieth, was my birthday. I had a late breakfast of scrambled eggs and poutine at a nearby restaurant. Poutine is a Canadian dish of French fries covered with rich gravy and cheese curds. It is salty and delicious, but not the least bit healthy.

Later Karl, Israel, and I walked around town purchasing some extras for our personal food larder. Karl and Israel bought chocolate and some groceries while I purchased additional hot chocolate. Karl and Israel both seemed to be concerned that they were spending more time on the trail than they had anticipated. At the local elementary school a teacher let us use a small, one-room library's computers to send e-mails.

FRED WRITES:

After breakfast I called CBC News–Talk Radio in Winnipeg. Damien Wall did a quick interview with me and asked that we keep in touch. He also gave me a stern warning about Lake Winnipeg's weather and waves. I knew that Winnipeg waters could be quite treacherous, but felt confident that we would make it intact.

Needing to exchange money, Charles and I headed to Pine Falls. The day was warm with little wind blowing as we crossed by the hydroelectric station. The bank was a couple of miles away. Even on this warm day it was a pleasant walk. For over a week our sole exercise was paddling, so it felt good to stretch our legs. On the way back we stopped at a hardware store to buy fiberglass and epoxy for the remaining hull repair. I figured that I could fix it on a down day once we were back on the water. Standing in front of me in line to pay was George Junkin. He gave us a ride back to camp. On the way we listened my interview with Damien Wall. Once again we said reluctant good-byes.

Next on the agenda was lunch. Jim Richards had recommended the Uncle Buck Burger at Charles Biggs, a truck-stop-style restaurant down the road. I had not had much for breakfast. It was midafternoon and I was hungry. The Uncle Buck Burger stands about eight inches tall, filled with one and one-half pounds of beef, ham, and bacon along with onions, tomatoes, lettuce, and cheese. Fries are extra. Normally it would have been far too much, but canoeing burns five to six thousand calories a day, so I deemed a hamburger meal overdue. Just like MacDonald's in Kenora, it wasn't a Bucky Burger, but it was a feast.

Doing my laundry later, I thought, *Pine Falls was a nice break.* It was a milestone. We were set for the rest of the trip, having repaired the stoves and the canoe. We had all our food. If we ran into trouble on Winnipeg, over thirty days of food was in our packs. If we were short provisions for the last leg on the Hayes, we could easily resupply at Norway House.

JAY WRITES:

We had taken a trail shower along for our personal use, but had not had time so far to use it. It's a thick black plastic bag with a small plastic hose and showerhead. The user fills the bag with water and then sets it out in the sun to warm the water. After several hours in the sun, the bag is hung for use. Fred and Charles had stretched our dining flies around some trees and bushes for privacy. After returning from the library I took a shower. It was only lukewarm but still felt good. Now I was ready to get back on the trail.

—CHAPTER XII—

PADDLE TO PRINCESS HARBOUR

If you want to hear de musique of de nort' win' as it blow
An lissen to de hurricane an' learn de way it sing
An' feel how small de man is w'en he's leevin' here
  below,
You should try it on de shaintee w'en she's doin' all
  dem t'ing!

"The Windigo"
by William Henry Drummond

[1 JULY 2008–7 JULY 2008]

FRED WRITES:

Portaging from our camp in Pine Falls to below the dam and subsequently having to skirt some strong rapids was going to require significant effort and time. Once again Ed stepped in. He took us in his truck to a public landing below the rapids. He was really a lifesaver. We all shook hands with Ed thanking him profusely and then headed out. Our plan was to paddle to Sturgeon Point for lunch. However, we stopped short of our goal on an island near Mitas Point. The first rocky island we picked turned out to be a bad idea. As we approached, hundreds of seagulls screeched overhead in an effort to protect several gray-downed

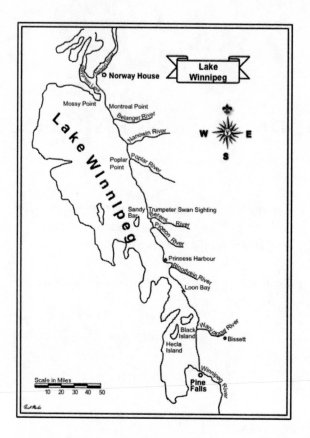

broods. Seagulls are filthy anyway so we would have moved on without their insistence.

JAY WRITES:

The sun was shining. It was the first of July—Canada Day. I felt a sense of accomplishment to finally be on Lake Winnipeg. As we paddled north, the wind picked up. Far to the west the opposite shore was either hidden by the horizon or by haze.

FRED WRITES:

After lunch we paddled on until three o'clock when the wind began to blow from the north even stronger. White, downy, pillow-shaped clouds floated overhead. The waves grew to about three or four feet. Karl abruptly turned toward a sandy shore shouting to the rest, "This wind is counterproductive. I am peeling off."

Winnipeg is a huge but shallow lake, so even a two-knot wind can produce large waves. I had paddled in similar winds on smaller lakes with no problem. I thought that we could go a little farther, but having no other choice we all followed Karl to shore.

We camped on a beach. For the most part it was unprotected. About twenty feet from the water's edge, a line of debris marked the last high water. Jay and I found a spot for our tent that was marginally protected from the wind well above the debris line. The rest of the crew set their tents up closer to the lake. I mentioned to Charles that it might be wise to move farther back. All four thought that they would be okay. Jim built a breakwater with some driftwood and deadfall. Again I commented on the prudence of moving back. In fact, Jay and I moved our tent even farther back as close to the tree line as we could get it. Finally, the rest took heed and did the same.

On the beach was another fresh set of wolf prints. His paws were also about the size of my fist. We had seen signs of wolves all along our route except in populated areas. Wolves tend to be shy, so you seldom see them unless they want you to or unless they might be curious about who you are.

The wind continued to build. We ate, cleaned up, and crawled into our tents for the evening. Over supper I offered to get up early to cook a hot breakfast. There was a wisp of low morale so I thought that something hot to start the day would lift our spirits.

It was again becoming difficult to remember the day of the week. As I dozed off I again resolved to write the day of the week down daily in my journal. I had become too lax.

I stirred several times during the night to hear the wind still blowing strong. There was not much rain, but the wind howled. Once I peeked out to look at the water. It had risen, but we were safe.

JAY WRITES:

I woke at five thirty a.m. All night the waves pounded the shore and the wind blew. This hinted that the wind would blow all day.

FRED WRITES:

When I woke the wind was still blowing steadily. Knowing that we had to be ready to leave, I packed. Even taking my time it only takes about twenty minutes to dress and stuff my gear into my dry bag. Our tent was well protected so I congratulated myself on selecting our spot. Looking down the beach I noticed that Jim's ersatz breakwater had washed away. Had the other four not moved their tents, they would have awakened in several inches of water.

As with most mornings it was cool, especially with a chilling wind blowing in off the lake. After waking the rest of the crew, I put on a pot of coffee and then made biscuits, gravy, and eggs. While cooking I kept looking out at the lake. Two-foot-plus waves were breaking on the shore. Even in a semi-protected area near our tent, launching would still be a challenge. Breakfast was well-received. Something hot besides coffee is always a great way to start the day.

After a second pot of coffee we finished packing, put on the spray skirts, and headed out. Spray skirts are basically cloth decks that stretch across the canoe to keep water out. At each end is a hole for the paddler. In a way, the canoe became a kayak with paddlers and gear protected from the waves and spray.

JAY WRITES:

We paddled into strong winds all day. Occasionally, waves lined up one behind another. As we topped each wave, the canoe seemed to list farther. I was quartering them as best as I could. Fred, being in the bow, caught the brunt of each cold splash as we dove into the trough. I had to improve my skills of quartering waves.

Crossing the waves at a ninety-degree angle, the canoe would break too deep in the trough with the next wave bearing down almost on top of us. Paddling parallel to the waves the canoe took the waves broadside. Both were unsafe propositions. With both the wind and waves fighting against me it was a struggle to keep the canoe at the proper angle. The goal would be to take each wave at a roughly forty-five-degree angle so as to glide over the crest and into the following trough without diving or splashing.

The spray skirts helped prevent water from splashing into the canoe. The water beaded up nicely and then poured swiftly back off into the lake. These spray skirts were absolutely essential on Lake Winnipeg.

Even with their spray skirt, Karl and Charles had to stop a several times to bail their canoe. At the end of the day, Fred and I had ankle deep water sloshing around, but never felt the need to stop and empty the canoe.

One of my concerns was the preservation of my maps. They were always wet. I thought privately, *I hope they last the trip.*

FRED WRITES:

Away from shore beyond some shoals the waves grew to about three to four feet. There were no whitecaps so I was grateful for that. We paddled on for about four hours, stopping for lunch on a leeward beach. After lunch the wind subsided and the sky cleared some. Intermittently, the sun warmed us as it skipped between and behind lazily floating clouds.

By five o'clock we could see Black Island on the distant horizon, signifying that we would soon be on Winnipeg's main waters. Ed, our Pine Falls friend, told us that we would find plenty of beach camps on Winnipeg. We camped almost exclusively on beaches. I missed our campsites high up on safe rocky points.

The group was settling in to a Winnipeg routine. It took longer to leave camp because we had to refit the spray skirts daily. I was glad to have them, though. Leaving camp was always the iffiest part of the paddle. Usually we had to walk the canoes out slightly from the shore, pointing the bow into the waves. Then, somehow, in one motion, we each jumped in, slid under the spray skirts, and began to paddle. Once we passed the breakers, though, we were in good shape.

JAY WRITES:

The next day we were on the water by eight a.m. The bugs were outrageous. They were so numerous that I had to wear my rain jacket and my bug net. I gobbled down my granola bars and then sipped my coffee through the bug netting.

That day's weather was better. It was a sunny, windy morning, but it was warm and the waves only grew to two to three feet.

FRED WRITES:

Jim and I paddled together. We were in the lead when Jim said almost casually, "Wait a minute. Karl and Israel swamped." We headed back along with Charles and Jay to help, but they were okay.

JAY WRITES:

According to Karl, they flipped over while they were crossing a submerged shoal. A rogue wave suddenly broke over them, swamping their canoe. Fortunately, even a quarter-mile from shore, they stood in only three feet of water. They were easily able to quickly upright and bail out the canoe. It was almost a non-event.

FRED WRITES:

Not much farther north we stopped for lunch on a beach. I ate quickly and then found a shady spot to lie back in. My back was aching. It had been bothering me for a while. I needed to stretch out, but hated to admit that I hurt. I must have dozed off because the next thing I heard was Israel telling me that it was time to go as he startled me awake by kicking the sole of my boot.

By now the wind had died considerably. It had also changed direction, blowing in from a southerly direction. With the wind's assistance, we paddled on until six p.m. Jim and I found that ideal rocky campsite that I had been missing. In the distance we could see Deer Island.

JAY WRITES:

Even with the morning winds we were able to tuck twenty-five miles under our belts. Navigation along a monochromatic shoreline frustrated me. I was used to obvious reference points that I could readily find on my maps.

FRED WRITES:

Once again after dinner I volunteered to cook a hot breakfast. Charles offered again to help. Over supper, the mosquitoes were tolerable, but when I woke up their numbers had increased exponentially. Our hot breakfast was cheese grits mixed with flying trail protein and topped with copious amounts of hot brown gravy.

With the mosquitoes and gnats swarming, we were anxious to get on the lake away from the bug infestation. Even though we were surrounded by high waves, the wind was favorable, blowing from the southwest. After lunch the waves grew considerably. Sometimes they seemed to hiss and spit like an angry feral cat. Maybe it was the horned *Mishi-bizhiw*, the water lynx, hissing at us as his spiked tail wagged, kicking up large waves. I was cognizant of the water and the hissing sounds as swells tried to break, but reasoned, "It's only a lake."

Out of the blue, interrupting our quiet paddling, Charles shouted. I don't recall his exact expletive. He suddenly looked over his shoulder from the bow with widening eyes, let out a deep roar, and started digging at the water with his paddle. I tried without success to turn into the wave. It was bigger than the rest. I can't say how big because it all happened so fast. In less than a blink of an eye I was looking up at a breaking, hissing wall of cold water. Then it was over. That feral wave engulfed us.

In one swift, smooth motion our canoe flipped and we were in the water. As my head broke the surface I reached for my paddle floating near my right hand. Charles was hanging onto the bow. "Are you okay?" he shouted.

"Yeah, but my boot is caught," I gasped, spitting water and still reaching for my paddle. I felt that I could free my boot, but didn't want to tear the spray skirt. Reaching down my leg, I tried to find what I was hooked to, but the water action prevented my efforts. Finally I reasoned that to get free I would have to go under or rip loose. Just then my right boot came unhooked. "I'm okay now. I'm free," I said as I grabbed the bow. Charles nodded that he understood and shoved the canoe forward so I could get my paddle.

JAY WRITES:

Israel saw them swamp first. Swamping is what I had earlier feared. Conditions were rough enough that it would be difficult to provide assistance. We turned around and paddled back to help. Charles was bailing rapidly, but the surging waves prevented any success. I was also concerned about the gear in the canoe. They assured us that it was well attached to the canoe. I was relieved to hear that, but knew that it was already soaked. The lake was too rough to attempt any sort of canoe-over-canoe rescue. We had to get to shore.

FRED WRITES:

The two other canoes came to help. Israel and Jay took my hat and paddle. After righting the canoe, Charles frantically tried to bail. As fast as he slung water from the bow, the canoe refilled from the stern. We were only 300 or 400 yards from shore, but it seemed like miles. Karl and Jim paddled to shore to unload.

After what seemed like forever they returned to help. They took our two food packs while we kept the gear pack.

In the meantime Jay and Israel hovered nearby for moral support. We tried in vain to kick and push the canoe toward shore, but were only tiring ourselves. Finally we decided to just hang on, try to enjoy the water, and let the lake do the work. It took about ninety minutes. Then, suddenly I was standing on a sandy bottom. It was the same feeling I had on the Rainy River. I was back in control.

I had expected when we swamped that hypothermia would be a problem. Winnipeg was surprisingly warm, or better said, "Surprisingly not so cold." On shore I pulled off my wet shirt and life vest and put on a dry rain jacket. Charles looked slightly chilled and said as much while we were still floating toward shore. Luckily the day was warm and sunny. Best of all I felt clean. I had not felt so clean since my shower back at Sommers.

Packing food for the trip, I had been well aware of the potential for moisture damage. Most meals were double- and sometimes triple-packed in plastic bags. The food survived. Some water seeped in but quickly dissipated in the warm sun. After a hot supper and warming up, we were as good as new.

JAY WRITES:

It was a sunny day, but Lake Winnipeg still stalled us. Charles and I were concerned about the much wider northern body of the lake. Fred thought he needed to read the waves a bit better and that the canoes all needed to paddle closer to the shore. I agreed. The safety of the shore can be more easily reached if you are near.

FRED WRITES:

Late that night the wind woke me. I got up to check the canoes, fearing that we had not pulled them up far enough. With no moon or stars, not even vague outlines of our crafts were visible. Eventually I could see that somebody had already moved the canoes—probably Karl. All I was wearing were trousers and a pair of moccasins. At first the wind felt good on my bare skin. Then I felt what I first assumed was windblown sand. Soon, I realized that it was actually thousands—or maybe only hundreds—of mosquitoes looking for a midnight blood-snack. I quickly got back in the tent hoping not to let any mosquitoes in. I was unsuccessful. Jay and I spent about an hour slapping and swatting at the dark at high-pitched, flying buzzes and whines.

Finally we dozed off waking after daylight. The wind was still strong. It worsened as the day wore on. I spent most of the day in the tent hoping that it would stop sooner or later. Early in the evening it did pause momentarily, but then abruptly picked back up. It howled through the night into the next morning. I woke the rest of the crew, describing the whitecapped waves on the lake. Large breakers roared when they broke on shore. I did not want to get out on it. I am not sure if the crew was resigned to being wind bound or glad for the extra rest, but each man rolled over and went back to sleep.

JAY WRITES:

Early in the morning, the wind increased to such intensity that my corner of Fred's and my tent came unstaked. I held it in place with my feet. The canoe over the food packs was blown over, leaving our supplies exposed. Charles and Karl had a tent pole break in the night. Somehow in the dark they managed to prop the tent back up by lashing a paddle to the tent pole. After sunrise Fred pulled out a spare tent-pole section he brought and quickly repaired the broken pole.

FRED WRITES:

I stayed up for a while looking out on the lake for a break in the clouds. There was none. When Lake Winnipeg is covered with storm clouds, everything has a lonely, hoary tinge. The water turns a monotonous gray and white. The green forest even takes on a dreary gray hue. Even the white sands are depressing. In the end I decided to go back to sleep in the event of a night paddle. We needed to move north.

I dozed on and off for a while when I heard Charles and Karl talking. Thinking that they were discussing the weather, I got up. It wasn't the weather they were talking about. A black bear had rummaged through our food. In the North Woods there is an expression—to be beared. We were beared. Luckily, mainly because the creature first found our garbage and because most of our food was in Kevlar bags, we lost very little. It took about an hour to sort through and separate our supplies, but we salvaged almost everything. Afterwards, I went back to my tent to get out of the wind and lay down. *Having been 'beared' means that we must move*, I thought.

JAY WRITES:

This was the first time that a bear had grabbed food on any of my canoe trips. He got a few dinners and then went through the garbage. It was a mess, but we saved almost everything

Lake Winnipeg was windy and choppy, but conditions were

good enough for us to get on the lake. Later on the wind picked up again. In the early afternoon while paddling into a headwind Karl said he could not go on. Charles and Jim were out of sight having already rounded a nearby point. Fred, Israel, Karl and I landed, bailed out our canoes, and waited for Charles and Jim to return. Eventually they came back. We ate a late lunch and then, during a lull in the wind, headed north again.

FRED WRITES:

Although overcast, a pleasant breeze moved in from the west. It blew cool on my face as we crossed Loon Straights. Reaching the south end of Loon Bay we took a short break. Then, with Jim and Karl leading the way, we headed north across Loon Bay. About a third of the way across the bay, the wind suddenly picked up and the waves grew. Out west on the lake the clouds blackened and became more menacing. There was no going back, though. What had been playful and pleasant waves turned rapidly into eight-foot hissing and spitting behemoths. I wasn't that surprised at the change in the water. I knew it could happen. Tom Copeland warned me when we were still planning the trek. Also, Damien Wall from CBC News told me the same thing. I wasn't worried for my safety, but was concerned for the equipment. If we lost any of it, the trip would be over.

Mostly Charles and I paddled at an angle across the waves. We paddled vigorously to the crest and then rapidly slid into the trough. Sometimes Jim and Karl disappeared below a neighboring crest if we were both in a trough. Behind us Israel and Jay maneuvered in and over the rough water. Being in the rear they were tough to keep an eye on. Regularly, waves broke across our spray skirt on our bow. At first it was just irritating, but soon I could feel cold water sloshing around my feet.

JAY WRITES:

The wind intensified as we crossed. Israel was now in my canoe. I would guess that the waves grew to about eight or ten feet. They seemed to come in threes. As the day wore into late afternoon they seemed to come in sets of four.

FRED WRITES:

Lake Winnipeg is known for its violent waves. The lake's freshwater sailors and fishermen call them the Three Sisters. They are actually are a succession of three waves. The first two are challenging, but the last one can kill. We crossed the Three Sisters several times. I had learned from our earlier swamping to paddle several waves ahead of the bow.

By now the water was sloshing up against my seat in the stern. Charles shouted, "Do we have enough freeboard?" His eyes were wide and white against his well-suntanned face. I knew that he could feel the water as well.

"We're okay," I answered. As we maneuvered over each wave's crest, I hollered to Charles, "We're good! We're good!" Under my breath I kept telling myself, "Don't mess up now." Actually, I think I used a different four-letter verb. Eventually—it was hours—with each stroke the shore became more clear. Several hundred yards north I could see two coves with calm water. We headed for the closest cove, but the wind and the water pushed us toward the farther one. Jim and Karl seemed to move toward the same goal. They entered, landed, and came out on a rocky point to watch us struggle slowly toward them.

By now our freeboard was only an inch or two. I kept thinking, "Don't mess it up now." I continued to listen for the waves' feral hisses that seemed in my mind to indicate impending danger.

Forty or fifty yards ahead I continued to scan the lake searching and listening for that third sister. If we broke deep, it would be over.

We came in just north of the cove, having to make a hard right. Our canoe had taken on so much water that I could not maneuver it alone. Charles helped by switching sides, now paddling hard on the left to push us to the right. Then we were safe. The water calmed. It was over. The trees broke the wind. Our canoe slid onto the coarse sand beach, stopping with a light jolt. Turning to my right I saw Jay and Israel entering the safety of the cove. Relieved, I thought, *We're safe.* What normally would have been only an hour paddle had turned into a three-hour battle. Once on the beach Jay got out of his canoe. Grinning with relief he shook everybody's hand, congratulating all of us on a safe crossing.

JAY WRITES:

We made it across Loon Bay. After we finally landed, my emotions were a mixture of elation, worry, and strong disappointment for continuing to paddle across when I should have turned around. Our GPS indicated we had paddled nine of the trip's toughest miles. It was nonstop paddling for several hours while watching for shoals and trying to read monster waves. I am sure that from above, our canoe climbing the waves looked like the fishing boat from the movie, *The Perfect Storm.* We struggled up the face of the wave, over the crest and then down into the trough. Then it was endlessly up, over, and down again and again and again and again. Often all I could see of the other canoes were two hats trying to negotiate the next crest. Each wave lifted our canoe's bow higher in elevation than my head. It was worrisome, but we had to get across.

It must have been worse in the bow for Israel. We frequently climbed waves that caused the bow to swing downwards through midair for a second or more before slapping the wave and racing violently into the trough.

A couple of times I was close enough to Charles and Fred that I heard Charles saying the Lord's Prayer, the Hail Mary, and some of the Psalms. He told me later that he was frightened and apprehensive about swamping. I don't blame him.

In retrospect, this was definitely a time we should have followed the shore instead of heading across a wide bay. I beat myself up about this as we crossed. I felt apprehensive even before we had reached bay. Even if it meant having to go a couple of miles out of our way, we would have avoided and unnecessary danger.

We made camp in the early evening, just south of Granite Quarry Cove. Despite becoming widely separated, we all had the same idea—like mental telepathy—about where to aim for a landing spot.

Sleep was difficult despite being tired from the day's exertions. However, today's paddle increased my determination to complete this trip and correct the error of ignoring and overruling my instincts.

FRED WRITES:

By morning the wind had died some. After a quick breakfast we paddled toward Princess Harbour. With the wind at our backs it was smooth sailing around Little Doghead Point. In fact, we tried sailing using the dining fly as a sail. The wind was just not strong enough.

In Bloodvein Bay we ate and then quickly headed north as the wind again picked up. Rather than taking the shortest route across, we paddled to the leeward side of some islands in the eastern part of the bay.

JAY WRITES:

In the distance a barge slowly worked back and forth on the western shore. It was still cold. The wind was not bad, but I would have felt better if we had followed the shore even more closely. The rain fell and cross winds blew as we started across the bay. We paddled for several miles and then took a rest break on a small rocky island. It was covered with gulls. When we had heard enough of their screeching, we paddled west to another island to regroup. Then we headed due north to shore.

There was a light, cold rain when we arrived at Princess Harbour. Since we had paddled in a relentless wind and pervasive rain for the past few days, our morales seemed to be down.

FRED WRITES:

Princess Harbour is a small community—population: eight. Although there is a winter road and a ferry, no summer paved or gravel roads service the community.

Jim and Israel found Ed Anderson, the part-time postmaster, outboard sales and service owner, and who probably took on a few other odd professions. He told us we could camp anywhere. He also showed us an abandoned cabin we could use to store our food and cook in. The cabin was a welcome reprieve from the weather. Wilderness rules are that if there is nobody to ask, then feel free to use the cabin. Just leave it in as good if not better shape than you found it. This one would be hard to leave in worse shape.

JAY WRITES:

The interior of the cabin was dirty and musty, but it sheltered us from the chilling, misty, early-evening air. Princess Harbour was small, but almost doubled in size with our arrival. Tomorrow's weather prediction, according to Ed, was more of the same— rain and wind. Lake Winnipeg sure is moody. It was nothing like what we had experienced prior to this trip.

FRED WRITES:

In the back room we hung up our wet clothes on a line stretched across several rusty nails. Outside, we pitched our tents on soft grass. Best of all, the land was flat. Even though the evening's cold worked hard to penetrate our clothes, we took pleasure in the small amount of heat from our cooking stoves. The steam and aroma from our bubbling chili dinner added marginal but appreciated secondary warmth. I sipped on a cup of coffee listening to the wind and quietly relished being dry. Absent-mindedly my thoughts wandered to our tent where a dry, warm sleeping bag anxiously awaited.

—CHAPTER XIII—

PRINCESS HARBOUR

On wan dark night on Lac St Pierre,
De win' she blow, blow, blow,
An' crew of de wood scow "Julie Plant"
Got scart an' run below—

> "The Wreck of the 'Julie Plant'"
> by William Henry Drummond

[8 JULY 2008–9 JULY 2008]

FRED WRITES:

In the morning my wet trail clothes were still wet. I hated to change out of my dry clothes, but knew the wet ones would probably dry once the sun came up. Karl got coffee going. The rest of the crew gathered. An annoying musty silence hung menacingly in the cabin as everybody sipped on their coffee trying to get warm and get something warm in our stomachs.

Snappishly and with a jagged, sharp tone, Jim verbally jabbed at me and Jay. "Everyone hates paddling with the two of you since we are all stronger paddlers."

I guess I was initially surprised, but shouldn't have been. My thoughts went back to some seemingly unrelated previous events. At times there seemed to be secretive conversations. I dismissed them as inconsequential. Sometimes the other four of us were moody, volatile, or aloof. I wrote this off a youthful incapacity to cope. There were other times that Jay or I was a target of sharp offensive comments that went far beyond friendly verbal sparring. This, too, I wrote off as insignificant. All of these events alone were insignificant. Now, combined with Jim's disparagement, they made sense.

"Okay, Jim, tell me what you want to do." I didn't want to hear the others' opinions. It was clear that they concurred.

"If we don't reach Norway House by July twentieth, I am quitting," Jim remarked in a dull, threatening tone. A day earlier Charles, too, told me that he was thinking of leaving if we got to Norway House after July nineteeth. His earlier comment now made sense.

I looked at Israel hoping to get some insight. He just shook his head saying, "Leave me out of this."

Karl added that none of them felt safe paddling with us as we took too many chances. I thought back. It was Karl and Jim who headed pell-mell across a large bay with bad weather looming.

Jay protested, "I thought that I was a strong paddler." He took it harder than I did. He didn't deserve those comments and would have never told any of the other four the same. Jay was simply better than that.

"If the mission is to drain the swamp, then the number and size of the alligators in the swamp do not change the mission." This is an old military maxim that fit the mood that morning. My mission was to paddle to Hudson Bay. I was determined to do so with or without the alligators.

After the exchange died, I finished packing and took the packs to the landing. Partly, our gear needed to be there. Partly, I needed to get moving to warm up. Partly, I was angry and needed to burn up some energy. At the landing, Karl was talking to Ed Anderson. Almost offhandedly, I asked what he was doing. I was mainly just trying to calm down the alligators. You can put a 'gator to sleep if you can turn it on its back and rub its stomach.

"I'm just checking out my options." After an almost imperceptible pause Karl added without a second thought, "I'm pulling out."

A ferry serviced Princess Harbour during the summer. We had seen it across from Loon Bay. The Canadian government operates it as part of the highway system. Being a part of the Canadian highway system, the ferry is free. You just have to call when you need it. Karl planned on taking it out and home.

Israel was standing nearby. He seemed to mentally retreat from my glare. In a resigned and almost apologetic voice he commented, "I'm leaving, too. I haven't felt good for over a week and don't think I can go on." I had known for several days that Israel had been ailing. I just figured that he could eventually shake it off.

The sky was gray. A west wind blew in cold air and a misty rain off the lake. I huddled up under the fish-processing building's narrow eaves in a protected corner. Jay quietly joined me. I told him what was happening and said, "No matter what they decide, I am still going to York Factory." It never occurred to me to do anything else but finish. I would have gone alone if I had to. I understood that was a rather high-handed thought, but I don't quit!

Jay looked straight at me. Without hesitation he said, "I am, too." I was not surprised and was extremely pleased to have him as a partner.

When Oberholtzer resolved to explore Nueltin Lake and the Thlewiaza River, he wanted Billy Magee to go with him. Billy was illiterate so Ober wrote Mine Centre and used an intermediary to ask Billy to join him. Billy's terse yet powerful reply was, "Guess ready go end earth."[44] So, too, Jay and I would continue to "go end earth."

The other four crew members were caucusing out of our sight. Charles seemed to chair the caucus. He acted as liaison between us and the other three crew members, providing updates on their decisions. "Karl and Israel are leaving. At this point Jim and I are still going, but we may drop out. If we do, I will help you reorganize for the rest of the trip." After this curt briefing he quickly turned and left.

Jay and I were still shivering in the cold mist and wind under the eaves. "I think he and Jim are quitting, too. Let's check the food to see what we are going to take," I told Jay as we both stared across Princess Harbour into the mist. Without any further words we headed back to the cabin. We quickly sorted through the food and then put our tent back up. It was obvious that we were going nowhere that day. The other four grouped together and then wandered apart several times. By now their tent was also back up. They lay down to nap while Jay and I discussed plans.

By noon the rain stopped and the weather was starting to clear. Karl cooked a big pot of oatmeal, offering us some. I was not hungry, so I thanked him but refused. Not long after lunch, Charles commented that the weather looked good for the next couple of days. I wanted a decision. All along Charles sounded

---

44 Keeper of the Wild, The Life of Ernest Oberholtzer, by Joe Paddock, 2001, Minnesota Historical Society Press, W. St. Paul, MN.

as if he and Jim had made up their minds with comments like, "What YOU need is—" All I wanted was for him to say, "We are quitting," or "We are going on."

"So, does the good weather mean you are going on?" I was blunt in my manner and meant to be. If I didn't get a decision, I was going to tell him that Jay and I were going on alone.

"Jim and I are not going. We are brothers and are sticking together." There was a pause. With a sense of personal anguish he added, "I'm sorry. . . . " His voice trailed off with an exasperated tone as if he were swallowing his remaining thought. His expression only slightly concealed that there was something else he wanted to say. I just didn't care to hear it.

"It's over." I was abrupt. I turned quickly and motioned to Jay. We headed back to the cabin to re-sort the food. Charles was true to his word, joining us to help. I had packed each meal separately so one package for six men would make two meals for Jay and me with some left over. The question really became, could we fit it all into a pack and get it into one canoe? I knew we would, even if it was a little cumbersome for a while. And it turned out we could.

JAY WRITES:

With the other four quitting, July eighth was a decisive and emotional day. Fred and I chose to continue without flinching. I had been dreaming of a trip like this for over a decade. That did not mean a half-trip. That meant completing a whole trip. I had also suspected that Fred was committed to completing the trip as well, prior to his asking me.

Looking back, I think that the other four men had been considering quitting for several days. Their morale was low. Several times Karl had admitted to fatigue. I knew that Charles had become scared while crossing Loon Bay. Crossing Bloodvein Bay, he evidently made up his mind. I thought back to times they had been unnecessarily curt or saturnine. In retrospect, feelings I had sensed earlier when they segregated themselves for quiet, secret conversations made sense. Israel's and Karl's money concerns in Pine Falls now fit into place.

For Fred and me, fewer people simplified the decision-making process. We were approximately 150 miles south of Norway House. Many large bays lay ahead. We needed to make distance when the waves and weather were right.

FRED WRITES:

While sorting through the food, Charles offered us his GPS, maps, and a few other items. It seemed to be an effort at redemption, but I think that he genuinely wanted to help. Charles and Israel had given Karl their Souris River canoe. This gave Jay and me the choice of the eighteen-and-a-half-foot Souris River or my Champlain. We chose the Souris River since it was six critical inches longer and had better freeboard.

As the afternoon oozed into early evening, I wasn't sure how to approach fixing dinner. In my mind I had already made the break. We were now two separate groups. I was ready to move on. The dinner dilemma was solved when Steve brought over dinner. Steve and Barry are two of the eight permanent Princess Harbour residents. They had come here from Georgia via a circuitous route through Vancouver. Barry was actually originally from Princess Harbour. The two had fixed a platter full of walleye fillets, cauliflower, potatoes, fresh melon, and homemade bread. It was the first home-cooked meal I had eaten since I left the Junkin's cottage on the Winnipeg River. It was a feast with smells that filled and warmed the cabin. Having skipped lunch, I was starving. That dinner was easily five stars.

After eating, everybody left except Charles and me. Some of the dinner smells lingered enticingly. The cabin darkened as the sun set. A wet chill crept through the partially open door. The time seemed right. "Tell me why you bailed," I said. I think it was more of a mild command rather than a request.

"The paddle two days ago scared me. First time I have feared for my life." Charles was quiet and calm with his answer. He acted as though he owed me the truth. He didn't say so, but I took it that he was also frightened for his brother. I also inferred from the way Jim had lashed out, that he, too, was frightened or at least overwhelmed by Lake Winnipeg. When we crossed Loon Bay, Charles' hyper-reactive demeanor and tone of voice made him seem frightened to me. In fact, I had said as much and told him that was the reason I repeated over each wave, "We're good! We're good!" At the time he denied it, so we settled on his adrenalin flowing extra fast. I was right on the first count. I felt a twinge of sorrow for him.

Charles and I then went down to Barry and Steve's house. They had only recently completed building it. It was warm and pleasant, although, being a California style, it seemed out of place in the North Woods.

Curled up in the kitchen was Soot. She was a six-month-old half black Lab and half basset hound. Actually the top half was Lab and the bottom half was basset hound. Barry and Steve asked us in. I thanked them both for the home-cooked meal.

"You looked like you needed something hot," Steve replied. He was built like an NFL lineman. "I enjoyed sharing with you." Somehow his size belied his ability in the kitchen. "Do you know what the small pieces of walleye were?"

"The cheeks," I answered. It was partially a question.

"You are right. They are the best part," Steve beamed.

After exchanging some pleasantries with Steve and Barry, Charles and I walked quietly back to our tents. The ferry was coming the next day—probably after lunch. The rest of the crew were already in their tents. After I zipped up my flap I heard Jim ask Charles, "What did you tell him?"

"I told him that I lost my nerve." The only noise after Charles's comment was a light breeze and the mosquitoes' incessant buzzing.

I knew that the others were planning to get up around nine thirty. Jay and I planned on being gone early so we would not have any discomfited good-byes. I got up at six to make coffee. Jay, unexpectedly, soon joined me. Next Charles and Jim came in and grabbed a cup of coffee. Although its subject was nondescript, the conversation was pleasant enough.

When I woke, the wind was up and there were whitecaps on the Lake. It seemed to calm a bit as the sun came up, but Jay and I could not decide whether or not to go. In a single canoe we had to be much more cautious. There simply was no room for any mistakes.

Soon, a sailboat pulled into the harbor. Its sole occupant was an older Canadian. He told me that he had come in to avoid a thunderstorm. The marine band radio had reported that early afternoon there would be a thunderstorm with a fifty-knot wind gust. That was enough for me. We would wait and see. Jay and I got a pepperoni sausage and some trail mix for lunch and settled in to wait.

JAY WRITES:

July ninth was the day the ferry came and our four crew members turned back. Charles and Israel were sorry to quit. I personally was sorry to see them go. Ironically, different from most days, it was a sunny, warm day. Almost all of the gear was dry. It finally felt like summer. I took the good weather as a positive omen now that Fred and I would be paddling alone.

FRED WRITES:

The weather report sounded foreboding, but the sky did not reflect the prediction. The sun was out and the wind seemed to be calming. Jay and I were packing the canoe when the ferry came. After some discussion, we had decided to at least leave Princess Harbour. As the ferry dropped its ramp we walked over to say good-bye. It just seemed to be the right thing to do. Karl and Israel wished us luck. Jim, too, wished us luck. He looked cold, though. His color was gone. His lips were tight and his eyes were hollow. He stood rigidly when he shook our hands. Maybe he was mad. Maybe the realization that he had quit and that there was no return had sunk in. I don't know. He just didn't look like himself.

Charles also wished us luck. Again, in a graveled, deep, almost hushed voice that seemed to trail off to deep down in his throat, he said, "I'm sorry."

I didn't reply. I don't think I even looked at him. I couldn't say it was okay because it was not okay. I had put too much time and effort into this trip and into preparation to say, "It's okay." I wasn't mad, but I was enormously disappointed. He was the first to say that he wanted to go. Now he was quitting.

Barry and Steve came down to say good-bye also. A friend of theirs on the ferry was the first mate. Soot waded in the water. She was definitely part Lab. In fact, she looked purebred with her bassett hound legs hidden in the shallow water.

As the ferry pulled out I again thanked Barry and Steve for their kind gift of a home-cooked meal. Steve said, "Listen for the crows. If they are cawing there might be a bear nearby." In the distance I could see Israel wave. Then the ferry was gone. It sailed beyond the point and was out of sight.

Jay and I finished packing the canoe. Everything fit. It didn't fit well, but it fit. We slid the canoe into the water and left. The sun was out and the water was calm. I was glad that we had waited.

JAY WRITES:

We followed the shore for twelve miles past the Bradbury River landing between Split Rock and Kanikopak Points. Both of us were glad to be back on the trail again. Winnipeg was finally being cooperative, allowing us to make good time. More days like this one would help us get to Norway House on schedule.

FRED WRITES:

That night we stopped at an abandoned fishing village near Kanikopak Point. There was a huge, comfortable, grassy spot for our tent. We cooked supper and cleaned up.

It was that night over supper when we decided to paddle the Hayes River and not the Gods River. Until that point it was debatable which route we would take to the Bay. All of our six predecessors had always paddled the Gods River. There was a simple reason why they did so. Eric Sevareid had paddled the Gods River when he had paddled from Minneapolis to York Factory back in 1930. The Hayes is actually the more historic river. It is not necessarily harder or easier. It is simply more historic. It is the river that the Hudson-Bay-Company York boats followed on their fur-trading trips. It is also a Canadian National Heritage River.

We went to bed. As I dozed off I thought, *Now, the adventure begins!*

PADDLE TO NORWAY HOUSE

Go easy wit' de paddle, an' steady wit' de oar
Geev rudder to de bes' man you got among de crew,
Let ev'ry wan be quiet, don't let dem sing no more
W'en you see de islan' risin' out of Grande Lac Manitou.

"The Windigo"
by William Henry Drummond

[10 JULY 2008–18 JULY 2008]

FRED WRITES:

For the first time in a long while the morning was calm—both
the weather and the mood. The four of our crew who had left
had become so intense and contentious that it was nice to be on
the water with only Jay. He is always upbeat. I felt peaceful.

JAY WRITES:

This was the kind of weather we needed. With about 130 miles
left on Lake Winnipeg, I knew that there was no margin for
error. We decided to paddle close to shore on the leeward side
of the numerous small islands and shoals. I pulled out my next

map, the Berens River map, and took heart being one map closer to Norway House.

FRED WRITES:

We left a little late. Now that it was only the two of us we had to figure out a different set of responsibilities and camp routines. We both knew it and had discussed our daily jobs. It would easily come with time.

Lake Winnipeg was covered in a fog. Ahead, just out of sight in the mist, you could almost see a voyageur canoe or maybe it was a York boat. If we could just paddle a little faster we might catch it. Whether York boat or canoe, its crew kept quiet, hoping we did not know that they were there. Unfortunately when the sun burned off the fog, it also burned off any ghosts hiding behind its misty curtain. Fortunately, what the sun left us was a smooth, windless lake. It remained that way until four o'clock. Paddling Lake Winnipeg, like any large lake, is like sitting down to eat a bull moose. You can gorge yourself, but you cannot finish it in one sitting. However, if you keep cutting off small slices, eventually you can eat the whole thing. Although we were both anxious to reach Norway House, we knew that we had to keep taking small bites.

When we reached Pigeon Point we found a pleasant camp. Checking the GPS, we were now only 123 miles from Norway House.

JAY WRITES:

This was our first full day alone on Lake Winnipeg. We paddled into the late afternoon, stopping at Pigeon Point. No pigeons were in sight but there were plenty of gulls to be found. Their cacophony of squawks and shrieks enveloped our campsite.

FRED WRITES:

In the morning the water spirits, the *Manitos*, were again kind to us. The wind came out of the east. Even with an easterly wind the waves precluded a direct and shorter crossing across Pigeon Bay. We paddled east and then, protected by the shore, headed north. Turning west we had a friendly wind at our back that helped push us to Flathead Point.

JAY WRITES:

We ate lunch at Flathead Point and quickly paddled on. Rain clouds floated on the horizon in several directions. We watched them closely as we crossed Peterson Bay headed for Sandy Bar. After we rounded Sandy Bar, the clouds, rain, and wind sauntered dangerously closer. It was late afternoon, so a combination of time and weather told us to look for a campsite.

FRED WRITES:

The water was starting to act up, so Jay, paddling stern, found a string of small islands to follow across the Peterson Bay and around Sandy Bar. Suddenly two grayish-red juvenile trumpeter swans flew over. From the noise you know immediately when it is a trumpeter. I think that the reddish color came from the sun. In normal light they are gray. These were last year's cygnets, as it was too early for this year's cygnets to be flying. Still, being gray they were under a year old. About a year after hatching they turn white. They were probably siblings, as they usually stick together until finding a mate. I've seen numerous bald eagles and always thought them to be and still consider them magnificent large birds. The trumpeter's size is even more impressive, being over two times an eagle's twelve to fifteen pounds. It was a great sighting. Their trumpeting was a thrill to hear.

We determined to paddle until five or five thirty if the weather permitted. Besides, there were not any readily obvious places to camp. Sandy Bar itself is narrow and wet. Beyond the point are marshes. We paddled on, but as the weather worsened we had to look for a campsite. After checking several sites, we chose a relatively dry, protected one situated about five feet above the water. Behind it was marsh, but it had all we needed—enough room for a tent and a dining fly.

JAY WRITES:

The site was about halfway to McKay Point. Before the rain could hit we quickly set up the tent and dining fly. While Fred was cooking, a chilling rain fell. We ate and cleaned up in the rain. I was soaked through my rain suit. The insects were horribly aggressive. Luckily I had my bug shirt.

FRED WRITES:

Already wet and cold, we got wetter and colder. The hot food helped, but we both wanted to get out of the cold and into the tent.

Both of us had become smug thinking that we had conquered Winnipeg. We were about one hundred miles from Norway House. There were only a few bites of our metaphorical bull moose left.

All night the storm raged. It did seem to let up around three a.m. I briefly had hopes of leaving in the morning, but soon the wind started blowing hard again. In the morning I looked out. Three-foot surf was hitting the shore. Some of it was lapping close to our tent vestibule. We had set up the tent about five feet above the lake, but Winnipeg rancorously reached out for us. I got out of the tent to check the canoe and pull it even farther up the shore. Then I fixed two small holes in the vestibule that were probably caused by falling or windblown debris.

JAY WRITES:

Almost the entire day was spent reading in the tent. Since the rain had stopped we hung our clothes on a line strung from the trees. With the strong wind, we hoped that even without the sun our wet clothes would go from soaked to only damp.

As the wind howled around the tent, Fred periodically looked out to survey the sky and the storm, trying to make some sense of when we would be able to resume our adventure. Late in the afternoon he figured that the next day did not look good. The storm would probably still be passing overhead for a while. I could not think of any objection to his assessment. We both resigned ourselves to spending more time at our tiny refuge wondering quietly how long we would be there.

Our site was at most six feet above the lake. As the waves broke and lapped up the shore, their foam reached our tent. The water made a hollow thumping sound as each wave pummeled the shore. I didn't say anything, but the thumping concerned me that the leading edge of the trees would yield to the waters. If they did, the marshy morass surrounding our tent might flood even worse. We would have no place else to go if that were to happen.

FRED WRITES:

There was no use to try to cook. We had little clean water. In fact, neither of us wanted to spend any amount of time outside with such a bitter wind. We had skipped lunch and breakfast. Back in on the edge of the marsh we had secured Kevlar food bags around some trees. Sooner or later one of us had to get out of the tent, so I pulled on wet trousers and boots and slogged back through the muck to our food. After some rummaging I found jerky and trail mix for dinner. It felt good to eat.

With the wind still, we settled in for the night hoping that the morning would be calm. I reread *Song of Hiawatha*. I always find a verse I have forgotten or something I never took note of. It is a grand epic. In the back of my mind I thought about Sevareid and Port. This was as far as they got on Winnipeg. Berens River was just south of us. That is where the two of them were storm bound. In those days, steamers ran the length of the lake. After several days in Berens River with no end in sight to the storm, the two accepted a ride on a steamer to Norway House. Sevareid commented that if they had moved on the day that they had planned rather than staying one more night, the storm would have ended their trip. I forced my mind to return to Hiawatha. Unlike Sevareid we would make it by canoe. With the steamers long since gone there really was no other choice.

In the morning there were still waves beating on the shore. They were not as bad as the previous day, but were too big for us to launch in. Off to the west was a blue sky. We again checked the equipment. It was all in good shape except for a couple of small holes in the rain fly. We patched these holes with some tent tape. I kept thinking of things we could, rather *should*, have done, as Winnipeg is one of the most treacherous lakes in North America. Number one—always get up as high as you can and then get up a little higher. Number two—bring a small marine band radio so you can monitor the hourly weather reports.

JAY WRITES:

Finally, we had a sunny but windy day on July thirteenth. Winnipeg was still too choppy to paddle. We prepared lunch outside of the tent. It felt good just to get outside and see a horizon without storm clouds and a lake without violent breakers. In some ways, being outside made the hot food taste better as we ate watching a sun we had not seen for over a day and a half. It continued to be breezy into the late evening, but at least we could enjoy being in the woods. We both looked forward to a calm lake. While residing in "Bug City" I was looking forward to arriving at Norway House.

FRED WRITES:

We had talked during the day of paddling in the evening if the weather let up. I think that we were both restless and ready to move after being cooped up in the tent for two days. By five thirty the waves were still too large. Reluctantly, we decided to wait until the morning. From our maps and from what we could see down the coast for several miles, there was probably no better place to stop. This part of Winnipeg's shore was mostly marshland.

By eight thirty the wind passed. The waves were down and we could watch a warm setting sun. Best of all our clothes were dry. We could leave in dry clothes.

Not wanting to unpack and cook, we ate corned beef and crackers for supper, then settled in confident that we were moving on in the morning.

All night I periodically woke and listened for the wind. It was calmer. Morning presented us with calm water. We were elated. After gobbling down a couple of granola bars, we left. To save on time we had no coffee. It had been three days without coffee, but with partly cloudy skies we knew that we had to take advantage of any time with smooth water.

JAY WRITES:

Departing on July fourteenth, we paddled ten miles stopping on a beach south of Mossy Point for lunch. Over lunch the wind picked up so we waited for it to abate. Strong winds created a whitecap-covered lake.

FRED WRITES:

It was a pleasant, clean beach beneath a high, grassy berm. We sat atop the berm behind a tree enjoying the shade and lunch. We decided to wait out the choppy water, hoping that it would abate by early afternoon or evening. The forced long lunch break gave us a chance to make a pot of coffee and enjoy the sun. After three days, some casual conversation over a hot cup of coffee was a welcome respite.

JAY WRITES:

There seemed to be yet even more flying rats. Actually, they are gulls. I call them flying rats because they to eat just about anything and leave filth everywhere they go.

FRED WRITES:

Seeing rain clouds in the distance, we decided to get the tent out and throw the bear ropes. Both of these decisions were just-in-case decisions and could have been easily undone. We were still hoping to get several more hours of paddling in, but the wind persisted. We ate supper and cleaned up. Finally at seven we said, "Let's stay."

JAY WRITES:

We were on a sand dune twelve feet higher than the lake so we would not be troubled by splashing water. It was still sunny after nine. I was happy to feel the sun's warmth and relax without a swarm of mosquitoes. I thought about how it should only be four more days until Norway House. Tomorrow's goal was Poplar Point.

FRED WRITES:

After laying the tent out to dry and securing our food and gear, we hiked north up the beach to check out an old board-and-batten cabin.

The cabin had been built too close to the water. Over the years storm surges had eroded the sand from beneath the building, so it tilted toward and was starting to slide down to the lake. Inside were three homemade wooden bunks. It probably was an old seasonal fisherman's cabin.

On the way we found wolf and wolf pup prints. Judging from their freshness of the tracks and the earlier storm, we concluded that the wolves probably came down to the lake that morning for a drink. I always enjoy finding wolf signs. In a strange way I have always taken solace knowing that the wolf is out there. At home I have an antique oil painting copy of Kowalski's *The Lone Wolf*. Kowalski's wolf stands under a blue-black, barely star-lit sky on a snow-covered Austrian alpine hill looking down at a small village. Kowalski may have wanted to portray the animal as threatening. On the contrary, I have always seen that lone wolf as a sentinel and a comrade, not a menace. When you hear wolves howl, it is strangely melodic. If you are lucky enough to see one—I have seen several—it is because the wolf wants you to see him. It is as though he is telling a stranger that he will share his domain for a while. It is a sense of serenity knowing that they are still there watching and raising new generations.

Returning, we set up a drier tent. Then with the maps we made plans for the next day. Poplar Point was about twenty-nine miles away. That was our goal. It was doable, but we knew we had to start early. To do so we would forgo coffee.

In the morning I woke and packed my personal gear immediately. Then I started gathering our Kevlar food bags. At night we tied the bags to trees so that if a bear found them he could not carry them off. By this time Jay was up and packed. We took down the tent, finished packing, and loaded the canoe. Now we could eat. Standing by a loaded canoe on the beach we gobbled down some granola bars and then left.

JAY WRITES:

We paddled nonstop to Big Stone Point where we stopped for a lunch of crackers, cheese, sausage, and dehydrated fruit. Even in this remote location our lunch site had trash lying around. Come to think of it, almost all of our stops had some sort of refuse. Frequently, it was empty marine-engine motor-oil containers or plastic bleach bottles that had been used for buoys.

During the afternoon, the wind picked up considerably. By now both of us had learned how to handle the rolling high water, but we still kept alert looking for that rogue wave.

FRED WRITES:

Jay did a masterful job maneuvering through the water. Aching in my lower back, I was glad to stop for lunch just so I could lean back. Our crackers were partially soggy so we ate what we could and gave the rest to Jay's flying rats.

On the beach were some moose prints. Following them I could see that he had been in the water getting a drink. There were no aquatic plants. After his drink he wandered north up the beach for about fifty yards and then disappeared into the woods.

After lunch we headed on toward Marchand Point, arriving there at four thirty. Being early, we stopped for a stretch but decided to go farther. Poplar Point was not far away and would put us in a protected area should the wind pick up the next day. For now the breeze was only a whisper so we might as well take advantage of the calm water.

By six we found a pleasant campsite and settled in for the evening. We had already learned to fill up our water bladders before even looking for a camp. It saved us time and with rough water we did not have to go back out for cooking water. With two-liter and five-liter bladders, we always had enough water for supper, coffee, and cleaning. This day's paddle changed our habits from morning coffee to afternoon coffee. Never again did we spend time making coffee in the morning. It simply slowed us down, and making coffee in the afternoon gave us something to look forward to.

We were sipping coffee sitting next to the stove where we were simmering a pot full of pungent smelling lentils and sausage when I heard a loud rattle behind me. Next to the canoe was a large black bear. It was big enough that it was probably a boar. Under the bow seat was a small bag of lunch garbage. I think that he was likely first enticed by the smell of our supper, but then stopped to check our garbage. I put my cup down, got up, and walked toward him waving my arms. Simultaneously I hollered, "Get out of here!" Behind me Jay reached for his bear spray.

Generally black bears are just as afraid of humans as we are of them. Luckily he saw me as a threat. With a sheepish look he turned immediately and left. Even wild bears have expressions. This was a pretty remote part of Lake Winnipeg. We had seen no people since Princess Harbour. My guess is that our bear had seen few if any people, so I was probably strange and maybe dangerous to him. Jay now had his bear spray but his quarry was gone.

Sometimes bears return. We ate, keeping an eye out for our friend. Then we made that extra effort to check and clean the area around our tent. We tied our Kevlar food bags an extra distance from the tent and hung the rest of our food doubly high in a large aspen tree. At ten o'clock the bear had not returned so we called it a day.

JAY WRITES:

In the morning the lake was calm. Absolutely flat water extended to the horizon. We pushed hard to take advantage of the still water. North of the Big Black River at Johnson's Point we finally stopped for the day. We were surprised to find that we were ahead of where we thought we were. We had paddled twenty-five miles. The change in the weather made a huge difference. Looking at the maps and measuring the day's distance,

I thought, *Only fifty-four miles to Norway House, as the crow flies.*

Red beans with sausage and rice was the dinner entrée, with seconds for each of us and some for the flying rats. Both Fred and I noticed that we were losing weight.

FRED WRITES:

The lake was glassy until after lunch when the wind picked up slightly. In the morning we saw four more gray trumpeter swans. They are an awesome sight and a memorable sound. Still, we had seen no white-feathered adults.

My back ached so I was glad for lunch and its short break. I was even more grateful for the end of the day. We both looked forward to a hot cup of coffee, but our efficiency destroyed that pleasure. In an effort to get things done, we had hung our unneeded food along with our coffee. Neither of us wanted to take it down. We had worked too hard in a swarm of mosquitoes and gnats to get it up.

The next morning was the calmest yet. There was no color differentiating the sky and the water at that point where the horizon should have been. They seemed to bleed into each other. The lake *Manitos* were most gracious, or maybe the *Mishi-bizhiw* was taking a well-deserved cat nap.

Earlier, just past Johnson Point, the pelicans seemed to disappear. Theretofore they had been ever-present. Summers they migrate to Lake Winnipeg to breed. Winters they migrate back to unfrozen environs. Then, suddenly thousands of them in a long, waving ribbon-like line flew by, disappearing over the southern horizon. Behind them was an equally long line of cormorants. They were the only blemishes on a perfect blue sky.

JAY WRITES:

Both Fred and I found these birds to be one of the more memorable sights of the trip. Flying with the other birds was a flock of geese. As they passed, we got to witness the lead birds at the point of the "V" being relieved and replaced by newly rested birds from the next row back. I had only read of that phenomenon in textbooks and this was the first time I saw it in action.

FRED WRITES:

By lunch the usual wind blew up three- to four-foot swells. There were no white caps. The waves did not hiss or spit at us. Off to the east were thunderstorms, but they were moving farther east.

JAY WRITES:

We kept lee of the shoals to protect our canoe from the waves. I thought, *Only one more day on this lake.* I was anxious—we were both anxious—to finally see the Winnipeg's north end.

FRED WRITES:

Late afternoon brought us to a sandy point across from the Spider Islands. This time we made sure that we had the coffee out. It tasted good over a hearty supper of chicken and dumplings.

JAY WRITES:

The next morning, July eighteenth, I arose at six a.m. I was excited, as this was to be the last day on large Lake Winnipeg.

Then, almost suddenly, I knew with certainty that the end of the lake was in sight.

FRED WRITES:

The morning was pleasant. We had a southeast breeze, but no waves. It was an easy paddle to Simpson Point and then on to Montreal Point. The crucial moment was at 9:05 a.m. It was then that Jay said, "There is the north end." We finally caught sight of land at the north end of Lake Winnipeg. Straight ahead was Little Mossy Point. To our northwest was Big Mossy Point

JAY WRITES:

At first it appeared like a mirage. Then I was certain we had reached the north end of Lake Winnipeg. Through the trees, faint power lines stretched across a channel between red- and white-striped poles. Inwardly, I felt a strong sense of accomplishment for having completed this segment of the trip. It was a fist-pumping moment of affirmation and happiness. I think I may have smiled to myself for several minutes, and could not help but think, *Holy Hell, we did it!* Even though the trip was not over, the end of this infamous, difficult, and demanding body of water was in sight and within reach.

Midmorning, we took a stretch break at Montreal Point's southern tip. Fred and I were delighted to be finished with Lake Winnipeg and all her mood swings. Ahead, Warren Landing's automated lighthouse marked the Nelson River Channel's western edge.

FRED WRITES:

With the north end in sight, we stopped just past Montreal Point for lunch and then headed for the Middle Channel, which was part of the Nelson River's headwaters.

JAY WRITES:

The wind began picking up and followed us along the Nelson River's middle channel, but the growing waves remained behind on the lake. It was as if Winnipeg were giving us one last taste of her fickleness.

FRED WRITES:

Winnipeg said good-bye by lashing out one more time. We had seen the worst and the best that Winnipeg had to offer. We finished off our last morsel of our metaphorical moose and as we made it to the north end.

Paddling through the Middle Channel was easy. It was narrow and calm, even though the wind was kicking up behind us. Knowing that there were probably no campsites on the Jack River, we decided around five o'clock to stop around Big Birch Island in Playgreen Lake. I was glad to stop, as my back was aching terribly. I had partially paddled through the ache either because it sometimes went away or because I was able sometimes to ignore it by concentrating on something more trivial. Two additional gray cygnet trumpeter swans flew overhead gracefully but noisily. In the distance under a clear sky to the west, several motorboats hummed as they sped north back to Norway House. Although they were far away, they were the first humans we had seen since Princess Harbour.

A cool breeze blew as, over supper, we congratulated each other on reaching the north end. Tomorrow we would be at Norway House. For me this was a big moment. Reaching International Falls, Kenora, and Pine Falls was satisfying, but I had previously been to all of those places. Granted, I went there by truck. The point is that Norway House, an unknown, would be a wholly new experience.

—CHAPTER XV—

NORWAY HOUSE

De place I get born, me, is up on de reever
Near foot of de rapide dat's call Cheval Blanc
Beeg mountain behin' it, so high you can't climb it
An' whole place she's mebbe two honder arpent.[45]

"The Habitant"
by William Henry Drummond

[19 JULY 2008–21 JULY 2008]

FRED WRITES:

Over breakfast Jay and I again discussed our route to Norway
House. We elected to paddle the Jack River. It was the shortest
route and would give us significant protection if the weather
acted up. We had talked about it before. Both of us had had
enough of big lakes. Compared to Winnipeg, Playgreen Lake
is small, but it is shallow and big enough to be treacherous in
bad weather. The shallows are a perfect backdrop for big waves.
Luckily, though, there was no wind. Under a clear sky we got
started around seven thirty.

---

45 An arpent is about 175 meters in length or about eighty-five percent the size
of an acre in area.

Paddling the Jack River was similar to paddling the Rainy River except that the Jack's banks were lined with First Nation[46] (Cree Indian) Reservation homes.

Paddling toward us were a couple of square back wood and canvas canoes, each with single occupants. Both men were using long, heavy, homemade oars. As we paddled down the river some of the Cree waved happily to us.

Just before leaving the Jack River we stopped for lunch on a large rock. I climbed up to a flat place. The heat reflecting back from the rock felt good on my face. On the other side of the river, white tanker trucks carrying water buzzed up and down a road behind the First Nation homes. Occasionally a pickup truck sped by. As we ate we both talked of being there. "We did it," was the topic of conversation. "We did it!!"

After lunch we headed under a bridge and around the point to the Norway House harbor. I had figured that the harbor would be the place to ask questions and find a Northern store for resupply.

Out on the lake was a York boat. It lunged forward over Little Playgreen Lake's choppy water with a dull thud after each tedious tug of the oars. In the rear a man stood at the tiller, shouting cadence to the oarsmen.

York boats gradually replaced canoes when George Simpson became the Hudson Bay Company Governor in 1826. He chose the York boat not because it was more seaworthy on Lake Winnipeg's mercurial waters. Simpson's decision was simple. With the same size crew as a large birch bark canoe—eight men—the York boat carried three times the cargo. They gained their name because their main destination was York Factory. Visually, especially when using a single sail, they resembled a

---

46 In Canada, Indian tribes are officially known as First Nation.

somewhat stubby Viking longship. In fact, the boat was based on an English design from Orkney in turn inspired by the longships. Thus, the Hudson Bay Company voyageurs became known as York Men. The boats remained in use until the mid-twentieth century.[47]

After watching the boat for a short while, we then paddled over to a tin building next to a Royal Canadian Mounted Police station with the letters "D.N.R." painted on the roof. We took it to mean Department of Natural Resources and decided to stop for information on campsites, telephone booths, laundry mats, and Northern store locations (Northerns are a chain of stores that service smaller North Woods communities).

We tied up at the dock and walked toward the building. Ken Simpson was the man on duty. I introduced myself to him and explained our quest. He was extremely helpful. His son-in-law was a river steward, but was off, so unfortunately we missed out on up-to-date information on the Echimamish and Hayes Rivers. But, Ken did give us directions to the Northern store and told us of some places where we might camp. He also offered some bottled water and the use of his phone.

I called Jean on my phone card. She knew that our group had broken up. Charles' father had called her. But, she was worried about me as I had not been able to call. Princess Harbour has a phone booth, but it sometimes doesn't work when it gets wet. The day I tried to call, it was wet. I was glad to hear her voice. Things had been chaotic at home, but Jean was fully in charge handling Sydney Rose.

Ken had already driven off so we didn't get to thank him again for his help. Following Ken's instructions, we paddled to a

47 Peter Newman, *Empire of the Bay* (Toronto: Penguin Group, Madison Books Press, 1989).

channel west and parallel to the Jack River. There, we found the Northern.

When the Hudson Bay Company recognized that it had to move inland with fur trade operations, the first trading post was Cumberland House in 1774. Norway House, because of its strategic location, followed in 1812. Norway House earned its name because it was built and initially settled by Norwegians. Access from Hudson Bay to Norway House was up the Hayes River. Although we may see the route as a challenge, the early traders and settlers were grateful for the Hayes River waterway to and from Norway House.

JAY WRITES:

Three early Norway House white clapboard Hudson Bay Company buildings still stand behind the Northern store. They have clearly seen better days. Vandalized metal historic markers tell a partial story. One building was a jail. One was a powder and ammunition magazine. The third was a warehouse. On the water was a dock that was obviously still in use as a place for boats to moor while their crews shopped at the Northern.

Originally the old Hudson Bay Post was at Warren's Landing, at the northern outlet of Lake Winnipeg. When it was flooded in 1814, the Hudson Bay Company moved to the present location in the early 1820s. After merging with the North West Company in 1821, Norway House became an inland meeting place and company headquarters second only to York Factory. Company principals met at Norway House to avoid trips down the Hayes River to York Factory. It also became the throat through which all goods were funneled from York Factory to the Canadian interior. Norway House's importance declined in the latter half of the nineteeth century with the arrival of the railroad to Manitoba.

FRED WRITES:

Inside, the Northern store reminded me of a mini Walmart. Although small, there was a wonderfully plentiful variety of groceries and, more importantly, gas for our stoves. Since we had quit using car gasoline, the stoves had not gummed up. I was intent on not chancing problems on this last leg so I was pleased to see the familiar red, camp gas cans.

Lloyd Nielson, the manager, spotted us and asked where we had started and where we were headed. "Lake Superior. We're going to Hudson Bay—York Factory." I don't remember which one of us answered. We talked for a while. I think that both of us enjoyed talking to somebody else for a change. Since we left Princess Harbour, our only human contact was with each other. Lloyd had worked for the Northern stores for thirty years. At one time the Hudson Bay Company owned the Northerns, but sold them off. Interestingly, the flag outside the Northerns, using a graceful script, has the letters "N W Co"—the North West Company.

Lloyd also gave us some good information on Hairy Lake, located about halfway up the Echimamish to the Hayes River. "Paddling east, on the right side, is a passage through the grass and cattails, worn open from years of First Nation use," He said.

I thanked him for the information. Paddling through reeds and lake grasses can be quite exhausting. It was nice to know that there was a path through them. We headed back up the river toward Gertrude Mietle's home. Ken had told us that she rented cabins and might let us camp on her property. On the way there was a house that remotely fit Gertrude's house's description. We decided to ask rather than miss our destination.

After tying up to the dock, we walked up the steps to the house. In the backyard next to a freshly painted forest green deck, an older man was relaxing in the shade of a tree. I have to be careful calling him older, as it turned out that he wasn't much older than I was. We introduced ourselves. He was Ed Campbell. I told him that we were looking for Gertrude's place.

"Sit down and talk for a while. I am just getting things spruced up for our fiftieth anniversary. Gertrude's place is farther down. Where are you going?" Ed asked with a rich North Woods accent.

"We're canoeing to York Factory. We're just planning to spend a couple of nights here, recoup, and resupply," I said. "We started at Lake Superior."

"Well, if you're only spending a couple of days here, you can stay with us. Let me go tell my wife." He said it as though we were not to argue. Ed walked with his cane into the house and returned with his wife Charlotte.

Introducing myself, I said, "I feel like we are imposing." I needed to make an objection. We really were imposing.

I was going to say that we were only looking for directions, but before I could say anything else, she said, "I'm Charlotte Campbell. We are North Woods aboriginal people and this is what we do." Her graciousness, smile, sparkling eyes, and warmth melted any other objections that Jay or I might have had.

They put us up in the den. There was a bed, sofa, and rollaway bed. I took the bed and Jay took the rollaway. First we put our food and gear in a dockside storeroom. Our personal pack we put in the den. Jay and I showered and took Charlotte up on her offer to use her washing machine. A shower never felt so good. I don't think that the sauna at Sommers felt any better.

Next Charlotte fixed a pot of Tim Horton's coffee. We had not fixed coffee that day, so a fresh cup of Tim Horton's was a special treat. It is strong, rich, and flavorful. My sister always brings me a can when she comes home to visit from Calgary. I only share it with special people. Starbucks could learn a lesson from Tim

Horton. Over coffee Charlotte asked where we stopped on Lake Winnipeg. "Princess Harbour," I said.

"Did you meet Ed Anderson?"

"We did. How do you know him?" I was surprised at how small the North Woods were.

"I grew up on Lake Winnipeg. Ed and I were the two tallest people so I used to go dancing with him. How is he doing?"

It was a small world. I told her that Ed seemed to be fine. She then asked if I had seen *Quest for the Bay*. *Quest for the Bay* is a Canadian Broadcasting Company documentary film with eight modern-day Canadian adventurers who row a forty-foot wooden York boat from Winnipeg to York Factory. The only trappings they could carry on the twelve-week trip were 1840 vintage gear and food.

"I have. In fact, a couple times. It is a great show. I wish that they would put it back on," I answered as I savored another sip of Tim Horton's.

"You know, it was a big event when they came through in their York boat. In fact, we knew one of the crew and met the others." She got out a thank-you note they had sent with all their signatures.

"There are two young men paddling from Minneapolis to the bay. Have they been through?" I had read about them on the Internet and was curious as to where we were in relation to each other. Actually, I hoped we were ahead of them.

"There were a couple of paddlers who were here ten or twelve days ago. I'll check. It may have been those two," Charlotte answered.

We talked for a while longer when I remembered Jeremy Kingsbury's letter for the Norway House piper. "Charlotte, is there a piper here?"

"No. If we need a piper then we bring him in. You know that

in two weeks will be our annual York Boat Days. People come in from all over. There is food, York boat and canoe racing. Ed will have to take you to see the York boats tomorrow." That explained what the York boat and the canoes were doing as we paddled in. They were training for the York Boat Days' races.

Ed and Charlotte left for Ed's sister's house. As they hurried off, Charlotte showed me some hamburger meat for us to cook for supper. Jay and I sipped on another cup of coffee while we waited for the laundry to dry. I called and left a message on Charles' voice mail letting him know we had made it to Norway House. He had asked me to do so and I had promised that I would. It had been a pleasant, yet eventful afternoon. Now, the food was safely stored. We were clean. Our clothes were clean. Our families knew that we were okay. Everything was done.

I was again overwhelmed by the North Woods hospitality. The Junkins, Barry, Steve, Ed Anderson, and the Campbells had all been most gracious. We need more people like them in the world. I was impressed. They had fed us and opened up their homes to us. Granted, we were doing something unusual, but we were total strangers. We also carried with us a strong trail odor of smoke and sweat. Yet, we were still welcome.

When Ed and Charlotte came back from his sister's house, we were able to talk. I learned more about them.

Ed is mostly Cree. His grandfather was a Scot who immigrated to Canada and went to work for the Hudson Bay Company. When he started work, he told his supervisor that he was hungry and asked where he could find something to eat. His boss gave him a rifle with three rounds and said, "Go kill something." He married a Cree woman. Their son, Ed's father, carried the mail and, like so many others, also worked in the fur trade. Ed's mother was Cree, so I guess that makes Ed three-quarters Cree.

As a teenager, Ed also worked in the fur trade loading large freighter canoes bound for Selkirk at Lake Winnipeg's southern end. They carried fur bundles that were later sent to Montreal. In fact, he loaded the last ten fur canoes to leave Norway House. I didn't ask him when that happened, but suspect that it was close to the time that York Factory closed in 1957.

Cree is his native language. Ed is fluent. When he was growing up, the schools didn't want the students to speak Cree. If teachers heard Cree being spoken, they "strapped" the offending boy. I took it that Ed meant he was hit with a heavy, thick, leather strap. Anyway, this Cree language prohibition and strapping was an understandable irritant. When Ed was sixteen, he had a teacher, German by birth, who was overly strict and cruel. This occurred at a time that the west was either still at war with Germany or had just defeated Germany. That spring, after school was out for the year, Ed and four or five of his friends found their German teacher and beat the living daylights out of him. Ed used some stronger words to describe their vengeance. He finished the story, chuckling, "I guess that word got around because none of the teachers ever strapped us again for speaking Cree. Eh?"

Charlotte is a retired nurse. That gave us some common ground because my wife teaches nursing. Charlotte started out working in a hospital and eventually went to school receiving her degree from St. Boniface in Winnipeg. She didn't talk much about growing up, but had an obvious strong affinity for her First Nation heritage and history.

Sunday morning, Charlotte fixed fresh poached eggs, sausage, and toast. After we'd spent almost two months on the trail, this meal was a real treat. A large pot of aromatic fresh coffee perked on the counter. Ed sat at his favorite place where he could see the river through the living room or kitchen window.

After breakfast Charlotte went to church. Ed turned on the

radio to the Cree station. The tunes were familiar, but I couldn't understand the language. As I listened I finally realized that they were old gospel and religious songs translated into Cree. I thought it was beautiful and said so.

Jay and I listened for a while and then went down to the dock to check the food. We had twenty-five days left of meals plus five pounds of grits and four or five pounds of Bisquick. We needed some more tortillas to use for sandwich bread for our peanut butter and jelly.

After Charlotte came back from church, Ed took us to the grocery and then over to Rossville where the York boats were docked. On the way he told us, "They make them out of aluminum now. When they first decided to have the York Boat Days, they couldn't find anybody who knew how to make York boats. So my father came back with his model of a boat and showed them how. They made them out of wood then. But, they didn't use the hardwoods that they used to use so the boats didn't last. Now they make them out of aluminum." Every other sentence ended with the Canadian North Woods "Eh." It was distinctive, charming, and almost contagious. I can still hear Ed talk, eh.

First we went to the old church. It was built in the 1840s by an English Methodist missionary, James Evans. Evans' story was inscribed on a nearby monument in English and Cree.

The Methodist Church posted him to Norway House in 1840. Realizing that English transliteration for the Cree language just would not work, he dove into creating a Cree alphabet based on English shorthand. He then built a printing press and began printing hymns for his congregation in his newly invented Cree alphabet. In the interim he translated the Bible into Cree. Finally in 1845 he was able to obtain a printing press from his superiors. Some of his Christian standards such as "Do not paddle on Sunday" got him in trouble with the then Hudson Bay governor,

George Simpson. The Hudson Bay Company saw him as interfering with commerce. Evans was charged with sedition, tried, and eventually acquitted. He died in 1846 in England.

Tied to the dock were two sizes of York boats. The large ones were for the adults and the small ones were for the children. Nine-man northern canoes were sitting nearby on trailers. These were basically the same design that the David Thompson Brigade used—sleek and large. I think Jay and I both secretly wished that we could stay for the York Boat Days, but knew that we had to continue on. In the north the summer grows short too quickly. As much as we were enjoying our trek, we both had to eventually go home.

Back at the Campbell's, Charlotte fixed supper. Then the two of them went to the bus station to pick up their granddaughter, Kristen. She was returning from a trip to Winnipeg to shop for a dress.

In the morning Jay and I had coffee with Ed, packed our canoe, and reluctantly said our good-byes. First we stopped at the Northern to get stove gas and then headed for the Department of Natural Resources building to find Ken and thank him for his thoughtfulness. We also needed to register our trip with the Royal Canadian Mounted Police in the event of a problem. Between Norway House and Hudson Bay, the only contact with civilization is Oxford House on Oxford Lake and North Star Lodge on Knee Lake. Registering our route would give the Mounties a starting point if we had problems. The duty sergeant was R.W. Batchelor. He was somewhat taken aback with our trip so far. After methodically taking down what he needed, we shook hands and he wished us luck.

We found Ken Simpson and again thanked him. He told us that he usually told people that they needed to allow twenty-one days to Hudson Bay. I thought back to the food. With twenty-five days worth, we had a sufficient amount. In fact, we had more than enough since we planned on less than twenty-one days. At least we hoped for less than twenty-one days.

Now we were again on the trail. The day was scorching hot. I had to keep dipping my hat and bandana into the water to cool off. By midafternoon we were at Sea Falls. I remembered the falls from *Quest for the Bay*. The old York boat used to run, but it was far too much for us especially with an overloaded canoe. We easily portaged around and then headed down the Nelson River looking for a campsite. Just past the ferry crossing we found one. It wasn't a great campsite, but it was only us and it was getting late. All around, the crows were making a racket. I thought back to what Steve had told us. "Listen for the crows. When they make a racket, there are bears around." His image whispered in my ear as we unloaded the canoes. There were no bears. I think the crows were just fussing at each other or maybe us. Anyway, I always check for signs of animals—scratchings on a tree, scat, or maybe a lie down. The island was small and didn't offer any food, so in spite of the crows we deemed it safe to stay. I proudly thought, *Tomorrow we will be on the Echimamish.*

CHAPTER XVI

PADDLE TO OXFORD HOUSE

But we'll not t'ink moche of danger, for de rapide she's
   no stranger
Many tam we're runnin' t'roo it, on de fall an' on de
   spring,
On mos' ev'ry kin' of wedder dat le Bon Dieu scrape
   togedder,
An' we'll never drown noboddy, an' we'll never bus'
   somet'ing.

"'Poleon Doré"
by William Henry Drummond

[22 JULY 2008–28 JULY 2008]

JAY WRITES:

We located the Echimamish's mouth, near a place called High
Rock. It wasn't more than thirty feet tall, but seemed high compared to the rest of the area. The numerous islands braiding
our meandering path made the GPS invaluable. It reassured us
that we were reading the maps correctly. The Echimamish River's name, meaning, "The River That Flows Both Ways," came
from local Cree Indians. Going toward Painted Stone Portage,

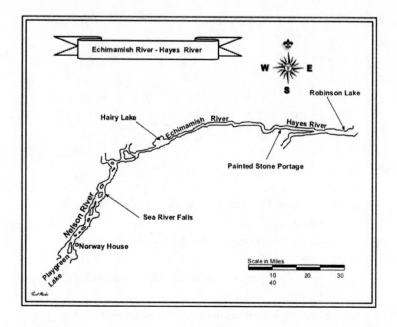

although the current is hardly noticeable, but you are paddling upstream. After Painted Stone Portage you are on the Hayes. There you portage over a hill, a minor Height of Land to begin the paddle downstream to Hudson Bay

FRED WRITES:

The first day on the Echimamish River[48] started out beautifully and remained that way. The river is attractive, looking more tropical than boreal. It may have seemed that way because the water was so high. It had been high the entire trip. At several points, people had warned us to be careful because of the high water. Ed Campbell told us that it would be easy going and that there were signs pointing the way to Oxford House.

---

48 The Cree I met pronounced it, "E-ka-maim-ish."

Roughly halfway to Painted Stone is Hairy Lake. We reached it at lunchtime. On a steep rock downhill from an abandoned cabin, we propped ourselves up for a quick lunch. From our vantage point the lake looked like it had a coat of fuzz. Remembering that Lloyd said that there was an open channel on the right, we kept close to the shore and then cut toward the center looking for the open water. We stayed surrounded by reeds. We then headed back toward the shore where we found it to be more open. Hairy Lake was not that big, so we could easily see the tree line marking the east end.

Early afternoon we reached where the Echimamish started again. Next to the river was a perfect campsite. "Do you want to stop?" I asked.

JAY WRITES:

At first I said, "No. Let's go on." Then on reflection I thought it prudent to camp here since campsites on the Echimamish were few. Ed had told us that there were only three. We, in fact, had not seen many sites on our way to Hairy Lake. I factored this into my reply to stay. The place was comfortable but messy. Strewn throughout the site was garbage from previous inconsiderate campers.

FRED WRITES:

The weather was beautiful that afternoon, so sitting in the sun was a treat. The wind picked up enough to keep the bugs down. We fixed a couple of pots of coffee. One of the stoves had started to act up, so I put our last generator on it. That solved the problem. Our personal gear pack, the gray whale, had a tear. That, too, I repaired.

We were both excited to be on the Echimamish. It was a place I had thought of for over a year. We both commented on the men who had paddled past this exact point. I think also that it was at this point that we both realized that we would finish our trek. It was not that we ever thought that we would not finish, but now we could see the proverbial light at the end of the tunnel. From this point on, nothing would or could prevent us from reaching our goal. We weren't smug, but confident.

We left Hairy Lake about seven thirty in the morning. Along the way were several prospective campsites. In fact, some were even marked with a black-lettered white sign saying, "Campsite." Toward lunch the banks became swampy with hordes of bugs. Finally we found a beaver run that was high enough to give us some less wet, firm ground. We stopped there long enough to eat and then left to escape the bugs.

About an hour up the river we found a rock to take a break on. It felt good to stretch out. My back was starting to bother me again. I could, to a degree, paddle through the pain, but relished the break. After about thirty minutes the rains came. It was not much more than a cold drizzle, but we moved on. If it is raining, paddle. In a cold drizzle, no matter what you do, you will get wet, but at least you'll be warm if you paddle.

JAY WRITES:

After twelve hours paddling we stopped about one mile from Painted Stone Portage. The two of us had covered close to thirty miles on a meandering river. The several times we had to pull our canoe over beaver dams were respites for our aching backs. I think that we were both glad to arrive and set up camp. It felt good to finally stand and stretch, as there were almost no places along the river to stop. It was a quiet paddle. We saw little wildlife. In places, the Echimamish was so narrow that it was hard to comprehend how York boats made it through. Even with the high water it was shallow and narrow—less than six yards wide in some places.

FRED WRITES:

Just as we finished the nightly chores and were crawling into the tent, the rain picked up. I dozed on and off. It seemed to rain all night.

The next morning as I crawled out of the tent there was a definite moist chill in the air, but the rain was gone. We canoed on to Painted Stone thinking that we would unload and cross. However, down a sloping rock to the Hayes was a large, slippery, oversized log ladder. Ed had described this structure, saying that all we had to do was slide down. With nothing to lose, we decided to give it a try. The canoe easily slid down over the rungs and happily splashed into the Hayes below.

We were there. We were in the Hayes River. There are times in a man's life that need to be remembered. This was one of those backslapping moments. Both of us marked the time. It was 8:10 a.m. on 24 July 2008.

JAY WRITES:

Painted Stone Portage derives its name from a narrow band of rock, between fifty to sixty yards wide. It is not very high, but divides water drainage to the mighty Nelson and the historic Hayes River. In the eighteenth and nineteenth centuries, the Cree Indians built a small stone "spirit Manitou" like an altar, here. White fur traders destroyed it, claiming that the Indians spent too much time at the altar and not enough time at their work assignments.

The Hayes River, named after Sir James Hayes, personal secretary to Prince Rupert, became the water route between Hudson Bay and the Canadian interior. The Nelson and the Churchill Rivers were simply too strong, difficult, and dangerous to navigate—especially with valuable cargos. The Hayes was the only one of the three rivers that could be reasonably negotiated upstream by canoe or York boat. To travel upstream, the men had to track with ropes. Some men pulled the craft upriver while others used their paddles to keep it in deeper water. Rapids were usually portaged around. I thought, *Hallelujah! We are now paddling the historic Hayes River.*

FRED WRITES:

We paddled in through an on-and-off cold rain all morning. On Robinson Lake we stopped for lunch. When it started to rain again we paddled on toward Robinson Portage. If you are going to get wet you might as well move. Between Norway House and Hudson Bay, Robinson Portage, one and one half kilometers long, is the longest crossing. People had warned us of it, but when they learned that we had walked eight and one-half miles along Grand Portage, they always said something like, "Well, then for you it won't be bad." For the York Men, though, it was their trial to determine if they deserved the title "York Men." First, they had to portage several tons of trade goods or furs and then their York boat. Some injured themselves bad enough under the York boat weight that this portage became their last.

Robinson Portage was one I looked forward to. I guess that the main reason was that for the York Men, it was an emblematic portage much the same as Height of Land was for the Nor'westers. Crossing it even without a York boat would mean that Jay and I had beaten all the challenging portages along both fur routes.

JAY WRITES:

The portage was basically an open, trouble-free trail. It was hilly, but mostly downhill. We had an easy time crossing Sea River Falls Portage and Painted Stone Portage. Robinson Portage was different. It was our first serious portage in several weeks and the first long portage since our crew had gone its separate ways. It was necessary to change who carried what. We quickly negotiated our loads. Each of us made two trips carrying more than a double load each time. With hands full, the mosquitoes and gnats that preceded us made it all the more unpleasant. Returning for the second load was even worse. I guess our insect friends just got stirred up by our first crossing.

FRED WRITES:

All along the portage were vestiges of what was probably portage machinery. The Hudson Bay York Men had even at one time used a rail to get their boats across. There were some narrow gage wheels at the east end. At places on the portage there were trail-wide narrow lumps that looked like ghosts of rotted railroad ties. Actually, they looked to be the same size as ties on Beatty Portage from Lac la Croix to Loon Lake.

We were now on Logan Lake. This is where our predecessors, those who began at Lake Superior, portaged over to Gods Lake. Near the base of Robinson Falls within view of the landing was a campsite. Still being early we decided to paddle on. The river channel wound about three and one half miles through a morass of tall grass, reeds, and cattails. I thought that we would never see the shore again. Soon, the reeds closed in around us and the channel disappeared. Then, thirty minutes later, just as suddenly as it had enveloped us, it opened up. There was a sign—or what looked like one—about a mile across the lake. This was not the first time we had seen a sign. There were a couple of signs on the Echimamish. We headed toward it. As we approached, both of us could see that it said what we knew it should say, "Campsite." It was about six o'clock. Jay and I were more than ready to stop.

JAY WRITES:

A Manitoba Ministry of Natural Resources river steward had placed the sign there. It may have even been Ken Simpson's son-in-law. We found a couple of these markers between Norway House and Oxford House, but none beyond Oxford House.

FRED WRITES:

By now we had our camp routine down pat. In fact, that really happened on Lake Winnipeg. Now we were almost working on rote. Jay secured the Kevlar bags and made coffee while I got the bear ropes in a suitable tree. Then I fixed dinner while we both enjoyed a cup of coffee. After dinner, Jay washed dishes while I got the small food pack ready to hoist up into the air. Sometimes circumstances dictated that we exchange tasks. When that happened, we each knew where the other needed help. We were a good team. It was a great day. We had finished our first full day's paddle on the Hayes.

In the morning I woke and checked my watch. I knew that it was early as it was still dark. I was right. It was four. Outside, the rain was falling. I lay there till five when the rain stopped. After I had packed, it started to drizzle. We left the tent up while we ate, hoping that the rain would stop. I hated to pack a tent in the rain. It was already wet and would just get more wet. As we looked down the lake, it became evident to us that the rain wouldn't stop, so we dropped the tent, packed, and left. We were now on a part of the Hayes where there were rapids that we either had to portage, run, or walk. We had long since decided that we would run a Class I, probably run a Class II, and portage anything else. With a full canoe we had little other choice.

At Oskatukaw Rapids we found a portage trail. Usually that is a dead giveaway to not run the rapids. Portages are there for a reason. Ohoomisewe Rapids were short. We initially thought of running them, then decided to walk the canoe down on the left. I think the main reason for our decision was that it had rained on and off all morning. We were already cold and wet. Neither of us wanted to chance swamping and getting more cold and wet.

JAY WRITES:

Walking and wading down Ohoomisewe Rapids' left side, we skidded and slid along algae and slime-covered rocks. The cold water stung and numbed me as we carefully inched along. Somehow we each managed to keep dry above the waist.

FRED WRITES:

The last rapids, Hell's Gates, flowed into Opiminegoka Lake. The first chute was a Class III. On the left was a portage marked with faded red plastic engineer's tape. At the landing on the down-river side, the current flowed fast. In lower water these would have probably been Class I rapids. In higher water it was just fast current. We got stuck on a rock. The canoe turned around threatening to swamp. I jumped out onto the rock and, with Jay's help back-paddling from the stern, managed to turn the canoe again. We were free. Down the river, next to a steep cliff, a man fishing from a red motorboat had been watching us. We waved but kept paddling down river.

About thirty minutes later the fisherman pulled up next to us in his red and silver Lund boat. The starboard stern gun'ale was bent pretty badly. I could hear him kill the motor, indicating he was stopping to talk. "Where are you headed?"

Jay proudly answered, "Hudson Bay—York Factory!"

The man offered, "Stop by and have a cup of coffee. I have a cabin down the lake. You can't miss it." He spoke quietly. I felt like I had to lean toward him to hear.

"I'm Fred. This is Jay."

The man pointed to himself, "Leon. Be careful on the lake with this wind. Nah, you two will probably be okay." Then, he started his motor, waved, and sped off.

The day was cold and overcast. Rain fell on and off. When it wasn't raining there was a mist in the air and a cold wind seemed to slap us in the face. Paddling bow, I turned to Jay and said, "We are stopping. I could use a hot cup of coffee." We had been wet and cold all day.

"No argument from me." Jay replied almost automatically.

As we crossed Opiminigoka, the wind picked up. Periodically the bow slapped hard, spraying me with cold lake water. "Sorry!" Jay hollered from the stern.

"It's okay," I came back. " Just part of paddling bow." The waves were about two feet now. We had seen worse on much bigger lakes.

At the far end of the lake we found Leon's cabin. It sat on an island where the Hayes began again. Outside was a generator, an American and a Canadian flag, five or six moose skulls and racks, an outhouse, a propane burner, and panoply of other high-tech backwoods equipment. Leon was inside sitting on his couch watching the Weather Channel on satellite TV. He was a heavy-set man—not overweight, but big. His black hair stayed crushed under a worn baseball cap. Leon had his boots off with his feet propped on a chair. He wore Levis and the obligatory North Woods plaid flannel shirt. Smiling slightly, he said, "Come in!" In the corner of his one-room living area under the window stood a propane stove. On top of it, coffee perked on the burner. The real benefit was that the stove comfortably warmed the cabin from the outside chill.

"Heat! I forgot that there was a thing called heat. Wah-chay! Wah-chay!" I commented as I shook Leon's hand. Ed Campbell had taught us that. In Cree it means roughly, "Hello! Come shake hands." I told Leon how I knew the greeting.

"I know Ed Campbell. He is a nice man," Leon softly countered.

Over a mug of hot coffee I asked where a good campsite was. Leon motioned at the cabin's front window and side wall. Then he offered his extra room, saying that he could not put us out in the cold. It was also misting slightly. He offered a hot shower. Even though both of us did not want to impose, the temptation of a hot shower for two cold, wet voyageurs was too much to refuse. We stayed.

The shower was primitive, creatively engineered, and hot. Like our friend Ed back in Pine Falls, Leon had that knack of making things work. We had not long been gone from Norway House, but I had forgotten what hot water and soap felt like. We hung our wet clothes in the back room on some nails to dry and changed into our one set of clean clothes.

Leon was caretaker and maintenance man for Moleson Lake Lodge. In the summers he lived in his cabin. In the winters he moved back to Norway House. Over coffee we learned that he was Ken Simpson's brother. The bush is a small world. It was comforting to have mutual acquaintances. Not long after we had our coffee, a float plane landed. Along with lodge supplies, it brought back Leon's girlfriend, Ruby.

Ruby fixed supper. Then she and Leon took off in Leon's boat on lodge business. There were cabins and fishing boats to tend to. Jay and I ate, watched TV until the generator died, and then went to bed.

In the morning Leon fixed eggs over easy, bacon, toast, and coffee. The bacon's smell was wonderful and that extra cup of coffee was even better. I hated to leave Leon's summer cabin, but knew that we had to keep going.

I thought back to something that Bob Cary had said once during staff training. "You know, the Indians laugh at us for calling this the wilderness. You know what they call it?" He was talking about the Ojibwe, but his question applies to the Cree also. Bob's eyes sparkled and his mouth broke into a partial grin. This was a trick question. His audience knew it was a trick question but stared blankly, searching in vain for an obvious answer. I am sure that I, too, gave him that blank stare. Bob never let his question linger too long. He was a master of the pregnant pause. "They call it home," he answered in a wry tone as his partial grin widened to a broad smile. His eyes sparkled while his look danced a jig and confirmed that we were all correct—the answer was obvious.

I thought back to Bob because this island that Leon lived on perfectly demonstrated what he meant. Many would call it the wilderness, but to Leon, this was home.

JAY WRITES:

Departing Leon's summer cabin, we paddled through Windy Lake. Surprise of surprises, we fought our way through healthy windy gusts. We only had to cross one bay but the blustery weather created two-foot waves. Finally, we were back on the Hayes Channel. After lunch we walked and waded through Hahasew, Moore, and Seeseep Rapids. The next fast water, Wipanipanis Falls, was another story.

The falls were in two sets. The upper falls rushed underneath a steel trestle bridge that was part of a winter road to Oxford House. A crooked rusty sign read, "Oxford House—65 km." We had to take care not to be caught in the current and get sucked under the bridge. First, we portaged over the winter road. This put us in still water. Then we finally located part of a trail only to find it flooded out. The actual portage crosses an island that divides the two main channels. This trail was out of the question for us. The water and current was too high and strong to land safely on the island. Eventually we found a way around on the left. It was getting late so we camped in a clearing toward the end of our bushwhacked trail. The rock we were on was covered with thick, soft reindeer moss. There was a tree for our food. Best of all, we had safely solved this challenge and were well-staged to paddle to Oxford Lake.

FRED WRITES:

At Wipanipanis Rapids we ran into Leon and Ruby in his Lund. Inadvertently, we paddled a more circuitous river channel allowing them to pass us. He said that he was fishing, but I think that he was just checking on us.

In the morning it only took us about thirty minutes to finish portaging downstream from the falls. Pushing out, we could better see the island's downriver portage landing. In the high water it, too, was turbulent. I was glad we had gone the other way. Next stop was Oxford Lake.

JAY WRITES:

Oxford Lake was originally named Holey Lake. For some lost reason, the British thought that the bottom was peppered with unfathomable, deep holes.[49] It was an easy paddle down the Hayes to Oxford Lake. We made it by midmorning. The rest of the day was spent paddling the lake.

FRED WRITES:

Oxford Lake is big, and big means that with the wrong weather the water can be bad. We certainly knew this from other big lakes. On this day we were fortunate. It was warm and the wind was absent. The sun actually seemed to burn me. Discussing our strategy on the way to Oxford Lake, our biggest concern was Jackson Bay. It was wide. With almost perfect weather, we opted to cross well to the north of Jackson Bay in a straight line to Eight Mile Point.

On the way I said, "You know what would taste good to me for supper?" It was a rhetorical question. "Eggs and biscuits." We were already going to brew a pot of coffee. Jay quickly agreed to my meal idea. I was glad. The sun was shining. I was dry for a change. I could taste supper. I had been thinking of eggs and biscuits all day.

We found a flat area high on a rocky ledge. As we set up camp and ate, numerous motorboats sped by from Oxford House heading back to the bush or to a nearby First Nation Reservation—back to their homes.

---

49 Robert Hood, *To the Arctic by Canoe: The Journal and Paintings of Robert Hood, Midshipman with Franklin*, ed. C. Stuart Houston (Montreal: McGill-Queens University Press, 1994), 3.

JAY WRITES:

Today marked two months on the trail for Fred and me. We observed this impressive milestone with a second and third cup of coffee. Over the rich brew under a warm sun we remarked on how far we had come, the challenges we overcame, and how well we adapted and improvised along the way.

FRED WRITES:

The fresh hot biscuits were topped with butter—lots of butter—and stuffed with scrambled, pepper-covered, powdered eggs. We washed them down with hot, strong, black coffee. Laying back on the rock with a refill of coffee to sip on, I relaxed in a pleasing breeze and a balmy sun.

In the morning we paddled to Oxford House. This would be our last chance to pick up any supplies. There were only a couple of things we needed, the main item being a scrub pad to wash pots. We had both figured that, with the previous evening's boat traffic, there would probably be a landing for the Northern store where we could tie up the canoe or beach it. The Northern was in a big, tin, industrial-looking building with green trim. Above the front door was a flag with the letters, "N W Co."

On the way into the store we met a young Cree, Lloyd. From our dress—we were wearing our PFDs[50]—it was obvious that we were canoeing. Lloyd asked where we were headed.

"York Factory." I don't remember which one of us answered.

"When you go through Knee Lake stop by the lodge and have a cup of coffee. I work there. Tell Ryan that I invited you." Lloyd was a fishing guide. He lived at Oxford House. Summers, he

---

50 Personal floatation devices.

worked for the lodge. Winters, like so many other people of that area, he trapped and found odd jobs.

"Thanks. We will," I answered. Jay and I looked around to see if there was anything we missed. As a special treat for ourselves, we bought a couple of oranges and brownies to add to our lunch. I knew that prices would be high. We spent seventeen Canadian dollars on the brownies, oranges, a couple of candy bars, and the scrub pads. Everything had to be flown in, so high prices were understandable.

While we meandered through the store, several of the Northern employees asked about our trip. I think that they were a little envious and would have preferred to be on the river with us rather than sorting produce and restocking shelves. It was also that Oxford House is a small, remote community. We were strangers. We were somebody different to talk to and about.

Jay and I called home. This was our last chance. On our way back down to the canoe, another man stopped to talk with us. He related that a couple of days earlier, a group of fourteen people had flown in and paddled off to York Factory. "You'll probably catch them," he said.

I was flattered at his compliment, but knew that protocol required we demur. "I don't know. Two days is a good head start."

"You'll catch them," he insisted.

We said good-bye, walked across the field down to the canoe, and left. It didn't take long before we were back on the Hayes River channel. It was around noon so we found an empty campsite for lunch. I don't remember what else we had, but I do remember the orange—a large, juicy navel orange, the most delicious one I have ever had. I am sure that I have had just as good quality. In fact, I know that I have had some Israeli-grown blood oranges that were fantastic, but after a couple of months without fresh fruit, this orange was a singular mouth-watering treat.

CHAPTER XVII

PADDLE TO KNEE LAKE

Out of the hitherwhere into the yon-
Stay the hopes we are leaning on-

> Out of the Hitherwhere
> by James Whitcomb Riley

[28 JULY 2008–30 JULY 2008]

FRED WRITES:

We were back on the Hayes River. Ahead were two sets of rapids. I kept thinking that we should come up on them at any minute. Approaching them, there was a muffled roar as an initial warning. We hit some swift water, but no rapids. The best we could figure was that high water covered what were only Class I rapids.

Soon we were at Kiasokanowak Rapids. When rapids have a name, they are often an obstacle to contend with. At least that was our philosophy. These rapids had a big, imposing, multisyllabic name. The river channel's drop was big enough, the water's roar was loud enough, and the rocks were numerous

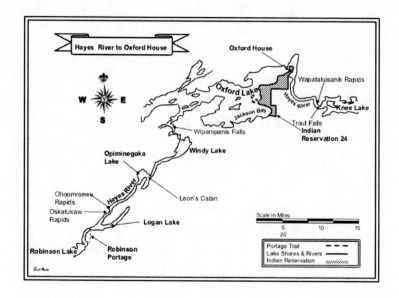

enough that we decided to walk down on a smaller left-hand channel.

Next was Knife Rapids. Jay was looking at his map searching for the portage as we floated closer, and we became caught up in some fast water. Finally I said, "Jay, we either need to go ahead and shoot these rapids or paddle out of this current."

"To hell with it. Let's shoot them," Jay shouted with bravado as we flew down.

I think that this was a knee-jerk reaction rather than a rational decision. But, we were safely through the first chute. We then paddled hard to a pool of still water where we found a portage around a rocky drop. From there we walked and ran the rest of the rapids. By the time we reached the end, we were both soaked from walking through the fast water and from an on-and-off rain. Knife Rapids, overall, are a Class III, so I was glad to be safely at its end.

JAY WRITES:

Knife Rapids is not a misnomer by any means. We stepped, slipped, and slid between numerous jagged rocks on our traverse down the river. The next obstacle, Wapatakosanik Rapids, came at the end of a long day. It was not marked on our maps, so it came as a kind of surprise. We slogged our way through. At a chute, almost at the end, the water was a little stronger than we felt safe walking through. After a bit of scouting we improvised a short portage. From Knife we headed to Trout Falls. On the way was one more series of Class II rapids that we walked and ran. It was now about six p.m. We found a good campsite and settled in for the evening. We would portage Trout Falls the next day.

FRED WRITES:

Once again I cooked while Jay made coffee. Being wet and cold, I pulled out some chili with cornbread dumplings. Between my chili and Jay's coffee, we quickly warmed up. The night was cold, but our sleeping bags and tent were warm. In the distance, Trout Falls' restful roar drowned out the buzzing mosquitoes. We would sleep well.

In the morning we got off early, portaged around Trout Falls, and were quickly in Knee Lake. Not long after entering the lake we met three men in a North Star Lodge motorboat. "Where are you going?" one asked.

"York Factory. Hudson Bay."

"Where did you start?"

"Lake Superior," I replied.

"Gees, that's on the other side of the world. Stop by the lodge— it's four or five miles down—and have some coffee."

We thanked them and waved as they sped off. Not long after that, another boat stopped. "Where are you headed?"

"Hudson Bay."

"Stop by the lodge. Help yourself to the food. Tell them that Ryan sent you." I figured that it was the same Ryan that Lloyd had told us about. They left so quickly that I didn't get to mention that we had met Lloyd.

We paddled on and then had an early lunch. I needed a break. My back was starting to bother me again. After lunch I could see the flash of a paddle in the distance. Before lunch, the weather had cooled down and clouded up, but by now the sun was peeking from behind some fluffy white and gray clouds. I thought, *Those must be the paddlers the fellow at Oxford House mentioned.* I could make out three or four canoes. They seemed to be zigzagging to the north of a distant island.

Suddenly it was in view: North Star Lodge was huge. The grounds were well kept. Individual log cabins lined the lakeshore. A large log cabin occupied the point. Numerous boats were tied to the pier. Two men in a golf cart were driving toward the shore. We paddled over to take up the offer of fresh coffee.

The men in the golf cart were Ron and Al. Ron was a bush pilot and Al was a fishing guide. Ron had done some adventure flying in Quetico, so he was intimate with that part of our route. Al, from Kenora, was familiar with our Lake of the Woods and the Winnipeg River legs. Al sent us down to the main lodge building. This was actually the office building and staff living quarters, but primarily the dining hall. We introduced ourselves to another Ryan, the assistant manager, who showed us around.

It was a huge, five-star, rustic dining room that would probably seat forty to fifty people. A fancy Victorian-style pool table occupied an ell. In another corner was a computer for the guests. On the wall were pictures of prize-winning fish along with a couple of mounted pike and walleyes. There are only two ways into Knee Lake. One is the way we came in—by canoe. The other is by charter plane. In effect, with the exception of the few canoes that come through going to Hudson Bay, North Star Lodge has exclusive use of the lake. They fly in their guests on a charter from Winnipeg and then treat them to the best fishing in the North Woods.

We thanked Ryan for his hospitality, the tour, and the coffee, and headed east again. On a high rock we found a good campsite. We lost time stopping at the lodge, but the hot coffee was worth the layover.

JAY WRITES:

Our original itinerary put us farther downriver. In fact, we should have been within two days paddle to York Factory. Obviously, being on Knee Lake we were still a long distance from Hudson Bay. I guess that we had been overly optimistic. On Lake Winnipeg we lost around five days of time. Part of this lost time, the first couple of days on Winnipeg, was a result of Karl quitting because of the weather. A couple of days were lost at Princess Harbour when the other four left. There were three times when we were wind bound. A couple of times we stopped early because we wanted to enjoy the day and an extra cup of coffee. With unpredictable events, it is important to keep a flexible schedule. I was hopeful that we would have no more unavoidable delays.

FRED WRITES:

In the morning, a thick fog covered the lake. We decided over breakfast that with the GPS we could easily get to the narrows by following the north shore. Just as we were about to enter the narrows, we ran across the group I had seen the previous day. It was fourteen people paddling collapsible canoes. Except for two adult leaders, they were all American and Canadian high school students. We talked briefly. They confirmed that they, too, were headed to York Factory.

We paddled away into the fog ahead of the other group. About the time we traversed the narrows, the fog lifted. Above was a blue sky. For a while the wind picked up. At lunch we stopped at a North Star Lodge site with a picnic table. After lunch it rained a little. When it cleared up, in the distance was a flat rainbow. I had never seen one that flat. Rather than a bow, it looked like a long, slightly-arched bridge resting just barely above the treetops.

JAY WRITES:

Knee Lake is long. In the distance was only a water horizon. In that sense it seemed a bit like Lake Winnipeg. As the afternoon progressed, we reached a point where a treetop horizon appeared. I could see where the Hayes River exited the lake. The staff at the lodge assured us that the trails and portages farther downriver were all in good condition. We would soon find out this was nowhere near the case.

FRED WRITES:

We stopped on a beach campsite at the lake's east end. Approaching, we found an eagles' nest in a large birch tree. A fledgling perched on a branch next to the nest. Above, the adults circled and screeched at us. I have been close to numerous nests in Quetico and the Boundary Waters. There, the eagles are much more casual. They at least do not see humans as threats. I took it that these two eagle parents saw few canoes. This was their home, so we didn't linger. When they saw us leave, the two adults immediately calmed down and then lit in the tops of a couple of trees to make sure that we didn't return.

The beach was not the best place we had ever camped, but it would be home for the night. In the morning we would be back on the Hayes. Knee Lake was the last large lake we had to cross. Until this trip the largest lakes I had paddled in Quetico or the Boundary Waters could be traversed in no more than a day. Bad waves were never more than a foot or so. Being able to see where the Hayes began again, we both knew that leaving early in the morning would give us time to cross the last open water before any late-morning or afternoon wind could kick up.

CHAPTER XVIII

PADDLE TO YORK FACTORY

Out of the hitherwhere into the yon-
Stay the hopes we are leaning on-

> "Out of the Hitherwhere"
> by James Whitcomb Riley

[31 JULY 2008–9 AUGUST 2008]

FRED WRITES:

We broke camp and prepared to paddle the last couple of miles on Knee Lake. Before we reached the Hayes, we picked up a headwind. It wasn't overwhelming, but it was strong enough to slow us down. Once we reached the river channel, the trees sheltered us so we started to make better time.

This part of the Hayes is surrounded by a marsh. That, along with the high water, left very few dry places to eat. The best we could do for lunch was to find a spot high enough to allow us to stretch our legs and eat quickly. The mosquitoes and gnats swarmed as we gobbled down our crackers, cheese, and some more winged trail spice. I think we had partially gotten used to

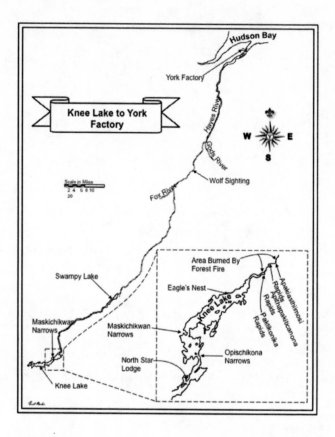

the bugs—both taste and sting. Their bites still smarted, but we didn't develop puffy places and itch as much as we did earlier in the summer.

After lunch we paddled on to Patikonika Falls. The portage was exactly where the map showed. It remotely reminded me of some of the Quetico portages—open and easy to follow. The next portage was gone. Not being able to see the end of the rapids, we decided to bushwhack around. It turned out to be about an eighty-rod slog.

JAY WRITES:

Downriver from Patikonika Rapids we entered an area destroyed by fire. Any indications of a portage were gone. Standing trees, blackened stumps, and charred deadfall covered the terrain. Around these obstacles, thick waisthigh grass and brush blocked our way. To get through, we first scouted the rapids to determine if we could run them. With the high water, the rapids were often violent enough that we decided not to run them. If we had to portage first, we had to scout and improvise a trail. For each portage we made three roundtrips—one to recon, and then two to carry our gear. Climbing with a pack or canoe over chest-high deadfall required a feat of agility.

FRED WRITES:

We easily ran the next rapids. From there it was a short paddle downstream where we had to bushwhack again. Being late, Jay and I decided to look for a campsite instead of portaging.

The previous summer's fire had not left much to offer in the way of a suitable tent pad. Finally, though, we found a place that would work. Not far from us was an eagles' nest with two dark-brown feathered fledglings. Not far from the nest a white-throated sparrow perched in the top of a leaf-barren, charred tree and sang plaintively, "Down to the river to pray."

The insects were so profuse that we decided to tie-off on a rock in the middle of the river for supper. There we shared crackers and peanut butter in a relatively bug-free, cool breeze. Afterwards we secured our food and gear and scrambled into our tent. It was nice to be away from the gnats and mosquitoes. The night was clear, but the hordes of insects sounded like a light rain as they crashed into our rain fly. This was one of my more restless nights. Underneath my shoulder blades was a tree root or limb I had missed when we set up the tent. As uncomfortable as I was, I preferred to writhe around the deadfall in search of the perfect sleeping position rather than fight the mosquitoes and try to remove it.

By morning I was glad to get up. I never did seem to find a restful position. The insect swarms were just as bad at sunrise as they were at sunset. We packed, quickly ate, and left. After bushwhacking our first portage, we ran the next rapids and then bushwhacked again. The forest fire had removed all traces of any portages.

I had scouted the first couple of portages. Jay scouted the next. The slow going was disheartening. Navigating the fire-wrecked, desolate terrain meant crawling under, climbing over, and inching around charred tree trunks and stumps. By the time we got to the end of the last portage we were covered in soot and looked like fire fighters who had lost the fight.

JAY WRITES:

Apithapakiticanona Rapids was one I scouted. We reached it just prior to lunch. Not far from the upstream landing we came was a wrecked half of a Kevlar canoe. An earlier group must have failed in an attempt to run the rapids. They left the remainder of their canoe tied upright like a monument as a warning to future travelers. The rapids were strong and raced sharply around a bend. We immediately heeded the warning. Fred stayed with the canoe while I disappeared into the bush to find and improvise a trail. Up in a charred tree on the crest of the hill, another eagles' nest had survived the earlier fire. Forcing my way through the brush I reached the other side and found a suitable landing.

FRED WRITES:

All during that morning the skies were cloudy. We were constantly surrounded with a light but cold mist. However, as we reached the next set of rapids the sky started to clear. We lined down and then paddled on to Swampy Lake. Not far from where the Hayes entered the lake was a campsite. Since the day had warmed up and we were both tired from the previous night's inferior site, we decided to stop. All around us the forest suffered from the fire, but we were in a Hayes River oasis under a couple of wonderful large shade trees. Our tent pad was flat. Best of all, bugs were nowhere to be found.

While enjoying a supper of summer sausage with black beans and rice, the crew of fourteen we had passed back on Knee Lake paddled by. They stopped for a short time to talk. We had talked briefly on Knee Lake. They were from Ontario. The two leaders were Sam and Claire. This was only a casual chat since it was getting late and they, too, had to find a camp. Sam told us earlier what their planned schedule was. If we stayed on our new adjusted schedule we would be at York Factory a day or two before them. That was the last time we saw them except from a distance. I was actually glad to have them behind us. If we ran into trouble we could wait for help.

The next day it took us about an hour and a half to reach the far end of Swampy Lake. Off to our right was the Ontario group. Judging from where they were and how long it took us to get there, they must have stopped at ten thirty or eleven.

Finally back on the Hayes, we paddled north winding through a series of islands that created numerous meandering channels. Seeing the channels narrow, I knew that we would have rapids to run sooner rather than later. First was a series of Class I rapids that we easily ran. Then Wetiko Rapids was next. It was a series of Class I and Class II chutes, all of which we effortlessly ran.

Next were some rapids that we walked on the right bank. Wading down a narrow channel we thought that we could probably get through. By the time it was too late to turn back, we were standing above a significant drop. Jay held the canoe while I tested the current trying to stand in it. It was far too strong. There was nothing left to do but find a path around. Behind us, the bank was three feet above the water. Jay held the canoe while I muscled the packs up from the bow. Then we switched. I held the canoe while he muscled the remaining packs up from the stern. Looking over my shoulder to the bank below the falls, it seemed open. Not more than a few rods away was a suitable landing.

Once across we immediately found a camp a few hundred yards downriver. By the time we finished supper and put up the equipment, a thunderstorm hit. I've always been in the habit of packing the equipment pack before turning in. It may seem like a small thing, but I have known crews to lose equipment not properly stowed. To the north, storm clouds were moving in. The storm hit sooner than we had thought. As the last pack buckle was fastened, the rain started. We hurriedly crawled into our tent for the night. The rain sounded good beating down on the tent. This time it was rain and not bugs. I slept soundly.

The evening rain seemed to clear the sky. The next day was clear and warm. We paddled to our first and second portage. Both were exactly where the map indicated. Next were some rapids with marked portages that we couldn't find, so we waded down. Our next portage was marked with some red engineer's tape. By this time it was getting late, so we found an island camp at the head of some rapids. After setting up, we discovered that the portage was through our camp.

When we left camp the next morning we had the intent of reaching White Mud Falls. That intent was based on portages being where they were marked on the map or at least just being there.

Whether you bushwhack around or line through an area, those methods take more time than a reasonably good portage takes. If you bushwhack your way through, you first have to scout the best way. It's useless to head through the woods with one hundred pounds plus on your back unless you know where you are going. If you wade, you still have to sometimes scout out where you can best get through. The trick seemed to be to make a decision. Scout a trail and bushwhack through or wade down picking your way as you go.

We waded some Class III rapids and then headed to High Hill Rapids. Jay had a portage marked on his map, but if it was there we couldn't find it. We saw some calm water on the south end of an island. From our vantage point it looked as if we could wade downriver on the island's east side. Approaching the island it still looked possible to wade down, so I got out to find a way. In fact, we could wade around part way. Then we had to portage through the island to the north end. The trail was great. When I told Jay I found a trail, he simply whispered an exasperated but appreciative "Thank you!" I think that we were both tired of having to clear our own portages.

Next we easily waded and paddled a couple of rapids. Katasako Rapids was next. As we approached, the water rushed loudly, but it looked like a good chute through the center. I shouted and pointed, "Jay, just go straight." The current was swift, but it looked like easy going the way we were headed. All of a sudden I could see that the water dropped several feet. To the right and left were some sizeable waves.

Jay hollered, "Are you sure?"

It was too late now. There was no way we could back up. We had to go. What I thought now didn't matter. I shouted back confidently, "Yeah, let's go." We shot through. The bow slapped down almost breaking deep as we went over the initial drop. We took on a couple of gallons of water. I got soaked with spray and splash. As soon as we were in, we were out. I quickly looked for whirlpools and eddies. There were none. The current was swift, but we were safe. It wasn't until much later that I saw on the map that these were Class III rapids. We weren't going to run Class IIIs, especially with a fully loaded canoe.

On a rock downriver we emptied the water from the canoe and paddled to the next rapids, Apetowikossan. They didn't seem bad, but I could not see the end. Finally we decided to paddle back up to the campsite at Katasako. It took us less than ten minutes to paddle downriver. To get back up took forty-five minutes. I couldn't help but think back to Ober and Billy and the voyageurs before them. It was quite a feat for any of them to paddle up the Hayes. It was tiring enough to go full force for forty-five minutes upstream. I couldn't imagine putting forth the same effort all day for weeks on end.

The campsite was ideal. Most of the day found us in a cold drizzle. In fact, we had to pull the dining fly over us at lunchtime to get out of the rain. After we got the tent up, Jay fixed coffee while I made supper. With rain clouds around us we put up the dining fly. Although we never needed it, it was comforting to have it available.

When we got up in the morning we were surrounded by black, ominous storm clouds. Not only did a storm loom, there was a definite chill in the air. I knew that we were going to have to walk the next rapids. Neither of us wanted to get wet and cold again. There were times walking through fast water that I would step off up to my neck. "When you are walking the bow through, it goes with the territory," I told Jay when he asked if I was okay.

"Let's stay. I don't trust this weather. Besides we could use a break," I said.

Jay agreed. So we unpacked what little we had already packed and settled in for a down day. It never rained, but it stayed cold. It felt good to be warm, to lie back, and to read and periodically doze off.

We had decided that we could only afford the luxury of one down day. No matter what the next day's weather was, we would reach and portage White Mud Falls. When we woke it was still cold and cloudy. Silently, we packed and headed downriver.

The previous day in between reading and sleeping, we had discussed that the best way down Apetowikossan Rapids was probably on the left. It looked to be the shortest route. Not being able to see around the bend, I got out to walk through the woods downriver. It was the best way down. In fact, there were scrapes from earlier canoes that had gone the same way. By the time I got back I was soaked from the rain and dew-sodden leaves. I thought, *I guess that I am meant to be wet today.*

We walked through in no time, then headed for Slanted Rock Rapids. Overall, Slanted Rock was a Class III with big white-water and numerous rock gardens. The rapids were aptly named, as they flowed down what seemed to be a long, gently sloping granite slab. We walked Slanted Rock, too, following the shore down on the right.

Next were a couple of Class I rapids. In no time we were at White Mud Falls. It is a Class III. Some crews run the falls. There is a chute on the right. We would portage. The landing was hidden, so Jay got out looking for the trail. He found it immediately. White Mud has a well-deserved name. The downriver landing was exactly that—the slippery mud was white, or more accurately, ecru. For both of us it was almost an anticlimactic portage. It was maybe thirty rods. Except for maneuvering through the white mud, it was a morning stroll. Now that we had crossed, we had mastered all of the Hayes River challenges. The map only showed one more set of rapids, Berwick Falls. With the high water, it was only fast water. We had made it. The rest of the trip would be easy paddling.

The only fear that I had left was of polar bears. In North America there are only two animals that consider people part of the food chain. One is the mountain lion and all his big cat cousins. The other is the polar bear. In fact, York Factory will not let anyone camp there because of the bears. We had a few miles left, though, before we had to be concerned. Using the GPS, Jay and I marked an arbitrary point thirty miles inland from York Factory that would be the closest we would go on the last night.

Down river from White Mud, the geology changed. Previously there were numerous boulders. Now there were none. The banks were tree-covered eskers left by the receding ice-age glaciers. Recent landslides told us not to camp at the base of a hill. Water oozed from the wet sand and gravel. After a couple of hours paddling, we found the first suitable place to camp. The riverbank was relatively flat and it was not under a hill. Not knowing how far the next campsite would be, we opted to stop. There were plenty of trees to tie our Kevlar food bags to. Best of all the sun was out and we could dry off and warm up.

We relaxed over a couple of pots of hot coffee before fixing supper. After cleaning up we crawled into the tent once again to escape the almost ever-present bugs. Outside I heard something splashing in the water. I peeked out, but saw nothing. It was probably a fish.

JAY WRITES:

August seventh was a good day. We covered about thirty-eight miles. The Hayes current was good and strong. By lunch we had paddled sixteen miles. The thirty-yard-high black-spruce-covered hills seemed to race by. I entertained myself watching the rocks on the river bottom zoom past in the fast current. We did some hard paddling in order to cover the distance.

FRED WRITES:

The first wildlife we spotted was a group of six geese on shore. When they saw us they started waddling quickly up the hill in a "V" formation as if to get away. It seemed a little comical because we could have caught them if we wanted to. For about a month in the summer, Canada geese shed all of their flight feathers so they are grounded and vulnerable for that period of time. At Grand Portage, the geese go to Grand Portage Island to molt. The Nor'westers and the Ojibwe knew the geese's routine, which made a ready source of fresh fowl for those willing to paddle out and give chase. I knew that the geese went through this phase, but had never seen it. The downside was that maybe the polar bears knew that there was a food source upriver.

After lunch we saw two adult wolves and three pups. We were far enough away at first that I thought that it was a black bear sow and cubs. They were black. When we got closer I could clearly see that it was a she-wolf and three pups. Then the male, a grayish-brown color, walked out of the bush. The pups played. The female watched us cautiously, but seemingly unafraid as we floated quietly by. The male walked down the riverbank as if to lure us away from his family. Every few steps he glanced over his shoulder to see if we were still following. After a hundred yards or so, he, too, disappeared into the waist-high bush. The female and pups watched from upstream and then followed suit, disappearing into the bush. I had seen wolves but had never seen the pups. I had hoped to see or hear some wolves before the trip was over.

JAY WRITES:

I have often heard wolves howling at night in the Boundary Waters and Quetico, yet this was the first time I had ever seen them in the wild. Most people never encounter wolves. I counted myself lucky to finally see some. It was the same scene that Indians and fur traders saw centuries past. The wolves were out on the riverbank only a couple of yards above the river. The adults watched while the pups played.

FRED WRITES:

We paddled until five thirty. On this part of the Hayes you camp where you can. Large stones don't make a good tent pad. Other places are just not level enough.

I fixed chicken and dumplings for dinner. Off in the north we could see rain moving east. It didn't look like it would affect us. After dinner we checked our maps again. We needed to get an early start so we could camp about thirty miles upriver on our last night.

By noon the next day we had paddled eighteen miles. The morning had been cold but clear. Clouds rolled in for a short time. Then the sky again cleared. With the sun, the day warmed up by about one thirty.

We found a camp almost exactly where we planned. High on a hill was a dilapidated emergency cabin. Inside, the builder had scribbled a note, "If your face is white, black, red, or yellow, you are welcome to stay." The floor was flat, so we set up the tent inside. Back down on the riverbank we made a pot of coffee.

While we were waiting for the water to boil, a green, motorized, wood-and-canvas cargo canoe with two men came down the river. They pulled in to talk. Both had jet-black hair. It looked unkempt, probably caused by riding hatless in an open boat. They wore blue jeans and North Woods plaid woolen shirts. We were unexpected, and strangers, so they were primarily curious. Jay and I introduced ourselves. The two men were Ernest and Abner from Shamattawa, a First Nation community upstream on the Gods River. Abner looked up to the cabin and said, "Didn't realize that it was still there."

"Who built it?" I asked.

"My uncle," Abner replied. He spoke with a heavy Cree accent combined with the North Woods, "Eh." "Where are you going?" he asked.

"We started at Lake Superior. We are headed for York Factory." At this point on the river, York Factory was the only place we could be going.

"Are you going to the Gathering?"

"No. I knew about it, but we are not going to it. Is that where you are headed? The Gathering?" The Gathering is an annual reunion sponsored by Manitoba Power. Many of the Cree who were displaced when York Factory closed, or their descendents, return to see old friends and to get in touch with their shared heritage. Sometimes the old themselves bring their children or grandchildren to show them how they lived and earned a living.

"How about a cup of coffee?" The water was boiling. I was glad for the opportunity to return some North Woods hospitality.

The two men smiled, gladly accepting the coffee. Glancing over to their canoe, I could see a twelve gauge and a couple of thirty-caliber rifles. Abner looked up at me and asked, "Have you seen any moose?"

"No, I've seen their sign. Why?"

"We are looking for meat," said Abner. "I want to shoot one."

I thought back to conversations with Ed. He talked of killing moose when he was younger. Abner's inquiry reminded me of how important the bush wildlife is to a First Nation diet.

"I had some friends who stopped at Shamattawa a few years back. They were paddling from Lake Superior too." Tom Copeland told me that he stopped there.

"I remember them. They didn't stay long." Abner looked at Ernest as if to remind him that they had met Tom. Ernest nodded that he, too, remembered. The two finished their coffee, thanked us, and said that they had to move on. We shook hands. They both had a warm, firm, friendly grip. Already being wet, I helped them push their canoe into the river. They started their motor, waved, and sped off downriver.

JAY WRITES:

I watched Ernest and Abner wind their way north until they disappeared around a riverbend. The boat's wake lapped lazily against the shore. Soon after they fell from sight, the rhythmic sputter of their outboard faded away. By now the Hayes widened to a couple of hundred yards. The current slowed noticeably. It was shallower with a course peppered by gravel bars. I think that I could have easily waded across.

FRED WRITES:

We made one more pot of coffee and then fixed supper. Both of us made an extra effort to get our camp straight because of our

---

proximity to the bay and the possibility of polar bears. We had camped high on the hill away from the river. We tied our Kevlar food bags to a log several hundred yards up the riverbank. I would have taken them farther if there was a place to secure them.

Although hardly a breeze blew, the next morning was chilled with a heavy fog that completely hid the river thirty or forty feet below. We had about a half a bottle of strawberry jelly and one bag of rye crackers left. Standing in the cold fog on Hayes' rocky bank, that was our last breakfast. Above us, the sun shone brightly. The opposite side of the river was hidden in the mist. We both found it hard to believe that we were almost there. Anxious to finish, we launched into the fog and headed north.

Before lunch we met a man and woman in a motorboat who were surveying the river for Manitoba Power. Farther on down the river we passed their campsite. By ten o'clock, the sun had burned off the fog.

We ate lunch on a big boulder at the south tip of Rainbow Island. It was the first time in several days that we ate lunch in a dry place. After a thirty-minute break, we resumed our paddle north. In our thoughts we could hear Hudson Bay's far distant echo. For the last year, its call had taunted me. Now I could hear it.

Jay and I paddled without a break. Just before three we rounded the last bend in the river. I dipped my fingers into the river to taste for salt. Directly in front of us north of Hay Island was Hudson Bay's vast expanse. Once more, and for the last time, we saw a watery, bowed horizon. Downriver on the left was a dock with a motorboat tied to it. About one hundred yards past that was a second dock.

Then we saw it. High above on the bluff stood a flagpole flying the Hudson Bay red standard with the Union Jack canton and the letters "HBC" in the lower right-hand corner. It fluttered lazily in the breeze off the bay. I think that both of our hearts were racing. We had made it.

As we neared, the wind picked up, creating some irritating one-foot waves almost as if to say, "Don't get cocky." Reaching the nearest pier, we jumped out and secured the canoe with a stern and bow rope. At the top of the stairs off to our right was the white clapboard depot building. It was the sole York Factory building still standing and looked so desolate in the field by itself, yet it was still an imposing structure.

CHAPTER XIX

YORK FACTORY

With such a comrade, such a friend,
I fain would walk till journey's end,

"A Mile With Me"
by Henry Van Dyke

[9 AUGUST 2008–10 AUGUST 2008]

FRED WRITES:

A raised, wooden sidewalk led to the staffs' house. Above us was a clear blue sky with a warm, bright northern sun. The north breeze cooled the afternoon. Jay knocked at the back door. Ian, the staff cook let us in and introduced us to Lisa and Larry. Both of them were attending the annual Cree gathering.

Jackie, a petite young woman from Winnipeg, walked in with a twelve-gauge shotgun. The gun was almost bigger than she was. Jackie and her husband, Doug, were the summer caretakers. In the winter, she was a kindergarten teacher in Winnipeg and Doug processed seeds for agricultural use. The side

York Factory

Silver Goose Lodge

Old Cemetery

York Factory
Depot Building   Cree Gathering
Kitchen

Cree Encampment

Boardwalk   New Pier

Work Shop   Gravel Air Strip

Park Personnel Housing

Hayes River

Hay Island

Old Pier

Scale in Tenths of a Miles

1/10 mile   2/10 mile

effect of their professions was that summers were free, so they-worked for Parks Canada at York Factory.

Lisa and Larry offered us a place for our tent with the Gathering. There could not have been a more perfect ending. Both of us gratefully accepted. We paddled down to the next dock and unloaded. What looked like surf hitting the pier was actually some of the children splashing and swimming in Hudson Bay. The water was cool, but the river being shallow kept it from being ice cold. Anyway, the day was warm and they were young. Larry met us with a four-wheeler with a trailer to carry our packs to the tenting area.

About 150 Cree had traveled from as far as Winnipeg to York Factory for the Gathering. The elders had all worked at York Factory in its waning days just prior to the mid-1950s. Their younger Cree children and grandchildren came to learn, explore, and play. For the Gathering, York Factory was alive again. New buildings had been constructed for a kitchen and for housing some of the elders. According to our friends, the Campbells, anybody over sixty is an elder and always gets waited on. I thought, "I guess that I am an elder, too, but I sure don't feel like it."

Larry found a safe place for our food pack. We found a comfortable place for our tent. Surrounding the tent area was a trip wire with flares to warn of any polar bear incursions. There had been a big boar a few days earlier. It reminded me distantly of our perimeter defenses when I was in Vietnam. Because of the bears, Parks Canada trained volunteers in polar bear watch procedures. At any given time there was a group of guards patrolling the encampment. Some had thirty-thirties, some had shotguns. Nobody wandered off without an armed guard.

Setting up, I warned, "Jay, if you hear gunfire during the night, don't sit up." "Why?" Jay asked almost absentmindedly. Before I could answer he got it. "I guess with people shooting. . . . " He droned off, but I knew that he understood.

While we were setting up, Lisa made a pot of coffee. True to our schedule, we had not had coffee that morning, so we greatly appreciated a fresh pot. Around the kitchen, generators hummed. Inside, Andrew, Sheila, and Irene, the encampment cooks, were taking their between-meal break. Periodically, children came in looking for something to snack on. There was plenty to eat. Sheila offered us some lunchtime leftovers. There were hamburgers, sandwiches, and sweets. There were even pecan tarts. I come from the home of the pecan. In fact, there are three pecan trees in my yard. So, a pecan tart was more than a welcome treat. We sipped coffee, talked, and were introduced to the men and women who came in.

I didn't see Abner and Ernest's canoe when we arrived at York Factory. Sheila said that they had been here, but camped on Hay Island across from the Depot. Today they were on their way up the Nelson River. It's a long trip, but you can get to Gillam by boat on the Nelson. In fact, that is how Larry and Lisa came to York Factory. I didn't ask, but figured that Abner and Ernest were headed toward Gillam. They seemed to be loaded for a jaunt longer than a day. I guess that the two men are still looking for their moose.

Jackie and Doug soon came down to the kitchen. First they took us to the depot for a tour. Jackie still had her shotgun. The riverbanks are eroding at about five feet per year, so in another fifty years if nothing is done to save it, the depot will be gone. To combat this threat, Parks Canada is conducting a long-term study to see if they can save the depot in place. If not, the question is, "Can we move it?" Boards have already been numbered.

Although it is one of Canada's most historic sites, the depot's remoteness limits visitors to about 300 a year. Half of that number is made up of Cree Indians who come for the Gathering. There are only three ways in. One is the way we came, down the Hayes River. Usually only about thirty people do that. The second is by charter aircraft. The last is by jetboat down the Nelson around the point into the Hayes. As a result, even though important, saving York Factory is not an immediate priority on Parks Canada's budget.

One of the problems encountered when building that far north is that you must build on permafrost. To me, permafrost is somewhat of a misnomer. Actually, the top of the permafrost melts and freezes with the seasons so there is some water flow and there can be some significant heaving from the ice. To counter these natural forces, the Hudson Bay Company built the depot like a ship. In fact, ship builders constructed it. If you look closely inside you can see joints that allow for movement. Being an amateur wood worker, I was impressed with some of the unnecessary details. All of the wallboards were tongue and grooved. The vertical board edges had a decorative bead. The corbels holding the joist for the ceilings were all made of huge tree roots. The curved grain allowed for perfect mounting and movement. They all seemed to age beautifully. In the glow of the afternoon sun they all had a mellow, golden hue.

In the courtyard is a newly discovered water collection pit. Archeologists dated it to about 1790. At some point it was no longer needed, so like many cisterns it was simply covered. Lining the square pit are 1790s logs. On each side is a square wooden, 1790s drainage pipe.

Upstairs rows of tables neatly display fur trade artifacts. Jackie commented that the best ones are on display in the Winnipeg museum. Occasionally fur trade-era carved graffiti highlights the walls. Probably the most engaging carving is a caricature of a man. I looked at Jackie and said, "I bet that he was a real person."

"You think so?" she quizzed.

"I do. Probably was somebody who worked right here."

We then climbed up to the cupola for the grand view. Off to our north was the encampment. To the east and the west was the empty northland. The blue sky eased some of the feeling of remoteness, but there was no doubt how isolated we were.

After the tour we headed for Doug's shop to get our paddles branded. When you paddle to Hudson Bay, the staff brands your paddle with the stylized York Factory, Y. It may seem inconsequential to some, but to the serious paddler it is important. Although informal, it is just as somber, solemn, and significant as the Height of Land Portage Ceremony.

Doug heated his acetylene torch and heated the brand to a

glowing whitish-red. I went first and then Jay went. Our wood paddles smoked and sizzled as the iron brand did its work. Afterward, Jackie walked us back to the kitchen. Some of the Cree asked to see our paddles. It was obviously as important to them as it was to us. If you have never paddled in the North Woods, it is hard to understand the importance of the canoe and the paddle. Canoes and rivers are simply central to Canada's history. Canada would not have been settled without the canoe. The First Nation peoples needed canoes to survive. I think that the Cree appreciated our journey.

We stayed up late talking, drinking coffee, and nibbling on some cookies. It had cooled down, but the kitchen was warm. One of the polar bear guards who came and went from the kitchen was Elton, a man about my age. I was glad to see another elder still out there. Finally, not because we were tired, but because we knew that we needed to sleep, we all eventually wandered off to our tents.

I woke early and went to the kitchen, partially to see if I could help and partially in hopes that there would be a pot of hot coffee. A couple of the graveyard-shift guards had come in to get out of the cold and wet. I joined the conversation, taking a couple of leftover sugar cookies. Soon Jay followed me in. Sheila and Irene came in next to fix breakfast and some coffee. In short order the kitchen was filled with the welcome aroma of cooking sausage and the crackle of hot grease. Next, diced potatoes were tossed into the grease followed by fresh eggs. On another burner, baked beans were warmed. Sheila sliced a loaf of bannock. Bannock has become a traditional bread for the Cree. We were going to have the North Woods version of a full English breakfast.

Over breakfast it stormed on and off. Our plane was coming around one o'clock. I thought quietly and hopefully that the weather would not delay our flight. After breakfast the storm abated, so I went to pack. Then Jay and I got a polar bear guard to walk us down to the depot for a couple of last pictures. On the way back we ran into Elton. He took us down to the old cemetery. On the way were the remnants of the York boat used in *Quest for the Bay*. It definitely had seen better days. I thought to myself that it would be lucky to make it through the next couple of winters.

The cemetery, although in disrepair, was a peaceful place, shaded by a grove of small spruces. Several of the factors from the 1800s were buried there. White wooden fences enclosed most gravesites. Elton was quiet as he somberly looked for some relatives' burial places. His brief act of pointing to a family gravesite here and there gave me a fleeting insight into the York Factory's former vibrancy and an appreciation of the Gathering's personal importance.

The morning slipped away. We headed back to take our gear to the landing. Doug and Jackie told us the day before that they would ferry us across to Hay Island to the landing strip. Down by the landing along with Doug's boat was the jetboat that Lisa and Larry had taken from Gillam. We loaded our gear. The young Cree boat driver laughed as he said, "Don't worry. It's not full till we load a dead moose."

The tide was out. You could almost walk to Hay Island at low tide. We raced across in the silver metal jetboat. As we neared the muddy shore, our driver cut the engine allowing the boat to slide through the seaweed across a muddy beach almost onto dry, rocky ground. We unloaded our gear onto another four-wheeler, then went to help Doug and Jackie unload. By now the sky was clear. In the distance we could hear the hum of the planes. They both landed without difficulty, but the pilots decided that taking off would be problematic. The morning's rain had flooded the gravel runway with deep enough puddles to make taking off hazardous.

Along with the pilots, Larry and Doug walked down to survey the runway. They determined that with some shovels and dirt that they could drain and fill the puddles. It was only a short delay. Soon we were loaded and airborne.

JAY WRITES:

On the morning the plane came, although I wished that I had used my camera more, I almost grudgingly took a few last photos. My mind was somewhat in a daze as I snapped shots of the depot and the vista looking out on the Bay. For over a decade I had dreamed of being right there, and now it was ending. In my mind I sorted through and organized my thoughts. There was the daily challenge to adapt, improvise, and overcome. We had to bust through overgrown or fire-ravaged areas. Rapids and waterfalls regularly blocked our way. Physically and psychologically there were days that we just had to just suck it up. I did not feel the metaphorical human soul's burning of "distant fires" that Scott Anderson wrote about, but there was a satisfying sense of triumph. We had succeeded in doing what few others had done.

Compared to our trek north, flying back to "civilization" was anticlimactic. It was so simple. For the first time in two and a half months, somebody else did the work. We shared the plane with three young Cree girls who came from Winnipeg to attend the Gathering. As they chattered, Fred and I sat hypnotically watching the land we had crossed slip slowly past.

FRED WRITES:

Even on a bright, hot day, the depot seemed even bleaker from the air. It was a beautiful building, but had a desolate appearance. To the west and north the mighty Nelson River shimmered and sparkled under a glaring afternoon sun. Comparatively, it made the Hayes seem like a small stream. Below us all around was the same kind of lonesome terrain that York Factory sat on. From the air I could see how secluded we were. Flying to Gillam, I thought, *It is over and sorrowfully we are on our way back to the twenty-first century. It is a place and a way of life that I have, on occasion, been able to break away from.* This escape was seventy-five days, almost 1,400 miles, over one hundred rapids, and eighty-five portages. But now I was reluctantly on my way back from a journey during which I was almost trapped in a long-ago time. Reluctantly, I was on my way back to the present.

> Out of the sound of the ebb and flow,
> Out of the sight of lamp and star,
> It calls you where the good winds blow,
> And the unchanging meadows are:
> From faded hopes and hopes agleam,
> It calls you, calls you night and day
> Beyond the dark into the dream
> Over the hills and far away.

"Over the Hills and Far Away"
by William Ernest Henley

ACKNOWLEDGMENTS
FROM FRED MARKS AND JAY TIMMERMAN

Thanks to all of the staff at Northern Tier who helped resupply us. They are great friends. Thanks also to Joanne Finstad for so graciously assisting us in International Falls. Our thanks also to the "Friendly Manitobans" who opened their homes to a couple of ragged, trail worn strangers. Wonderfully warm Canadians like Ed and Charlotte Campbell at Norway House, George and Charlene Junkin on the Winnipeg River, Steve and Barry at Princess Harbour, and Leon Simpson on remote Opiminegoka Lake all gave us a welcome respite from the trail. Finally, only because our meeting came at the end of the trip, our hearty thanks to the men and women of the Fox Lake Band of Cree. Without hesitation, they welcomed two scruffy strangers to their Gathering at York factory.

APPENDICES

—FAJITA STEW—

• INGREDIENTS •

3 lbs stew meat

3 potatoes

¾ lb carrots

1 bell pepper

1 onion

1 c freeze-dried black beans

2 c freeze-dried corn (Note: If you can take cans, you can substitute
   them for the freeze-dried vegetables. Or, use frozen vegetables since
   this is a first-night meal.)

3 pkgs fajita seasoning

Oil

2 pkgs flour tortillas (or enough tortillas for two pieces per person)

1 bottle salsa

1 small tub of processed cheese or 1 small bag of shredded cheese

1 to 2 cloves garlic

Salt and pepper to taste

• INSTRUCTIONS •

Slice carrots into ¼-inch slices and sauté in oil with one bag of
seasoning. When done, put into stew pot with 3 cups of water to
simmer with the diced garlic cloves. Next, cube the potatoes and
sauté with second bag of seasoning. Sauté meat with remaining
bag of seasoning mix. You may either dice the onion and bell

pepper, adding directly to the water in the stew pot, or sauté with the potatoes. Add water if necessary. Lastly, add beans and corn to the stew. Let simmer for 30 to 45 minutes until done.

Serve by placing tortilla in bowl. Scoop stew on top of tortilla. Garnish with liberal amounts of salsa and cheese.

Comments: Serves 9. Unless you are taking an ice chest, freeze the meat the night before. It should not completely thaw before you are ready to cook supper. If you have an ice chest, then sour cream is great on top instead of salsa.

—CHILI WITH—
CORNBREAD DUMPLINGS

· INGREDIENTS ·

1 pkg Wyler's Mrs. Grass 3-bean chili mix
1 15-oz can chili w/o beans
4 oz beef jerky
1 pkg instant tomato soup or dried tomato paste
1 pkg chili seasoning
6 c water (more if using dried tomato sauce)
1 pkg cornbread
4 oz lentils (Lentils cook in the same amount of time it takes for the chili mix.)

· INSTRUCTIONS ·

Boil 7½ cups of water and add lentils, chili mix, tomato sauce, chili seasoning, and beef jerky. When almost done, the lentils will be tender. Add the can of chili without beans. Let simmer.

Mix the cornbread following package directions. If it is plain cornbread, add cumin and chili powder to the mix. When the chili is almost done, drop the cornbread by a tablespoon onto the chili. Cook 10 to 15 minutes covered.

Alternatives: Add dried garlic and onions. For a hungry group of four, add 1 package of Mexican rice and 2 extra cups of water and 1 extra can of chili. Use microwaveable containers if there is a restriction on cans. Instead of microwaveable chili, summer sausage can be substituted; however, additional chili seasoning will be needed.

Comments: Serves 6. If it is a hungry group of six, add an extra container of chili and a package of Spanish rice. Add extra water to account for rice.

—CURRIED CHICKEN—
AND LENTILS WITH RICE

· INGREDIENTS ·

3 c lentils

½ c soy sauce (either a few soy packages or repackaged soy in plastic
    bottle)

½ c crunchy or smooth peanut butter

2 cubes chicken bouillon

2 large pouches of chicken

4 tsp chopped dry garlic

4 tsp ginger powder

2 tbs curry powder

2 c rice

2 oz dried carrots

· INSTRUCTIONS ·

Boil 6 to 8 cups of water. Next add lentils. Let lentils cook for
about 5 minutes. Add chicken, bouillon, garlic, ginger, soy, curry
powder, and peanut butter. Simmer for 15 to 20 minutes or until
lentils are tender.

While lentils are cooking, in a separate pot boil six cups of water.
When water reaches a hard boil, add 3 cups of rice. Lower heat
and let simmer until done. Serve rice over lentils or lentils over
rice.

Alternatives: Curry dishes are usually hot, so red pepper flakes would be in order. Summer sausage or jerky can also be added. Leftover raisins and peanuts are great sprinkled over the top.

Comments: Serves 6.

—CHICKEN & DUMPLINGS—

• INGREDIENTS •

*1 envelope or 2.4 oz Knorr Kosher Vegetable Soup or equivalent amount
of instant vegetable soup*
1 10-oz can and 1 4-oz can chicken
1 pkg chicken gravy
1 pkg white country gravy
3 c of dry noodles
1 pkg pizza dough
*Pepper to taste (Salt may not be necessary, as gravy mixes usually have
enough salt.)*
1 tsp dried sliced garlic cloves
7 c of water (4 cups for the soup and 3 cups for the noodles and gravy)

• INSTRUCTIONS •

Boil water with vegetable soup, noodles, and gravy mixes. (Depending on soup mix, you might have to add or subtract water.) Turn camp stove down to low heat, stirring occasionally. When done the noodles will be tender. Add chicken. Prepare pizza dough mix according to package directions. Roll out on fillet board. Cut into strips or squares and place on top of chicken mixture. Cook uncovered for 10 minutes, then cook covered for about 10 minutes on low heat.

Alternatives: Freeze-dried vegetables may be substituted for the soup mix. Mushrooms may also be added. Freeze-dried chicken can be substituted.

Comments: Serves 4. If it is a hungry group of four, add more noodles and chicken and adjust the amount of water.

—CHICKEN SPAGHETTI—

• INGREDIENTS •

1 pkg Lipton's vegetable soup
2 pkg Lipton's Alfredo noodle mix
2 small pouches chicken
6 oz summer sausage
1 small pkg real bacon bits
6 oz Velveeta cheese
3 oz Parmesan cheese
1 pkg powdered milk
Dehydrated mushrooms
2 to 3 tbs dehydrated onions
1 to 2 cloves garlic

• INSTRUCTIONS •

Boil enough water to cook Alfredo noodles. Cut summer sausage into bite-size pieces and add to water along with mushrooms, onions, and garlic. When water boils, add Alfredo noodles. Stir and turn down heat. When noodles are almost done, add soup and milk. Add enough water to hydrate soup and milk. When noodles are done, add chicken, cubed Velveeta cheese, and Parmesan cheese. Sprinkle bacon bits on top. Let sit for 5 to 10 minutes and serve.

Comments: Serves 4.

—BANNOCK MIX—

• INGREDIENTS •

1 c white flour
1 c whole wheat flour
2 tsp baking powder (always use good baking powder)
½ tsp salt

• INSTRUCTIONS •

At Home: Mix ingredients together in a plastic bag. Use on trail with water or milk to mix into a dough. Some of the old-time bannock concoctions on the trail use leftover bacon grease for extra flavor and an egg. If you don't have bacon grease, add a couple of tablespoons of oil. To make drop biscuits, use just a little extra water. Use less water for a heavier biscuit. Flatten the dough on a cutting board to about ½-inch thick, then cut into equal portions and bake for 15 to 20 minutes.

Comments: Serve with a strong brown gravy or syrup or jelly. Serves 9 or more.

THE WINDIGO

·

by William Henry Drummond

Go easy wit' de paddle, an' steady wit' de oar
Geev rudder to de bes' man you got among de crew,
Let ev'ry wan be quiet, don't let dem sing no more
W'en you see de islan' risin' out of Grande Lac Manitou.

Above us on de sky dere, de summer cloud may float
Aroun' us on de water de ripple never show,
But somet'ing down below us can rock de stronges' boat,
W'en we're comin' near de islan' of de spirit Windigo!

De carcajou may breed dere, an' otter sweem de poole
De moosh-rat mak' de mud house, an' beaver buil' hees dam
An' beeges' Injun hunter on all de Tête de Boule
Will never set hees trap dere from spring to summer tam.

But he'll bring de fines' presen' from upper St. Maurice
De loup marin an' black-fox from off de Hodson Bay
An' hide dem on de islan' an' smoke de pipe of peace
So Windigo will help heem w'en he travel far away.

We shaintee on dat islan' on de winter seexty-nine
If you look you see de clearin' aroun' de Coo Coo Cache,
An' pleasan' place enough too among de spruce an' pine
If foreman on de shaintee isn't Cyprien Palache.

Beeg feller, always watchin' on hees leetle weasel eye,
De gang dey can't do not'ing but he see dem purty quick
Wit' hees "Hi dere, w'at you doin' ?" ev'ry tam he's passin' by
An' de bad word he was usin' , wall! it offen mak' me sick.

An' he carry silver w'issle wit' de chain aroun' hees neck
For fear he mebbe los' it, an' ev'ry body say

He mus' buy it from de devil w'en he's passin' on Kebeck
But if it's true dat story, I dunno how moche he pay.

Dere's plaintee on de shaintee can sing lak rossignol
Pet Clancy play de fiddle, an' Jimmie Char-bonneau
Was bring hees concertina from below St. Fereol
So we get some leetle pleasure till de long, long winter go.

But if we start up singin' affer supper on de camp
"Par derriere chez ma tante," or "Mattawa wishtay,"
De boss he'll come along den, an' put heem out de lamp,
An' only stop hees swearin' w'en we all go marche coucher.

We've leetle boy dat winter from Po-po-lo-be-lang
Hees fader an' hees moder dey're bote A-ben-a-kee
An' he's comin', Injun Johnnie, wit' some man de lumber gang
Was fin' heem nearly starvin' above on Lac Souris.

De ole man an' de woman is tryin' pass de Soo
W'en water's high on spring tam, an' of course dey're gettin' drown',
For even smartes' Injun shouldn't fool wit' birch canoe,
W'ere de reever lak toboggan on de hill is runnin' down.

So dey lef' de leetle feller all alone away up dere
Till lumber gang is ketchin' him an' bring him on de Cache,
But better if he's stayin' wit' de wolf an' wit' de bear.
Dan come an' tak' hees chances wit' Cyprien Palache.

I wonder how he stan' it, w'y he never run away
For Cyprien lak dog he is treat heem all de sam'
An' if he's wantin' Johnnie on de night or on de day
God help heem if dat w'issle she was below de second' tam!

De boy he don't say not'ing, no wan never see heem cry
He's got de Injun in heem, you can see it on de face,
An' only for us feller an' de cook, he'll surely die
Long before de winter's over, long before we lef' de place.

But I see heem hidin' somet'ing wan morning by de shore
So firse tam I was passin' I scrape away de snow
An' it's rabbit skin he's ketchin' on de swamp de day before,
Leetle Injun Johnnie's workin' on de spirit Windigo.

December's come in stormy, an' de snow-dreef fill de road
Can only see de chimley an' roof of our cabane,
An' stronges' team on stable fin' it plaintee heavy load
Haulin' sleigh an' two t'ree pine log t'roo de wood an' beeg savane.

An' I travel off wan day me, wit' Cyprien Palache
Explorin' for new timber, w'en de win' begin to blow,
So we hurry on de snow-shoe for de camp on Coo Coo Cache
If de nor' eas' storm is comin', was de bes' place we dunno.

An' we're gettin' safe enough dere wit' de storm close on our heel,
But w'en our belt we loosen for takin' off de coat
De foreman commence screamin' an' mon Dieu it mak' us feel
Lak he got t'ree t'ousan' devil all fightin' on hees t'roat.

Cyprien is los' hees w'issle, Cyprien is los' hees chain
Injun Johnnie he mus' fin' it, even if de win' is high
He can never show hese'f on de Coo Coo Cache again
Till he bring dat silver w'issle an' de chain it's hangin' by.

So he sen' heem on hees journey never knowin' he come back
T'roo de rough an' stormy wedder, t'roo de pile of dreefin' snow

"Wat's de use of bein' Injun if you can 't smell out de track?"
Dat's de way de boss is talkin' , an' poor Johnnie have to go.

If you want to hear de musique of de nort' win' as it blow
An' lissen to the hurricane an' learn de way it sing
An' feel how small de man is w'en he's leevin' here below,
You should try it on de shaintee w'en she's doin' all dem t'ing!

W'at's dat soun' lak somet'ing cryin' all aroun' us ev'ry w'ere?
We never hear no tonder upon de winter storm!
Dey're shoutin' to each oder dem voices on de air,
An' it's red hot too de stove pipe, but no wan's feelin' warm!

"Get out an' go de woodpile before I freeze to deat'"
Cyprien de boss is yellin' an' he's lookin' cole an' w'ite
Lak dead man on de coffin, but no wan go, you bet,
For if it's near de woodpile, 't isn't close enough to-night!

Non! we ain't afraid of not'ing, but we don't lak takin' chance,
An' w'en we hear de spirit of de wil' A-ben-a-kee
Singin' war song on de chimley, makin' all dem Injun dance
Raisin' row dere, you don't ketch us on no woodpile—no siree!

O! de lonesome night we're passin' w'ile we're stayin' on dat place!
An' ev'rybody sheever when Jimmie Char bonneau
Say he's watchin' on de winder an' he see de Injun face
An' it's lookin' so he tole us, jus' de sam' as Windingo.

Den again mese'f I'm hearin' somet'ing callin', an' it soun'
Lak de voice of leetle Johnnie so I'm passin' on de door
But de pine stump on de clearin' wit' de w'ite sheet all aroun'
Mak' me t'ink of churchyar' tombstone, an' I can't go dere no more.

Wat's de reason we're so quiet w'ile our heart she's goin' fas'
W'y is no wan ax de question? dat we're all afraid to spik?
Was it wing of flyin' wil' bird strek de winder as it pass,
Or de sweesh of leetle snow-ball w'en de win' is playin' trick?

W'en we buil' de Coo Coo shaintee, she's as steady as a rock,
Did you feel de shaintee shakin' de sam, she's goin' to fall?
Dere's somet'ing on de doorway! an' now we hear de knock
An' up above de hurricane we hear de w'issle call.

Callin', callin' lak a bugle, an' he's jompin' up de boss
From hees warm bed on de corner an' open wide de door—
Dere's no use foller affer for Cyprien is los'
An' de Coo Coo Cache an' shaintee he'll never see no more.

At las' de morning's comin', an' storm is blow away
An' outside on de shaintee young Jimmie Charbonneau
He's seein' track of snowshoe, 'bout de size of doulbe sleigh
Dere's no mistak' it's makin' by de spirit Windigo.

An' de leetle Injuin Johnie, he's all right I onderstan'
For you'll fin' heem up de reever above de Coo Coo Cache
Ketchin' mink and ketchin' beaver, an' he's growin' great beeg man
But dat's de las' we're hearin' of Cyprien Palache.

THE WRECK OF THE "JULIE PLANTE":

A LEGEND OF LAC ST. PIERRE

•

by William Henry Drummond

On wan dark night on Lac St. Pierre,
De win' she blow, blow, blow,
An' de crew of de wood scow "Julie Plante"
Got scar't an' run below–
For de win' she blow lak hurricane,
Bimeby she blow some more,
An' de scow bus' up on Lac St. Pierre
Wan arpent from de shore.

De captinne walk on de fronte deck,
An' walk de hin' deck too–
He call de crew from up de hole,
He call de cook also.
De cook she's name was Rosie,
She come from Montreal,
Was chambre maid on lumber barge,
On de Grande Lachine Canal.

De win' she blow from nor'-eas'-wes',–
De sout' win' she blow too,
W'en Rosie cry, "Mon cher captinne,
Mon cher, w'at I shall do?"
Den de captinne t'row de beeg ankerre,
But still de scow she dreef,
De crew he can't pass on de shore,
Becos' he los' hees skeef.

De night was dark lak wan black cat,
De wave run high an' fas',
W'en de captinne tak' de Rosie girl
An' tie her to de mas'.
Den he also tak' de life preserve,

An' jomp off on de lak',
An' say, "Good-bye, ma Rosie dear,
I go drown for your sak.'"

Nex' morning very early
'Bout ha'f-pas' two–t'ree–four–
De captinne—scow—an' de poor Rosie
Was corpses on de shore,
For de win' she blow lak hurricane,
Bimeby she blow some more,
An' de scow bus' up on Lac St. Pierre,
Wan arpent from de shore.

MORAL

Now all good wood scow sailor man
Tak' warning by dat storm
An' go an' marry some nice French girl
An' leev on wan beeg farm.
De win' can blow lak hurricane
An' s'pose she blow some more,
You can't get drown on Lac St. Pierre
So long you stay on shore.

'POLEON DORÉ

•

by William Henry Drummond

You have never hear de story of de young Napoleon Doré?
Los' hees life upon de reever w'en de lumber drive go down?
W'ere de rapide roar lak tonder, dat's de place he's goin' onder,
W'en he's try save Paul Desjardins, 'Poleon hese'f is drown.

All de winter on de Shaintee, tam she's good, and work she's
      plaintee,
But we're not feel very sorry, w'en de sun is warm hees face,
W'en de mooshrat an' de beaver, tak' some leetle swim on reever,
An' de sout' win' scare de snowbird, so she fly some col'er place.

Den de spring is set in steady, an' we get de log all ready,
Workin' hard all day an' night too, on de water mos' de tam,
An' de skeeter w'en dey fin' us, come so quickly nearly blin' us,
Biz—biz—biz—biz—all aroun' us till we feel lak sacrédam.

All de sam' we're hooraw feller, from de top of house to cellar,
Ev'ry boy he's feel so happy, w'en he's goin' right away,
See hees fader an' hees moder, see hees sister an' hees broder,
An' de girl he spark las' summer, if she's not get marieé.

Wall we start heem out wan morning, an' de pilot geev us warning,
"W'en you come on Rapide Cuisse, ma frien', keep raf' she's head
      on shore,
If you struck beeg rock on middle, w'ere le diable is play hees
      fiddle,
Dat's de tam you pass on some place, you don't never pass before."

But we'll not t'ink moche of danger, for de rapide she's no stranger
Many tam we're runnin' t'roo it, on de fall an' on de spring,
On mos' ev'ry kin' of wedder dat le Bon Dieu scrape togedder,
An' we'll never drown noboddy, an' we'll never bus' somet'ing.

• • •

Dere was Telesphore Montbriand, Paul Desjardins, Louis Guyon,
Bill McKeever, Aleck Gauthier, an' hees cousin Jean Bateese,
'Poleon Doré, Aimé Beaulieu, wit' some more man I can't tole you,
Dat was mak' it bes' gang never run upon de St. Maurice.

Dis is jus' de tam I wish me, I could spik de good English—me—
For tole you of de pleasurement we get upon de spring,
W'en de win' she's all a sleepin', an' de raf' she go a sweepin'
Down de reever on some morning, w'ile le rossignol is sing.

Ev'ryt'ing so nice an' quiet on de shore as we pass by it,
All de tree got fine new spring suit, ev'ry wan she's dress on green
W'y it mak' us all more younger, an' we don't feel any hunger,
Till de cook say " 'Raw for breakfas'," den we smell de pork an' bean.

Some folk say she's bad for leever, but for man work hard on reever,
Dat's de bes' t'ing I can tole you, dat was never yet be seen,
Course dere's oder t'ing ah tak' me, fancy dish also I lak me,
But w'en I want somet'ing solid, please pass me de pork an' bean.

All dis tam de raf' she's goin' lak steamboat was got us towin'
All we do is keep de channel, an' dat's easy workin' dere,
So we sing some song an' chorus, for de good tam dat's before us,
W'en de w'ole beez-nesse she's finish, an' we come on Trois
    Rivieres.

But bad luck is sometam fetch us, for beeg strong win' come an'
    ketch us,
Jus' so soon we struck de rapide—jus' so soon we see de smoke,
An' before we spik some prayer for ourse'f dat's fightin' dere,
Roun' we come upon de beeg rock, an' it's den de raf' she broke.

. . .

Dat was tam poor Paul Desjardins, from de parish of St. Germain,
He was long way on de fronte side, so he's fallin' overboar'
Couldn't swim at all de man say, but dat's more ma frien', I can say,
Any how he's look lak drownin', so we'll t'row him two t'ree oar.

Dat's 'bout all de help our man do, dat's 'bout ev'ryt'ing we can do,
As de crib we're hangin' onto balance on de rock itse'f,
Till de young Napoleon Doré, heem I start for tole de story,
Holler out, "Mon Dieu, I don't lak see poor Paul go drown hese'f."

So he's mak' beeg jomp on water, jus' de sam you see some otter
An' he's pass on place w'ere Paul is tryin' hard for keep afloat,
Den we see Napoleon ketch heem, try hees possibill for fetch heem
But de current she's more stronger, an' de eddy get dem bote.

O Mon Dieu! for see dem two man, mak' me feel it cry lak woman,
Roun' an' roun' upon de eddy, quickly dem poor feller go,
Can't tole wan man from de oder, an' we'll know dem bote lak
    broder,
But de fight she soon is finish—Paul an' 'Poleon go below.

Yass, an' all de tam we stay dere, only t'ing we do is pray dere,
For de soul poor drownin' feller, dat's enough mak' us feel mad,
Torteen voyageurs, all brave man, glad get any chances save man,
But we don't see no good chances, can't do not'ing, dat's too bad.

Wall! at las' de crib she's come way off de rock, an' den on some way,
By an' by de w'ole gang's passin' on safe place below de Cuisse,
Ev'ryboddy's heart she's breakin', w'en dey see poor Paul he's taken
Wit' de young Napoleon Doré, bes' boy on de St. Maurice!

An' day affer, Bill McKeever fin' de bote man on de reever,
Wit' deir arm aroun' each oder, mebbe pass above dat way—
So we bury dem as we fin' dem, w'ere de pine tree wave behin' dem
    An de Grande Montagne he's lookin' down on Marcheterre Bay.

You can't hear no church bell ring dere, but le rossignol is sing
    dere,
An' w'ere ole red cross she's stannin', mebbe some good ange
    gardien,
Watch de place w'ere bote man sleepin', keep de reever grass from
    creepin'
On de grave of 'Poleon Doré, an' of poor Paul Desjardins.

Note: A Tale of the Saint Maurice

De Habitant

·

by William Henry Drummon

De place I get born, me, is up on de reever
Near foot of de rapide dat's call Cheval Blanc
Beeg mountain behin' it, so high you can't climb it
An' whole place she's mebbe two honder arpent.

De fader of me, he was habitant farmer,
Ma gran' fader too, an' hees fader also,
Dey don't mak' no monee, but dat isn't fonny
For it's not easy get ev'ryt'ing, you mus' know—

All de sam' dere is somet'ing dey got ev'ryboddy,
Dat's plaintee good healt', wat de monee can't geev,
So I'm workin' away dere, an' happy for stay dere
On farm by de reever, so long I was leev.

O! dat was de place w'en de spring tam she's comin',
W'en snow go away, an' de sky is all blue—
W'en ice lef' de water, an' sun is get hotter
An' back on de medder is sing de gou-glou—

W'en small sheep is firs' comin' out on de pasture,
Deir nice leetle tail stickin' up on deir back,
Dey ronne wit' deir moder, an' play wit' each oder
An' jomp all de tam jus' de sam' dey was crack—

An' ole cow also, she's glad winter is over,
So she kick herse'f up, an' start off on de race
Wit' de two-year-ole heifer, dat's purty soon lef' her,
W'y ev'ryt'ing's crazee all over de place!

An' down on de reever de wil' duck is quackin'
Along by de shore leetle san'piper ronne—

De bullfrog he's gr-rompin' an' doré is jompin'
Dey all got deir own way for mak' it de fonne.

But spring's in beeg hurry, an' don't stay long wit' us
An' firs' t'ing we know, she go off till nex' year,
Den bee commence hummin', for summer is comin'
An' purty soon corn's gettin' ripe on de ear.

Dat's very nice tam for wake up on de morning
An' lissen de rossignol sing ev'ry place,
Feel sout' win' a-blowin' see clover a-growin'
An' all de worl' laughin' itself on de face.

Mos' ev'ry day raf' it is pass on de rapide
De voyageurs singin' some ole chanson
'Bout girl down de reever—too bad dey mus' leave her,
But comin' back soon' wit' beaucoup d'argent.

An' den w'en de fall an' de winter come roun' us
An' bird of de summer is all fly away,
W'en mebbe she's snowin' an' nort' win' is blowin'
An' night is mos' t'ree tam so long as de day.

You t'ink it was bodder de habitant farmer?
Not at all—he is happy an' feel satisfy,
An' cole may las' good w'ile, so long as de wood-pile
Is ready for burn on de stove by an' bye.

W'en I got plaintee hay put away on de stable
So de sheep an' de cow, dey got no chance to freeze,
An' de hen all togedder—I don't min' de wedder—
De nort' win' may blow jus' so moche as she please.

. . .

An' some cole winter night how I wish you can see us,
W'en I smoke on de pipe, an' de ole woman sew
By de stove of T'ree Reever—ma wife's fader geev her
On day we get marry, dat's long tam ago—

De boy an' de girl, dey was readin' it's lesson,
De cat on de corner she's bite heem de pup,
Ole "Carleau" he's snorin' an' beeg stove is roarin'
So loud dat I'm scare purty soon she bus' up.

Philomene—dat's de oldes'—is sit on de winder
An' kip jus' so quiet lak wan leetle mouse,
She say de more finer moon never was shiner—
Very fonny, for moon isn't dat side de house.

But purty soon den, we hear foot on de outside,
An' some wan is place it hees han' on de latch,
Dat's Isidore Goulay, las' fall on de Brulé
He's tak' it firs' prize on de grand ploughin' match.

Ha! ha! Philomene!—dat was smart trick you play us
Come help de young feller tak' snow from hees neck,
Dere's not'ing for hinder you come off de winder
W'en moon you was look for is come, I expec'—

Isidore, he is tole us de news on de parish
'Bout hees Lajeunesse Colt—travel two forty, sure,
'Bout Jeremie Choquette, come back from Woonsocket
An' t'ree new leetle twin on Madame Vaillancour'.

But nine o'clock strike, an' de chil'ren is sleepy,
Mese'f an' ole woman can't stay up no more
So alone by de fire—'cos dey say dey ain't tire—
We lef' Philomene an' de young Isidore.

I s'pose dey be talkin' beeg lot on de kitchen
'Bout all de nice moon dey was see on de sky,
For Philomene's takin' long tam get awaken
Nex' day, she's so sleepy on bote of de eye.

Dat's wan of dem ting's, ev'ry tam on de fashion,
An' 'bout nices' t'ing dat was never be seen.
Got not'ing for say me—I spark it sam' way me
W'en I go see de moder ma girl Philomene.

We leev very quiet 'way back on de contree
Don't put on sam style lak de big village,
W'en we don't get de monee you t'ink dat is fonny
An' mak' plaintee sport on de Bottes Sauvages.

But I tole you—dat's true—I don't go on de city
If you geev de fine house an' beaucoup d'argent—I rader be stay
    me, an' spen' de las' day me
On farm by de rapide dat's call Cheval Blanc.

THE VOYAGEUR

·

by William Henry Drummon

Der's somet'ing stirrin' ma blood tonight,
On de night of de young new year,
Wile de camp is warm an' de fire is bright,
An' de bottle is close at han'
Out on de reever de nort' win' blow,
Down on de valley is pile de snow,
But w'at do we care so long we know
We're safe on de log cabane?

Drink to de healt' of your wife an' girl,
Anoder wan for your frien',
Den geev' me a chance, for on all de worl'
I've not many frien' to spare
I born, w'ere de mountain scrape de sky,
An' bone of ma fader an' moder lie,
So I fill de glass an' I raise it high
An' drink to de Voyageur.

For dis is de night of de jour de l'an,*
Wen de man of de Grand Nor' Wes'
T'ink of hees home on de St. Laurent,
An' frien' he may never see
Gone he is now, an' de beeg canoe
No more you'll see wit' de red-shirt crew,
But long as he leev' he was alway true,
So we'll drink to hees memory.

Ax' heem de nort' win' w'at he see
Of de Voyageur long ago,
An' he'll say to you w'at he say to me,
So lissen hees story well
I see de track of hees botte sauvage

---

* New Yer's Day

On many a hill an' long portage
Far, far away from hees own village
An' soun' of de parish bell.

"I never can play on de Hudson Bay"
Or mountain dat lie between
But I meet heem singin' hees lonely way
De happies' man I know
I cool hees face as he's sleepin' dere
Under de star of de Red Riviere,
An' off on de home of de great w'ite bear,
I'm seein' hees dog traineau.

"De woman an' children's runnin' out"
On de wigwam of de Cree
D leetle papoose dey laugh an' shout
W'en de soun' of hees voice dey hear
De oldes' warrior of de Sioux
Kill hese'f dancin' de w'ole night t'roo,
An de Blackfoot girl remember too
De ole tam Voyageur.

De blaze of hees camp on de snow I see,
An' I lissen hees "En Roulant"
On de lan' w'ere de reindeer travel free,
Ringin' out strong an' clear
Offen de grey wolf sit before
De light is come from hees open door,
An' caribou foller along de shore
De song of de Voyageur.
If he only kip goin', de red cinture,
I'd see it upon de Pole

Some mornin' I'm startin' upon de tour
For blowin' de win aroun'
But w'erever he sail an' w'erever he ride,
De trail is long an' de trail is wide,
An' city an' town on ev'ry side
Can tell of hees campin' groun'.

So dat's de reason I drink to-night
To de man of de Grand Nor' Wes',
For hees heart was young, an' hees heart was light
So long as he's leevin' dere
I'm proud of de sam' blood in my vein
I'm a son of de Nort' Win 'wance again
So we'll fill her up till de bottle's drain
An' drink to de Voyageur.

CHIBOUGAMOU

·

by William Henry Drummond

Did you ever see an air-hole on the ice
Wit' de smoke a risin' roun' about it dere?
De reever should be happy w'ere it's feelin' warm an' nice,
But she t'ink she ought to get a leetle air.

An' she want to be a lookin' on de sky
So of course de cole win' hit her on de nose-
"I'll come up again," she say, "on de spring tam, bimeby,
But I'm better now below," and off she goes.

Dat's de way I feel mese'f on de farm a year ago,
W'ere ev'ryt'ing should be a pleasan' dream;
Lak de foolish reever dere, I'm not satisfy below,
So I got to let meoff a leetle steam.

Den a man he come along an' say to me, "Look here—
Don't youi know that place dey call Chibougamou
W'ere de diamon' lie aroun' like de mushroom on de groun',
An dey're findin' all de gole an silver too?

"W'at's de use of stayin' here den? Did n't Johnnie Drutusac
Lif' de mor'gage off hees place an' buy a cow?
Only gone a leetle w'ile—hardly miss heem till he's back;
He's easy worki' man too, an' look at Johnnie now?

"Well enough, ma frien', you know I can never tell de lie
W'en I say de gole is comin' t'ousan' ounces on de ton,
Am' de solid silver mak' you feel funny on de eye,
Lak de snow-blin' on de winter w'en it shine de morning sun.

I s'pose you won't believe, but you know dat gravel walk
Ma fader got it facin' on hes house at St. Bidou-

But w'at's de use of spikin', w'at's de use of talk?
Dat's de way you see de diamon' on dat place Chibougamou.

"Course you got to go an' fin' dem quickly, or de stranger man
Come along wit' plaintee barrel an' you 're never knowin' w'en
Couple o' Yankee off the State, he was buyin' all de Ian';
Affer dat an' w'ere 's your gole an' silver goin' den?

"So, Bateese, get up an' hurry, sell de farm, mon cher ami,
Leave de girl an' bring provision, pork an' bean, potato too,
Leetle—w'isky, an' I'll put heem on de safe place under me'
Wile I sit an' steer you off to dat place Chibougamou. "

Oh! de day an' night we 're passin', me dat never was before
On de bush, except w'en heifer go away an' den got los';
Oh! de pullin' an' de haulin', till I 'm feelin' purty sore,
But of all de troub an' worry, de skeeter, he 's de boss.

Beeg? lak de leetle two-mont' robin. Sing? lak a sawmill on de spring.
Put de blanket roun' your body an' den he bite you troo.
Me, I never tak' hees measure, but I t'ink across de wing
He 's t'ree inch sure dem skeeter, on dat place Chibougamou.

De man he 's goin' wit' me, never paddle, never haul,
Jus' smoke an' watch an' lissen for dat ole Chibougamou ;
I s'pose he can't be bodder doin' any work at all,
For de feller tak' you dere jus' have not'ing else to do.

T'ousan' mile we mak' de travel t'ousan' mile an' mebbe more,
An' I do de foolish prayin' lak' I never pray at home,
'Cos I want a chance to get it, only let me see de shore
Of Chibougamou a little w'ile before de winter come.

No use prayin', no use climbin' on de beeg tree ev'ry day,
Lookin' hard to see de diamon', an' de silver, an' de gole
I can't see dem, an' de summer she begin to go away,
An' de day is gettin' shorter, an' de night is gettin' cole.

So I kick an' raise de row den, an' I tole ma frien' lookout
Purty quick de winter's comin' an' we 'll hurry up an' go;
Never min' de gole an' silver diamon' too we'll go widout,
Or de only wan we're seein', is de diamon' on de snow.

Mebbe good place w'en you get dere, w'at you call Chibougamou,
But if we never fin' it, w'at 's de use dat place to me?
Tak' de paddle, for we 're goin', an' mese'f I'll steer canoe,
For I 'm always firse-class pilot on de road to St. Elie.

Oh! to see me on de mornin', an' de way I mak' heem sweat,
You can see de water droppin' all aroun' hees neck an' face;
"Now, Chibougamou," I tell heem, "hurry up, an' mebbe yet
You'll have chance again to try it w'en you leave me on ma place."

So we have a beeg procession, w'en we pass on St. Elie,
All de parish comin' lookin' for de gole an' silver too,
But Louise, she cry so moche dere, jus' becos she's seein' me,
She forget about de diamon' on dat ole Chibougamou.

After all is gone an' finish, an' you mak' a fool you' se'f,
An' de worl' is go agen you, w'at's de medicine is cure
Lak de love of hones' woman w'en she geev it all herse'f?
So Louise an' me is happy, no matter if we're poor.

So de diamon' may be plaintee, lak de gravel walk you see
W'en you're comin' near de house of ole Telesphore Beaulieu,
But me, I got a diamon' on ma home on St. Elie
Can beat de pile is lyin' on dat place Chibougamou.

INDEX

CPSIA information can be obtained at www.ICGtesting.com
Printed in the USA
LVOW091120120812

293983LV00002B/18/P